CW00523992

DUCHESS MATILDA AND HER HOLY CRUSADE

BOOK ONE: THREE UNLIKELY HEROES

AUTHOR: RICHARD GILES

A HISTORICAL COMICAL DRAMA TOLD IN TWO BOOKS ABOUT A STRONG-WILLED AND POWERFUL WOMAN WHO WILL STOP AT NOTHING TO ENSURE HER HUSBAND, WILLIAM, DUKE OF NORMANDY, BECOMES KING OF ENGLAND. SHE BELIEVES GOD WILL SEND HER THREE MEN TO ACHIEVE HER GOALS. IS THIS THE END OF SAXON ENGLAND, OR CAN HAROLD GODWINSON AND OTHERS SAVE ENGLAND?

See the last page for unbelievable fake reviews that are not to be taken seriously!

DUCHESS MATILDA AND HER HOLY CRUSADE
BOOK ONE: THREE UNLIKELY HEROES

NOW AVAILABLE:
DUCHESS MATILDA AND HER HOLY CRUSADE
BOOK TWO: FOUR MEN, ONE ENGLISH CROWN

COMING SOON:

The comical historical saga,
THE REVOLTING ENGLISH SAXONS

And a trilogy of modern-day mystical comical thrillers,
starting with the soon to be published:
RICHARD HENRY FIGHTS EVIL
BOOK ONE: THE FRENCH COLLECTOR AND ODIN

All characters, apart from the obvious historical figures, in this publication are fictitious and any resemblance to real persons, alive or dead, is purely coincidental.

FRONT COVER IMAGE
The copyright of the image displayed on the front cover of this book belongs to Reading Borough Council that in turn owns Reading Museum. The Museum has granted formal permission of its use in this publication.
It is a copy of a part of The Bayeux Tapestry depicting the English Earl, Harold Godwinson, in Normandy, swearing his oath before Duke William of Normandy.

Copyright © Richard Giles 2022

THE BAYEUX MUSEUM, NORMANDY, FRANCE

It was twenty-five minutes to midnight on October 13 2026 at the Bayeux Museum. Richard Henry Owen sat alone, admiring the ancient needlework known as the Bayeux Tapestry. It showed scenes from the epic story of William, Duke of Normandy's attempt to become King of England. The saga's climax was the Battle of Hastings, fought on English soil on October 14, 1066. The young Englishman, a full-time student of British medieval history at Oxford University, began reading his research notes again. He had just finished his second year and was considered one of the University's brightest scholars. He had decided to spend his summer break learning as much as he could about the Bayeux Tapestry and the events between 1064 and 1066. This would form the basis of his final year thesis. When his tutor had contacted both the Bayeux Museum and London's Victoria and Albert Museum, they had agreed that Richard Henry, known to his friends as Henry, could have full access to the Bayeux Museum *if* he became the night cleaner and guard and shared his completed research in full. It was clear to Henry that his tutor had a great deal of influence over certain people in authority. Indeed, he had noticed that some of the French officials that he had met over the last few weeks became rather nervous whenever his tutor's name was mentioned and Henry wondered whether he had some sort of hold over them.

Young Henry had already found some important documents in the archives of several museums in both

England and France. A few of these had remained unread for centuries. In the French papers were some clues as to the whereabouts of the missing final scenes of the Bayeux Tapestry and yet another unknown tapestry, made at about the same time, one that gave another version of events. It seems this missing tapestry included the actions of Matilda Duchess of Normandy, her spy network, and two mysterious twins named Richard the First and Richard the Last. Henry was determined to find these lost items.

The sound of his mobile phone startled him. He sighed as he saw who it was, and then answered. 'Hello Mother!'

'Richard Henry, are you awake?'

Henry knew when she used both of his given names that she was not happy with him. He sighed, 'Yes Mother.'

'I had one of my funny turns!'

'I'm not coming home Mother!'

'But I'm all alone!'

'Good bye Mother, I'll phone you tomorrow.'

'Is she with you, that girl?'

'No, she's in Bristol, and she has a name, it's Elizabeth.'

'It's Elizabeth Harlot!'

Henry smiled - he knew what the consequences would be if Elizabeth met his mother. It would definitely be a close contest. Elizabeth was no pushover. 'No Mother, it's Elizabeth Falaise, and she's related to the royal family so let's have some respect please!'

'Oh, well, when am I going to meet her? You shouldn't have gone to that Glastonbury Festival - it's just an excuse for an orgy. Days of loud music, sex and drugs!'

Henry smiled again, remembering the festival. 'I've got to go.'

'Let me speak to her!'

Henry raised his phone up and moved the screen so she could see the room. 'Look, I'm all alone!'

His mother let out a sharp scream. 'What's that coming out of the tapestry? It looks like small wisps of mist! Yes, it um, yes, now it looks like small ghostly souls emerging from the pictures! You'd better leave and come home; the museum is haunted and you're in danger!'

'Mother have you been downloading horror films again? You know they're no good for your nerves!' Henry looked at the tapestry. 'It's just a trick of the dim light. Nice try Mother. I'm safe - the museum is securely locked.'

'Richard Henry, listen to your mother. Father Rodut said that you—'

Henry interrupted. 'Good bye Mother.'

'Henry dear, do you have the cross he gave you?'

Henry felt for the cross around his neck. 'Yes Mother, good night!'

'Richard Henry, I must tell you something that I should have told you many years ago, and I must warn you that you are—'

Henry's phone went dead. He knew it wasn't the battery. *How strange* he thought.

He walked over to the tapestry and studied it in detail. It was now one minute to midnight. A strange atmosphere had descended upon the room. The air was unnaturally cool and a freezing mist seemed to be forming in front of his eyes. He breathed in deeply. The frigid air hurt his lungs. He exhaled and he could see his breath, as if his soul had just vacated his body. Henry shivered. He felt a strange unearthly sensation, as if ghosts were materialising before his tired eyes.

He sat down on his camp bed and took tight hold of the cross around his neck. He closed his eyes and tried to think of other things to distract his racing imagination. He asked himself, *what were these people like in real life, and what role did they play in the events leading up to that famous battle? There were the main characters, King Edward the Confessor, Duke William, and Earl Harold of course but what of these others such as Bishop Odo, Archbishop Stigand, Queen Edith of England, King Harald Hardrada of Norway, the Norman knights Wadard and Vital, Harold's brother Tostig, and a dwarf named Turold? Finally, there were those mysterious and obscure twins, the two Richards, rarely mentioned in any historical documents – were they real or just legends?*

Henry's tiredness, together with the oppressive atmosphere in the room, was too much for poor Henry. As he inhaled more of the mist, he laid back on his bed and fell asleep and was soon immersed in a strange dream, created by the souls who had now materialised in the room.

The souls, representing those principal characters from the events that had culminated in the Battle of Hastings 960 years ago, were all gathered at their reunion. God, it seemed, had allowed them to meet together every 120 years. Each time they met, they failed to agree about those events and this led to many arguments that would have caused much bloodshed, had they had any blood. This year they had the unique opportunity to use Henry's dream to play out their saga. They all knew that his ancestry made him an ideal spiritual conduit. They, and God, hoped that this would show, once and for all, exactly what did happen all those years ago. God hoped this would allow the troubled souls to finally rest in peace.

DUCHESS MATILDA IIAS A DIVINE VISION

It was the year 1064, the feast of Easter had come to an end
and the last mass had taken place. It was late at night and
Matilda, Duchess of Normandy, sat alone in the new abbey
at Caen. All was quiet, just as she liked it, when she wanted
time with God, Jesus, and the apostles. To say that she was
a devout Christian would be an understatement. Some
would even say she was an extreme zealot. Although well
loved by the general population who considered her a
living saint and the mother of Normandy, many at court
feared her. She was the undisputed power behind Duke
William. Her personal bodyguards stood outside the main
and side doors on full alert. Over the years since her
marriage to Duke William she had become as paranoid as
her husband. In his case it was only to be expected, since
from the age of eight when he became Duke of Normandy,
until the age of about twenty, there had been numerous
attempts to depose and even murder him. Many of his
bodyguards and advisors had perished during these years. It
was only when, at the age of twenty, he led his army and
defeated his enemies and the rebels that he was able to end
the insecurity. Now he was feared throughout Europe. His
enemies called him 'William the Bastard' - not only
because of his 'low' birth mother, but because he could
unleash terrible retribution on those who opposed him.
Matilda, on the other hand, was from one of the greatest
noble families in France, but as a woman in a man's world
she had quickly learned how to survive and wield subtle

power without antagonising her husband. She looked like a small, pretty, defenceless woman, but behind that exterior was a woman with character equal to any king in medieval Europe. Even her father, Count Baldwin, the true leader of France, was afraid of her.

At the age of twelve, Matilda had started having visions about her future and these had led to her agreeing to her marriage to such a man as Duke William. As she sat and meditated, she started to consider the doctrine of the trinity - the Father, the Son, and the Holy Spirit – the three cornerstones of Christianity. What was God trying to reveal to her? Why was three so important? She closed her eyes and waited. Yes, a vision was forming. She could see three grey clouds that gradually formed three distinctive shapes. They were three people, but who were they? One was small and the other two were tall. Colours started to emerge and then the detail. All were Norman men with their distinctive Norman haircuts. The small man was well built and dressed as a jester, or jongleur as they were known as in France, and the other two looked like twins dressed as Norman soldiers.

She was sure she could hear God speaking to her: 'I will send you three men. You will know them by their names - Turold, and the twins called Richard. They will come to you by the day of Ascension. Be ready. They are my gift to you, my beloved Matilda.'

The vision suddenly disappeared.

Matilda broke down and sobbed. She could not believe it. The time was near. Her holy crusade to save the English peoples would soon begin. She let shout, 'Hallelujah! God be praised.'

Outside, her guards heard her, and rushed into the church thinking that she was in mortal danger. Master Jedick was first to reach her, and instinctively grabbed her and held her close to protect her from any assailant.

Matilda was not amused. 'Remove your unclean hands and body from my person immediately.'

Master Jedick knew only too well that he must obey even though he was enjoying the embrace. 'Your Grace, we thought your, um, most regal person was under threat. You know we would all rather die than see you come to any harm.'

Matilda rearranged her dress and hair, calmed down and smiled at her most valued agent. This startled Master Jedick, as a smile from Duchess Matilda was like a snarl from a lion just before it was about to pounce. 'Dear Jedick, my most loyal spy, sit and pray for the rest of the night, and consider carefully your numerous sins, and my command never to touch me again on pain of death. Only my husband may touch my person.'

She turned to the other guards, 'Please escort me back to the castle. I feel unclean and sullied and in need of a bath. You, Master Jedick, can stay here and reflect on your sins. You are very lucky that I am in a good and forgiving mood!'

Master Jedick sat alone in the abbey, thanking God that he was still alive. He had indeed learnt an invaluable lesson that night. His dear Duchess Matilda had a very desirable body but it would never be in his arms again. Love was indeed bittersweet, but in his case more bitter than sweet. He had to agree with her that he did have many sins to confess, but then God already knew that.

KING EDWARD AND TUROLD-A BRIEF HISTORY

Turold was the principal jester at King Edward's English royal court. King Edward had met Turold's Norman-born father, Dwarf Rollo, while exiled in Normandy. Dwarf Rollo was a leading exponent of the art of being a court jester or as they were called in Normandy, a jongleur. Edward was exiled there and under the protection of the Duke of Normandy, having fled the Danish invasion that saw the Danish Viking King Cnut take the throne of England. Prince Edward spent many miserable years there with his brother Alfred, while his Norman-born mother, Queen Emma, married Cnut following the death of her English husband and the boys' father, King Ethelred. Edward grew attached to Dwarf Rollo and often said that he was the only ray of sunshine in his world of despair. Of course, Dwarf Rollo's comical skills as court jongleur helped. He added comedy, sparkle and colour to all formal proceedings and events. What a jester he was. His singing of exciting and bloody tales and sagas, his tricks and bawdy jokes, certainly amused Edward.

In the summer of 1040 Edward's half-brother, Harthacnut, became King of England on the unexpected and sudden death of King Harold Harefoot. In 1041 King Harthacnut invited Edward to return to England and help him rule the country. His mother, Queen Emma, was behind the reconciliation. Edward brought a household including Dwarf Rollo, his family, and many Normans. In 1042 Harthacnut died suddenly at a wedding feast, and poisoning was suspected although never proved. Edward denied his involvement but the rumours continued throughout his reign. Only Edward, Bishop Stigand (later archbishop of Canterbury) and God knew the truth.

Edward's reign was not easy. One English lord had been a real problem - the Earl of Wessex, Lord Godwin. He was, as the saying goes, as sly as a fox and as slippery as an eel. He had been the close advisor of both King Cnut and his bastard son, King Harold Harefoot, and was complicit in the death of Edward's poor brother, Prince Alfred, when both he and Edward had undertaken their ill-fated project to take the English throne by force in the year 1036. Edward escaped with his life but Alfred was captured after being betrayed by Earl Godwin. His fate was even worse than his guards' who had been brutally slain in Surrey after being wined and dined by Earl Godwin and then captured as they slept unarmed in their beds. Prince Alfred, in contrast, had been taken to Ely where he was tortured and had his eyes plucked out before being murdered. It had been a warning by the brute King Harefoot to Prince Edward. This greatly affected the pious young Edward. Edward knew those to blame were of course King Harold Harefoot and Earl Godwin, and swore an oath before God that he would revenge his brother's torture and murder.

How the fortunes of Edward had turned. He was now King of England and the son of Dwarf Rollo, Turold, was the court jester and a great friend and advisor of Edward's. Certainly, God had decided to reward Edward despite his sins. Edward's rule had been generally a peaceful one and this stability had made England richer than ever before, but Edward still had severe problems.

Although initially banned from the kingdom, the Godwin family had returned with a large fleet and army. They were too powerful to be repulsed by King Edward especially as Earl Godwin was well supported by the English earls who resented all the Normans at court. Edward was forced to return Godwin's lands and titles, and to marry Godwin's daughter, Edith. Edward could not love Edith as a wife so the two of them agreed that he would treat her as a daughter and she would think of him as a father. Edward told Turold that he could not face having sexual relations with the daughter of a murderer. He added that whenever he had taken hold of her naked body, and looked to kiss her lips, all he could see was Alfred's bloody face with two empty sockets where his eyes should have been. He had therefore remained without issue, and this was a problem.

There were many who thought themselves heirs to the crown of England. The main claimants were King Sveyn of Denmark (a descendant of King Cnut) and the bastard son of Duke Robert, Duke William of Normandy. They both wanted to wear the English crown. Edward had underestimated Duke William. He had befriended him during his long exile in Normandy and had listened to William's case for becoming King of England due to being related through no other than Edward's mother, Emma. In addition, in 1051, William further argued that his new young wife, Duchess Matilda, also had a blood claim through being related to Alfred the Great himself. According to the duke, Edward had originally agreed in 1040 that William would become the next King of England following Edward's death if Edward became king and had no legitimate son. Edward disputed that such an agreement existed, although he admitted he had written a letter in 1051 indicating that such an arrangement might be possible. William had a good memory, ambitions above his birth, and an extremely determined and influential wife.

Coincidentally, Edward had become extremely friendly with Matilda over the years, since they saw eye to eye on most religious matters. Their friendship came to a head in 1051 during William's visit to London, where he had sworn his support for Edward and promised military help if required. Matilda had also visited England, but in secret. Matilda and Edward had several lengthy theological discussions, and their mutual love of the bible had led to something more physical during one particular night, with fateful consequences. Both had felt so guilty that Edward swore to God that he would never lie with another woman and Matilda made a solemn vow to God that she would never return to England nor betray William again.

TUROLD'S TROUBLED EVENING

It was a lovely spring early evening in the year 1064. Turold whistled as he walked down the lane leading to his small home. He was composing a bawdy song about the Danes and a bloody saga about the Viking gods, that for some strange reason, given Edward's pious nature, seemed to continually amuse him. Such songs and sagas were always well received by the Saxon royal court.

His walk was more of a sequence of skips, jumps, sways, and bounces. This was the dance to go with the new song, along with synchronised juggling of his jangling balls. In addition, he would enact King Cnut's attempt to hold back the tide, which would end in one very soggy Turold and hopefully a great deal of laughter.

He may have been less than four foot tall but, being part of the royal court, he had a high social standing in the community. He was now in his mid-twenties and, other than his height, was well built, with nice rounded features, a lovely smile, and good teeth. His father, Dwarf Rollo, had often said to him that he was not ugly enough to be a great jester, but Turold made up for it in skill and personality along with heavy cosmetics. He was an expert in creating a pox-holed face using masses of makeup and pottage. He waved at his neighbours as he continued his tune and dance. The onlookers just couldn't help loving this strange foreign man. He was generally well liked and respected by all who knew him.

Everything in London was in hues of brown. *Very depressing,* he thought as he whistled. The houses were brown and the mud-covered potholed clay roads and lanes were brown. The water in the deep potholes was brown, even the people were brown, all dressed in coarse brown cloth with matching dirty faces. *There is only one colour throughout London Town,* he thought. London Town was very drab. This was in sharp contrast to the vibrant colours at the royal palace. He looked down at his clothes. *Yes,* he thought, *I blend in alright.* Light brown linen shirt (it should be white but where can Londoners find any clean water?), a brown knee-length woven tunic tied with brown cord, brown leggings, socks, and shoes, all covered with a dark brown cloak. He was starting to feel depressed. *And another thing,* he thought, *everything and everybody is smelly and dirty.* Turold's problem was that he had seen and smelt a better world being court jester, and that had made him realise that there was a clean world beyond the slums of London. He was not contented and ignorant like his small-minded neighbours. *And what about the external and internal parasites?* He was getting depressed.

'No, no, NO!' he cried, thinking of the brightly coloured clean clothes in the bag that he carried over his shoulder. He had a fine life compared to most, due to the generosity of Edward. *I have a lot to be thankful for and nothing is going to spoil my good mood.* He was wrong as usual.

By now he had reached the small one-roomed house provided by the king. A typical peasant-style London dwelling, it was a squat thatched rectangular cottage, its one room warmed by a central fire supplemented by a rotting smelly warm pile of straw in a small pit in one corner. The walls were oak timber-framed with a London clay infill. He pushed the front door open and it fell with a clatter on the floor, just missing the dog.

'Blast,' he muttered, putting the door back into the void, 'I should have fixed that by now.'

The dog turned and growled. Inside the home, from the dim evening light coming through the south facing windows (another standard feature of peasant housing so as to avoid the worst of the weather), he could just make out a small woman stirring the contents of a large cauldron on the firebox.

'Where's my supper, wench?' Turold asked his wife as he entered the hovel, falling over the dog, which gave his leg a nasty nip in retaliation.

He picked himself up off the clay floor and brushed the straw off his clothes and onto the dog.

'You're late, you wastrel, so it's in dog Lowell's stomach,' replied his wife, Megan.

Turold scowled at Lowell and said, 'Then put the dog in the cooking pot. I'm famished.'

Megan and Turold loved each other but they both had wicked tongues. She called him her 'little rabbit' because of his large ears (and other things) and he called her 'my sweet sow' because of her snoring. Turold looked at the dog and it snarled at him. It had never liked Turold, ever since he had kicked it in the soft parts for mauling his equipment. The feeling was mutual. There was something about Turold that brought the worst out of most four-legged animals. He could never understand it.

Megan pointed to the shelf in the corner and replied, 'There's some three-day-old bread and cheese that just needs its mould cut off over there,' and continued knitting some woollen tights.

'That dog eats better than me.'

His wife laughed. 'I know he does. He doesn't splatter food all over the walls like you do, and he doesn't release wind at the table.'

Turold nodded. He had to admit that he got a lot of new entertainment material from his wife. In fact, he often thought that they ought to be a double act, but at four foot three she was just too tall, and she might outshine him and that wouldn't do at all. Turold sat down on the sleeping bench. He looked at the tapestries hanging on the wall. *She has a point,* he thought, as he recognised some of his past meals on them.

'Look, Megan, about my flatulence,' he tried to explain, 'that's just artistic expression, it's an art form, and part of my craft and I have to practise daily.'

Megan nodded. 'And you certainly stink this place out on a regular basis that's for sure!'

Turold went on. 'Well, dear Megan, in any case, what's in the pot over the fire? I'll have some of that.'

'If you wish. It's your shirts. You can get your teeth into them if you want.'

Turold knew he stood no chance of getting any food. 'Well, I'm off to the alehouse for some ale and a meat pie.'

'Oh, leaving me again, are you? Have you ever found any meat in one of those unique pies?' she asked.

'No,' he replied, 'but I live in hope, you have to at my height.'

'Well, just think on this, my dearest heart, there's a lot of people dying in this town but very few graves. If you see any bits of clothing in those pies, be warned. And on the subject of health and safety, just make sure you whistle as you walk in the dark or you may get stepped on.'

He couldn't think of a reply and the dog was looking longingly at his leg again so he left, pursing his lips, and whistling.

Turold pondered, *today is proving difficult*. Old Edward was more depressed than usual and had found no comfort in Turold's craft; his comic song about Harold Harefoot (the devilish progeny of King Cnut) and the sheep had fallen on deaf ears. Turold had taken over duties from his father upon his death. His father had had a large funeral, but small coffin. Turold had inherited his equipment and had promised to continue the traditions. Unfortunately for Turold, Edward was preoccupied with the completion of Westminster Abbey and the saving of his soul. He was nearing the end of his life and wished its dedication as soon as possible. He had made an oath to God to build a magnificent abbey and he had to keep it or be damned for all eternity. As a pious man, Edward found some consolation in his bible, saying, although not as funny as Turold, it still gave him great comfort, especially at night. Turold had always felt very sorry for Edward as he could think of much better things to do during the hours of darkness. Edward had read the bible to Turold many times, translating it into French, as the dwarf had no understanding of Latin. The Christian Church was a significant part of everyday life in England at that time. Each man and woman tried to take extreme care of their souls, thinking more about the afterlife than life on earth. However, many took out protection insurance by continuing to practise paganism. Religion was indeed taken very seriously, especially if it meant a great number of saint days involving drinking, feasting, and cavorting.

Tomorrow was going to be an important day. Edward was going to have an audience with Earl Harold Godwinson, son of the late evil Earl Godwin, and he wanted Turold's presence. Edward was increasingly reliant on the dwarf's honesty and large well-tuned ears. Harold was one of the few happy things in the old man's life. Following the death of his father, Harold had grown into his role as protector of the interests of the realm, and as a relatively honest man, helped rule the country and increase its prosperity and the popularity of Edward. Edward now thought of Harold as the son he would never have.

As Turold walked down the street he suddenly realised how late it was, and the risk he was taking in being outside just before most folks went to bed. He was too late to take evasive action as the contents of a bucket were thrown out of a hovel's window and landed on his head.

'Shit,' he swore, and he was right.

Turold chastised himself for walking on the north side of the road. This was usually a good choice at night since the dwellings on the north side had their windows looking onto the road and therefore gave out dim lighting in the dark. However, one needed to avoid certain times of the night. He had debated with a friend whether it was better to have little rooms with buckets installed in houses but they finally agreed that the smells and flies were best kept outside. Luckily Turold was near a horse trough and although the water looked extremely unhealthy, he plunged in for a soak.

Later, as he stood next to the alehouse fire, his clothes steaming away as they dried, and looking for non-existent meat in his pie, he had to agree that God was not smiling on him at present. The pie had been invented by the current owner. It would be another 300 years before pies became a popular form of food throughout England. The English were all very conservative when it came to their diet. Anything new or foreign was looked upon with extreme suspicion. Turold thought, and decided that tonight he would pray for his king and himself. He would ask for good fortune, but knowing his luck he would probably wake up tomorrow one foot taller and therefore an unemployed giant jester.

By now he was talking to himself, 'It's all the will of God I'm told, but I think it's extremely unfair if you have no knowledge of Latin to read the bible, and no money to offer to God for forgiveness or help. The path to the afterlife for those who are uneducated and poor is very precarious. It does seem to me that the rich and educated have an advantage in such matters.'

No-one was listening but many noses smelt the pong. Suddenly his fellow drinking companions picked him up and took him outside.

'Come on headbutt, let's get that nasty niff sorted out, it's souring the drink,' exclaimed Svien, holding his broken nose as he spoke.

Turold had to agree, so into the horse trough he went, but this time Ivar Onefoot poured the remains of his flagon of ale over Turold's head and gave him a good scrub. Turold thought: if he wore his facial hair like the English, he would soon have both curly hair and a moustache. But he kept his hair in the Norman tradition, shaved at the back and short on top. It was the family custom, made him stand out from the crowd and added to his appearance during his performances. It also kept down parasite infestation to manageable levels.

'Alright Frenchie, let's all get back inside, drink ale, and you can tell us some of your colourful stories!' shouted Svien.

Turold's face went bright red as he shouted, 'I'm not French! I'm Norman and don't you forget it!'

Svien laughed. 'Don't blow your head off, Norman Turold or you'll do yourself a mischief.' Svien put his arm around his friend's neck and they walked back into the alehouse.

The owner was always pleased to have Turold's presence. Turold was a legend in the area, not only because of his knowledge of the royal court but also because of his storytelling and skills. Drunkards would travel miles just to hear his jokes and his songs. This meant good business for the owner and free drinks and meatless meat pies for Turold. A good arrangement for all concerned. Turold had now mastered the English language and had recently been experimenting with adding certain French words to his stories, such as beufe, porc, and such like, and gradually the locals had been accepting these words and using them in everyday conversations to the confusion of those from outside the area. *Who knows*, Turold thought, *this could lead to people being able to have reasonable conversations, not limited to the English language, which often led to misunderstandings and fights. I'll get these English civilised if it kills me.*

After his stories, there followed the English telling their jokes which, quite frankly, went over Turold's head (not that difficult considering his height). Finally, the ceremonial alehouse brawl ensued and Turold's legendary groin head-butting won the contest. Then they all said their farewells, and left for their own hovels where wives, children and dogs were waiting. Some to shout and moan, some to cry, and some to bark and bite. Turold staggered home, drunk but worried and in a bad mood.

Meanwhile, his wife considered her life as she sat by the fire. The dog was licking its bits and pieces and she looked at it and thought, *I wish my husband could do that, it would make such a difference in bed.* The dog growled since it could smell Turold at 500 paces. The twins slept soundly in their sleeping drawer in the cupboard, save for occasional wind (they were their father's sons alright). *He's a funny little Norman, but he's faithful, and we're well off compared to most people. And although my husband is small, he's well-built and often makes me laugh and giggle at night. Let's hope he's in a good mood when he gets back.* She was going to be disappointed.

WORRIED HAROLD GODWINSON

Earl Harold Godwinson was worried. He had an important meeting with King Edward, at his king's insistence. *What's that going to be about?* he wondered. He reflected on how he'd achieved his current position. He knew he had no imagination or political awareness but he was strong, was one of the best warriors in the country and could organise and inspire an army. This he'd shown at the battle against the Welsh in 1063 when he and his brother Earl Tostig had defeated King Gruffydd. He had then returned to London and presented the unfortunate former King of Wales to King Edward, minus his body. This had naturally rather upset the Queen of Wales and the Welsh. Harold laughed. His reflections continued.

He came from a noble family, royal blood flowed through his veins and he was well admired and liked by many English men and women, although more so in the south of the country. He was aware of his faults and weaknesses, especially when dealing with conniving and untrustworthy men. Being honest and true came with its drawbacks. However, Edward was now treating him as his own son, and by the will of God, things looked well set for him. But he had a family issue to discuss with the king that required Edward's permission for him to leave the country. Harold had sworn an oath to God, and it was time for him to carry out the required task. He could not go back on his oath without bringing the wrath of God down upon him and his family. So was the will of God. He looked lovingly at his mistress, Edyth Swanneck, as she lay next to him. They were married in the eyes of the law but not those of the English Church or God. She was the best thing in his life, along with their dear sons. He would give up his life for them. Yes, Harold was indeed worried. He had had a bad dream the previous night where God had deserted him in his hour of need. What did it mean? What did the future hold for him? What had God in mind?

'Well, my love, I must depart now and leave your soft warm embrace for I have an appointment with King Edward.'

'Can you not stay and kiss me just one more time before you leave?' she replied.

'A mere kiss, yes, but anything else will surely make me late, and that would certainly displease Edward.'

'You must either displease him or me as I will take no less than a kiss and a cuddle.'

Harold, it seemed, would arrive late for his meeting.

OLD KING EDWARD

An old man sat on his throne in his palace at Westminster, and pondered. At least, he thought, he had survived the harsh winter and now it was early summer. But how many more summers did he have left? It was May 1064 and King Edward was feeling his age. He has been King of England for over twenty years. Unusually, England had seen comparative peace and prosperity and good government. He had been blessed with Harold, the son of that murderer, Earl Godwin, who had met his rightful fate, thanks to the will of God, helped by the hands of men. Yes, Harold was the son he never would have. Due to his issues of intimacy with his wife, the couple remained childless. He had never had a mistress, in fact the only sexual experience he'd had was that one night of passion with a certain duchess, and that had only led to a great deal of guilt and a vow of celibacy. In his twilight years he'd contented himself with his friends, Harold, and his jester, Turold, and his closeness to God. His current project, the construction of Westminster Abbey, was going well, although he was deeply concerned that he may not live to see it finished.

Meanwhile, Queen Edith was entertaining Earl Edmund in her bedchamber.

He exclaimed, 'What a wonderful jewel sitting so sparkling on your throat!'

'Yes, it is. It's part of the royal jewels handed down from queen to queen over hundreds of years. However, it comes with a terrible curse.'

'Oh, and what is that my precious?' questioned Edmund while holding her tenderly and stroking her hair.

'A decrepit and senile King of England,' she replied.

They both laughed.

'You are more of a daughter to him than a wife.'

'Well, I certainly do not do with him what I'm about to do with you!'

The Royal Palace of Westminster was a kaleidoscope of colour and such a contrast to brown old London Town. Common people who visiting could not believe such colours existed. Indeed, any new servants of the palace who ventured into the highly decorated and furnished rooms for the first time were often unable to move, as if blinded by what their eyes were gazing at. Turold, however, was used to it all. He hardly noticed the colourful woven tapestries on the walls, and the bright red furniture. Turold had changed into his costume for the day, vivid red velvet trousers, curled up green shoes with bells on the end, numerous other bells about his person, a nearly-white shirt with embroidered lions, a patchwork cloak with deep pockets for his equipment, and a floppy yellow hat festooned with stuffed black birds. He was ready.

Turold entered the throne room. 'Good morning Your Grace, where is that Earl Harold Godwinson?'

'He is late, Turold, probably on some important official assignment or other,' Edward replied.

'You're right, I heard that he often has to satisfy the requirements of a local large white bird before coming to the palace.'

The king laughed. 'We all have our weaknesses for the wild life of England, and a certain swan is his. Mine, in contrast, is hunting as you know, although these days I'm not sure whether I could mount my horse or let loose an arrow without someone's assistance.'

Harold blustered in. He could not think of an excuse, having no imagination, but then none was required. King Edward struggled to his throne, sceptre in hand, with all the looks of an old, lanky, bearded druid dressed in robes of green and gold and wearing a weighty gold crown and a large sapphire ring on his right hand.

'Come near to me, Harold, I must talk quietly to you on an important matter.'

'Yes, Your Grace,' Harold replied, 'but does this Norman jester have to be here in our presence? He could be a Norman spy. No offence, Turold.'

'None taken My Lord.' Turold jangled his bells.

The king looked at the two of them, so different in every way. *If you combined them*, he thought, *you could make one great man.* 'Firstly, please both drop this "Your Grace" when we are alone; we are all friends here.'

Harold turned and glared at Turold and in retaliation Turold jangled his bells noisily again, which he knew would annoy Harold.

Edward continued, 'My faithful friend the jester acts for my failing ears. They are indeed large enough, and his mind is as sharp as any at remembering conversations which, unfortunately, I easily forget these days.' Edward winced as he adjusted his seating position. *This throne*, he decided, *needs extra padding for my piles and anal tear*.

Edward closed his eyes, then following the sound of more bells, refocused his sluggish mind. 'Well, Harold, as you know I treat you as my son, and you have treated me both as rightful King of England, and as a father following the unfortunate death of yours.'

'Yes,' Harold replied, 'in that you are correct, and it was such a coincidence that my poor father perished at that Easter feast on the very anniversary of the death of your brother, Alfred, betrayed by my father, and then so horribly mutilated by that devilish Danish king.'

Edward looked uncomfortable, and coughed. 'Eh, yes, a great coincidence indeed.'

Turold noticed Edward's unease, so jangled his bells again.

Harold continued to speak. 'And then there were the sudden deaths of both those Danish kings of England, Harold Harefoot and Harthacnut!'

Edward coughed again, this time more severely, gazed heavenward, and whispered something, and gave the sign of the cross with his ring finger. He moved quickly on. 'Don't dwell on the past, Harold my boy. We must look forward. Now listen to me, Harold, this is the matter to hand. I am old and dying, but have no direct heir. This will surely lead to trouble. As you know, your sister Queen Edith and I have problems and we seem unable to carry out the required act and bear fruit, although I understand she can get great satisfaction elsewhere. What you might not know is that I may have made a foolish promise, though no oath, to that dastardly Duke William, the promise being that he would become King of England upon my death if I had no sons. He has a large army and many allies. He has the mind of a devil snake and will surely consider the bargain sealed. These Norman men are descended from Vikings and cannot be trusted to uphold English law and justice. In addition, his wife is a fervent Christian who seems heaven bent on cleansing the English Church through some sort of holy crusade. I have thought long on this and prayed to God and believe that it is His will that you, dearest Harold, and not William, who should become King of England upon my death.'

Edward sat back and closed his eyes, it had been a long speech, and a great strain on his increasingly feeble brain. For once, a clear thought came to his mind. *Yes, that one night of true passionate and spiritual union between Duchess Matilda and me is the main cause of Normandy's threat to England, not Duke William*. Not only had guilt been behind his promise to William, but his solemn vow of celibacy had led to there being no son to inherit the throne of England. God had indeed punished him for his sin.

Harold was taken aback by the news. He was dumbfounded. Turold broke the silence by jangling his bells again.

Eventually Harold spoke. 'Your Grace, I mean, eh, Edward, I had no idea that you would consider me worthy.'

'Ah yes, that is your weakness, you've no real ambition or imagination.' The sickly old man cackled, coughed, and spat in his spittoon. He looked carefully at the colour of its contents, which showed some blood amongst other things slithering and diving amongst the dark sludge. *That doesn't look too good* he thought. 'Well, that is my decision and I will not change my mind,'

Harold could only reply, 'By God's will Your Grace, oh damn, sorry, Edward.' *But is it the will of God*, he thought, *or just the will of a dying old man?*

Harold started pacing up and down. He was both excited and worried. Edward had originally chosen his half-nephew Edward (many royal families had no imagination when it came to names), to be the next king. He had been saved from the Danes by being sent into exile in Hungary with his family. He was known by the English as 'Edward the Exile' since the English too had little imagination when it came to nicknames. It had taken three years to persuade his nephew to return to England, together with his family and wealth. The young prince had been uneasy when he'd stepped ashore in 1057, and as it turned out, he was correct to be so reluctant, because within days he dropped down dead at a feast. Poison was suspected, but by whose hand? Many thought that the Duke and Duchess of Normandy were behind it, given their agenda. Duke William had visited England in 1051 for discussions with Edward and no doubt had planted many spies and agents there. In addition, William went on to dispose of another contender in 1063, Edward's French nephew, Walter. Both Walter and his wife mysteriously died in Norman custody while having a meal. Eating was indeed a hazardous activity during these times. William suggested it had been some terrible accident due to some bad mussels or oysters, but most believed otherwise. Harold mused. *What would God have in store for me if it were known that I was next in line? I must accept that when the fateful day finally came, the Witan (the English Council) would have the final say and they would prefer the strong hand of the wealthiest and most popular Saxon man in England. In other words, poor me. Edward must have concluded that I was indeed the best option.*

He stroked his fine Saxon moustache and continued musing. *There will be many powerful, dangerous, and ambitious men around when Edward finally died. It would be a miracle if I remained king of England for more than a year. By God's will however, I, Earl Harold Godwinson, would do my duty and survive.*

Edward had been sleeping while Harold had been pacing up and down and thinking, but as soon as he started snoring, Turold gave him a prod with his jester stick.

Edward woke with a start and gathered his wits. 'Ah, yes, Harold. Now I understand that you wish to discuss a project with me, so be quick as I'll need my mid-morning prayer, confession, and sleep soon.'

'Yes, Your Grace, sorry, Edward, as you're aware, my brother and nephew are both held by Duke William. They were sent there by you and held on your command to ensure the good conduct of my father.'

Edward sighed, then coughed, and spat in his spittoon. 'Yes, and I'm truly sorry for my action. I think William now sees political gain in continuing to keep them as hostages.'

'Well, I've sworn an oath to God and it is time for me to go to see him and demand their release.'

Edward nodded. He'd never seen Harold so resolute, and considered his reply. Turold gave a comical birdcall, representing a raven, the bird of impending doom. 'Beware, Harold. You would be his equal on the battlefield, but he and his wife will surely tie you up in knots due to their political cunning before you know it. You will be so bound that you will be unable to free yourself or your kin without giving something important to Duke William in return. Heed my words beware Duke William's wife, Duchess Matilda. She sees most of the English as pagans or at best, lapsed Christians, in need of saving, and believes that God wishes her to launch a crusade so that she may save the souls of my subjects from the Devil himself. I warn you not to go. She told me in a recent letter that God Himself has promised to send her three men in order that she may carry out His will. You must abandon your kin and be content with your current prospects.'

Harold sighed. 'No, I cannot. I have sworn an oath before God and must go.'

'Then go sir, but I foresee that this adventure will lead to nothing but danger and trouble, for you, and your family, and for my kingdom.'

Edward shut his eyes and sighed. Suddenly he received an inspired thought, as if from God. 'If you must go, take Turold with you. He is Norman by birth and speaks French. He also has a good brain and large useful ears. He will certainly be of help to you.'

Turold was crestfallen. He did not want to go on such a perilous journey. He and water were not good bedfellows and he suffered badly with seasickness. Harold was not too pleased either. He could never understand the performances of the dwarf, and what pleasure could be gained from someone jangling bells loudly or juggling his noisy balls?

However, Harold could not defy Edward. 'I will lend Turold my son's pony Thor for the journey to the port of Bosham on the Sussex coast. We will set sail after our prayers at the church there and our feasting at my manor house.'

Turold continued to worry. He and horses just didn't get on at all. However, he also could not defy Edward. 'Oh good,' Turold interjected, 'At the feast, I will give you a performance to be remembered for years.'

'That will not be necessary,' Harold curtly answered.

Well, this is going to be a happy journey indeed, thought Turold, *I hope there will be lots of ale and food.*

Edward was now asleep, snoring and dribbling, so the unnatural allies left as silently as they could, but with Turold's jingling and Harold's armour and sword, this was still a noisy exit. However, Edward's ears had shut down, so he was oblivious to the noise. He was now dreaming of God again and confessing his crimes against Harold's father, two Danish kings, and others, hoping that God could see the bigger picture, forgive him, and not punish England. Luckily for Edward, most of England considered him a devout and almost saintly man as no-one, other than Stigand the Archbishop of Canterbury (Edward's confessor) and of course God Himself, knew of his sins. Regarding his sins, Edward hoped that God would be satisfied with his sincere confessions and the building of Westminster Abbey.

It was God who would decide the fate of England. The Church of England and the English people still had a chance to tip the scales in their favour, but time was surely running out as Edward neared the end of his life. Earl Harold therefore had to be very careful that his actions did not antagonise God during this precarious period.

TUROLD'S LAST NIGHT IN LONDON

'Hello wench Piggy, I'm home!' exclaimed Turold as he stepped over the door and dog.

Lowell growled and Megan jumped, knocking over the log pile, which ended up on Turold's feet. He let out a yelp and the twins replied likewise as they played hunt the flea. It was strange but true, the twins saw very little of their father and too much of the dog, and as a result related more towards the canine, spending most of their time out of their drawer on all fours, playing with the dog, learning how to scratch off fleas and how to eat them. The dog, on its part, loved them as if they were his pups, and had become very possessive as a result, resenting any contact Turold had with them. This was increasingly a problem.

'Watch my feet ye witch!' Turold shouted.

Megan replied, 'Why so early? Have you been dismissed by the king? I told you that your comic rendition of miniature maypole dancing would not go down well as we English have no sense of humour when it comes to the sacred art of English dance routines.'

'No dearest, Edward is badly unwell today and has fallen asleep, and in any event has volunteered me to accompany Earl Harold to Normandy.'

'Eek!' Megan yelled. 'Don't go to Normandy my dear, they are not English, they smell funny, eat strange food and have a habit of poisoning any guest just for sport.'

'I don't want to go, but must, and as to poisoning, I think we in England are just as guilty. Why just think what happened to Earl Harold's father and that Edward the Exile, let alone the two previous Danish kings of England!'

'I thought it was just too much strong wine and rich food that led to their hearts stopping.'

Turold laughed. 'Let's just agree that their hearts did indeed stop but in very suspicious circumstances.'

Megan thought quickly and decided on tonight's events. 'Well, as you are home early and I may never see you again, eat your tea, play with the twins, then satisfy my desires, and not necessarily in that order.'

Turold mulled over the night's activities. 'What's for tea?'

'It's pottage,' Megan replied.

'You mean leftover bits and pieces?'

'That's right.' Megan giggled.

'Well then, feed it to the dog and I'll play with the twins, then play with you, and hopefully have time for a quick meat pie and ale as I'm feeling lucky tonight. This may be my last night in England so I might as well get as much done as possible.'

Once Lowell had been pacified by giving him a bone, Turold's playtime with the twins commenced. That consisted of sitting them in their drawer and pulling them round the back yard, putting them in their litter tray, and finally, bouncing them on his knee. They loved this and let out little yelps of delight. As was the custom in England, neither had yet been named just in case they did not survive the next plague. It had been over four years since the last one, so the next was surely overdue. While merriment ensued, Lowell finished his bone, and started growling loudly at Turold. This turned into snarling and gnashing of teeth, so since Lowell was bigger than him, Turold kissed the boys goodnight and placed them softly in their drawer, making sure the dog did not take advantage of his exposed rear end. The 'pups' settled down, had a scratch, and a lick, and after a few gentle yelps were fast asleep save for a few farts (a parting gift no doubt for their real father). The dog settled down too, next to the fire.

Now, thought Turold, *what's next on the list? Ah yes.* 'Dear Megan, do you feel tired?'

Megan looked at him, giggled and replied, 'I'll let you decide how I feel.'

All became quiet except for the occasional giggle from the sleeping-bench.

After his exertions, Turold slipped out of the bed while his wife snored contentedly. Down at the alehouse he had his pie containing one piece of meat together with something that looked suspiciously like a piece of linen, washed down with a flagon of ale topped with fly sprinkles. He then said goodbye to his friends.

'What, going so early?' Edgar, the rat catcher, questioned. 'You'll miss the brawl!'

'Yes, I must. I have to leave early in the morning with that idiot Earl Harold Godwinson.'

Turold continued, telling Edgar the latest news.

Edgar looked like the victim of many a plague. He had lumps and bumps all over his body, and while others had fallen arches, he had a bad case of a fallen chest, where his chest had ended up in front of his stomach. Edgar blamed the last plague caused by a surfeit of rats, flies, and fleas, but Turold thought it more likely to be because of a surfeit of meat pies and ale since he'd never seen Edgar outside the alehouse. Indeed, he believed he lived in that very dark corner of the establishment which was inhabited by the largest rats in England. It was said that once a knight entered the alehouse, and after agreeing to tackle the creatures, was allowed by the alehouse owner to become a permanent resident, in return for the supply of the main meat ingredient of the famous and unique Bow Bells pie. For some reason, Edgar was extremely interested in any royal court gossip, and would even sometimes take down notes. Turold had therefore concluded that Edgar must be a lost but well-educated knightly historian and rat catcher.

Turold returned home, only to find that Megan was awake and ready. *This has turned into a very eventful day indeed, a day to remember*, he thought. *It must surely be the will of God. For once He must be smiling on me.*

Unfortunately, he never did, nor would, understand God.

THE NORMAN SPY

Meanwhile, a shadowy character dressed in a black cloak swept into the alehouse, and sat in his usual seat near that dark, dank corner. It was indeed strange that he always appeared as soon as Turold left. Edgar approached this Norman spy carefully, as he was never sure what mood this strange man would be in. He was definitely a person not to be trifled with, especially given the situation Edgar's poor mother was in. Normandy was not the place for such a frail old lady.

'Well, mon Edgar, report, silver plate, immediatement,' the man hissed, or that's what Edgar thought he said, although he'd never understood what this rich man's tableware had to do with anything.

'Turold's going with Earl Harold Godwinson to see your master. They ride in the morning to Bosham,' Edgar whispered.

'Zut alors, I must send word to Normandy and report this before Harold Godwinson gets there. Duchess Matilda will surely find this pre-warning of great use. I will leave as we say, toot sweet, this will be of great importance, just like the news you gave me a few years ago about a certain exile returning to England. Well done mon ami.'

'How's my mum?' Edgar enquired.

'She is as we say, tres bonne, and here's her latest letter for you to read.'

With a puff of dust the spy was gone, leaving Edgar to read his mother's letter, supposedly dictated by her and written down by a Norman priest (as she could not write a word). Edgar was always amazed at her improving use of the English language - they must surely be teaching her well during her time in captivity. He hated the things he had to do to preserve her health, but you've only got one mum, and so she must come first.

His mother looked down from heaven with tears in her eyes. 'He was always a stupid lanky idiot!' she said to Mary as she strummed her harp. Joseph nodded as he sang a psalm.

STRANGE EVENTS AT GUILDFORD

'Well, we're on our way to Bosham, men. We'll soon be smelling the salt of the sea.'

Turold thought, *Harold was always one for the obvious!* Turold hated the sea. In his experience the sea meant the smell of seaweed and being bombed by seagulls the size of swans, and being seasick. *Harold looked a right fool on his small horse, his reins in one hand and a great big brown hawk on the other.* Turold could never understand falconry, although he knew Harold was one of the best at the so-called sport. Turold had thought it would be very comical to do an act with a talking stuffed hawk, but he'd heeded Megan's warning. She had thought it unwise since the English took the pastime of falconry as seriously as they did their maypole dancing. Turold did, however, have an act consisting of many birdcalls, including birds of prey, and on several occasions received standing ovations from the noblemen, especially when once he was attacked by a peregrine falcon while doing an impression of a great bearded tit. He rubbed the scars left by the claws. *I don't think I'll do that one again without checking first for any loose birds of prey.* Turold was positive that at last God was with him, and he hoped for once the seas would be calm. Even his little pony was well behaved, although it had to be given a flagon of beer before it let Turold sit on it.

Harold had been asked by Edward to break the journey at Guildford. Edward had requested that prayers should be said at the place where Harold's father, Earl Godwin, had betrayed Edward's brother, Alfred, and also at the field where all of Alfred's men had been executed. Edward had also asked Harold to inspect the Guildford Royal Mint. There were discrepancies between the amounts of precious materials used in the production of coins and the number of coins produced. Following some forceful interviews, the culprit confessed and was sent back to London for public punishment, which was another well-loved English pastime. After these tasks, the group stayed the night in an establishment for travellers on the Harrow Way, an old Roman road connecting the ancient towns of Winchester and Canterbury.

Everyone spent a peaceful and uneventful night except Turold, who was given the task of looking after Harold's hawk. The hawk spent the first hour glaring and squawking at Turold from its cage. Eventually Turold was forced to put a sheet over the cage and shove it in the darkest corner of his room. He was then able to settle down for the night, eventually dreaming of his two brave sons in their drawer.

About two hours later, his door opened and a shadow swished in. Someone whispered, 'Excusez-moi.'

Turold, three quarters awake, mumbled, 'Un grand verre de vin, s'il vous plait.'

He then rolled over and continued to sleep. This time it was Megan who was the subject of his dream.

The tall Norman silently searched the room and found the sheet in the corner. 'Ah, qu'est-ce que c'est?' he whispered.

Turold replied in his sleep, 'Et des mussels s'il vous plait.'

The spy then made the wrong decision and lifted the sheet. The bird awoke, glared at him, and started squawking loudly. It had heard the homing messenger pigeon that the spy was carrying under his black cloak. 'Zut alors.' The spy made it to the door in four seconds and had left the room before Turold had even opened his eyes.

Two minutes later Harold rushed in, exclaiming, 'What are you doing to my bird Alfonso? I give you one simple task and you end up upsetting my little precious. He'll be off his food for days now, he's sensitive you know.'

Harold picked up the cage, whispered some consoling words to the bird and stormed out of the room with it.

Turold was still coming back into the real world. He sat up and scratched his head and buttocks. 'What in heaven is going on?' He said out loud. He had no idea. All he knew was that the bird and cage had disappeared. Discounting the probability that the bird had just extended its wings through the bars of the cage and flown out of the window, and considering the commotion and the human voice, he decided that it must have been stolen. *I must tell Earl Harold*, but then he thought better of that idea. *No, I'll break the news to him in the morning*. Still half asleep, he turned over and went back to snoring, mumbling, 'It must have just been a nightmare.'

Meanwhile, the spy had dashed outside, written a short message, tied it to the pigeon's leg and released it. 'Voler vite, mon ami.' The pigeon cooed at his owner and headed south, its destination, the headquarters of Duchess Matilda's spy agency, special branch, in-coming post division. The spy mounted his horse and headed off in the direction of Bosham, thinking that just one last mission remained before he could relax and return to his family in London. Agent Cecil was one of Matilda's most valuable spies, and the network of spies that he had managed to create in England was formidable.

Turold awoke at daybreak. *Now where is that stupid bird?* He searched the room: no cage, and no bird. *It wasn't a dream and this is a nightmare,* he thought, panicking. He went next door to Harold's room and tapped lightly on the door. He could hear nothing but snoring. So, he opened the door, and was met by a pair of glaring eyes behind cage bars. Turold scratched his head, and other parts, as he left quietly, shut the door, and went downstairs for a call of nature. He couldn't understand it but there it was. He decided that he would not say anything about last night unless tortured.

When Harold and his guard arose an hour later, he had a lot to say to Turold about mistreating poor defenceless birds. 'You're on a final warning,' Harold concluded.

The day was bright and breezy as they set off on the next half of their journey to Bosham. Nothing untoward happened as they travelled southward towards the coast.

Harold was in a better mood as they passed the old Roman town of Chichester. 'Men, and dwarf, the weather is set fair for our journey to Normandy. God is indeed with us.'

As they eventually neared Bosham Church, the wind picked up. Surely a storm was brewing, thus proving that weather forecasting was not one of Harold's strengths.

FESTIVITIES AT BOSHAM

Harold jumped down from his horse. 'Look after my horse and bird while I pray, Turold.'

Great, Turold thought, *I like neither and they despise me*. Well, that was not quite true, horses loved kicking him and birds of prey enjoyed getting their claws into his flesh.

'I'll try My Lord, but a lot depends on their attitude.'

Harold turned to him as he entered the church. 'I suggest more beer, but just a few drops for Alfonso or he'll fall off his perch.'

Turold felt the hawk glaring at him through its eye covering, while Harold's horse seemed to be daring him to jump off the pony and come over and stroke his mane.

Harold and his party of knights clanked into the church. Harold knew the church well, as he had attended services there since he was a baby. Its claim to fame was that it was the resting place of King Cnut's young daughter, who at the tender age of eight had drowned in the millstream behind the church. As was the tradition, being lord of the manor, he said a prayer at her tomb. He continued kneeling as he thought about those care-free times with his brothers. As boys, they loved visiting Bosham. A sudden thought came to him. *What if the Danes still ruled England rather than Edward? Is there any truth to the rumours that Edward was behind the deaths of the last two Danish Kings of England? Surely, one way or another if it was not for Edward the current problem of Duke William wouldn't exist! Yes, it's Edward that has caused the Norman threat! If it was not for Edward, England would be safe from invasion by any foreign power!*

Harold sighed deeply, and stood up. 'Come men, let's get down to our prayers so that we can move on to my manor house for a good honest English feast before our journey to Normandy, where the food is inedible and the women ugly.'

In his sermon, the priest reminded the congregation of the story of St Wilfred who brought Christianity to Sussex so long ago. He advised all present to be as faithful and generous as they could, and to aspire to be as godly as St Wilfred was. He reminded them that the church roof needed repair and that there was a donations bowl just to the right of the door, and that all contributions would be well received in the eyes of God. The priest then concluded with suitable prayers, and Harold and his men left in an upbeat mood, with both lighter souls and purses. As they approached Turold he handed over his drunken charges and thanked God for his deliverance.

Harold was livid. 'Turold, look at my dear Alfonso, he's sleeping upside down in his cage! If he gets the mange, there'll be hell to pay! I warned you! I'll have to think of an appropriate punishment.'

Bosham Manor was a great English house. The ground floor was used by the servants since it was susceptible to flooding from the high tides, and the first floor was used by the Godwin family and guests. It was made up of a large feasting room and several bedrooms. The feasting room had large windows looking over the lovely sheltered harbour. Bosham was well favoured by the English for the start of any boating expedition due to its location, ease of access, and secluded inlet. The party arrived in good spirits, and jumped off their horses. Turold jumped more quickly and further than the others so as not to get a parting kick from his pony. It had been an uneasy truce between the two of them, but after the initial few kicks from both the ridden and the rider, Turold and the pony had come to an understanding. A flagon of beer every day was Turold's fare. The pony seemed to be looking at him and thinking *next time it'll be different as I'll be taller and will not miss.*

The hunting dogs that accompanied the party were intent on getting up close and personal with Turold, but were eventually bribed with some scraps of meat and taken away. With a swirl of cloaks, they entered the manor house and settled down in the hall. The servants quickly poured wine and ale in drinking horns and cups, and the feasting began, with toasts to God, King, England, and Harold. While this was going on, Harold had arranged for his ships to be made ready for the morning tide.

Harold felt pensive as he studied his food and drink, then a thought came into his mind. 'Turold!' he shouted, 'Come here my man.'

Turold wandered over slowly, thinking, *I'm not HIS man, I'm here to keep an eye on him and to report events to my king.*

'Come quick you slug!' Harold shouted even more louder. Harold was not used to anyone being below his best when doing his bidding, and he was getting annoyed.

Turold finally arrived, and Harold continued, 'Your usefulness is being underused, especially as I have already arranged tonight's entertainment and it does not involve you. So, I have decided that you will serve me more usefully as my official drink and food taster. It is an important job, although the length of your employ could well be short. At least while in this employ, your appetite will be satiated and if anything untoward does happen to you, your body and your family will be well provided for.'

Turold could not believe his large ears, but thought quickly before replying. 'This is indeed an unexpected honour My Lord, but I must decline on the grounds that I am a vegetarian.'

'Pigswill!' Harold shouted, 'The matter is settled. Now start your services immediately.'

What could Turold do? Looking at things optimistically, perhaps his stomach could endure any poison following years of eating alehouse pies and Megan's cooking. Also, it might be safer than being told to mind the horses or birds or the hunting dogs. He sat down next to Harold, his head just reaching the height of the tabletop. *This is what must be meant by the term sitting at high table*, he thought. Turold sighed loudly.

'Three cushions for my food taster!' Harold commanded.

With these in place, Turold could now manage to carry out his new duties. The wine and ale were top quality with hardly any foreign substances in them at all. A real treat, he was starting to enjoy this.

But Harold had other ideas. 'Just take a sip and stop gulping it down, you lowlife. Stop for one minute to see what happens, then pass the rest to me. The same goes for the food.'

The feast continued with much animated conversation and discussion regarding the journey to Normandy. However, Turold was finding it difficult to drink and eat much. Harold just snatched anything that had passed the 'Turold test'.

To make matters worse, the entertainment was provided by a troop known as 'The Pius Pipe Playing Pilgrims of Pevensey'. Turold could not believe it, English entertainment was so grey, no colour at all. He sulked and slurped Harold's ale loudly during the quiet bits. *If this is the best of what Pevensey can offer, then there's no chance that it will ever prove of any historical importance*, Turold thought.

Wrong again, God thought, as He chuckled.

Turold was stopping Harold enjoying the show and this annoyed Harold, who was trying his best to understand this Godly but boring performance, so he kicked Turold in the intermission. Turold thought, *this was all for God's benefit. Harold was trying to show to God that he was a true believer of the faith. However, God will not be so easily fooled.* It had all turned into a nightmare. *Things can't get any worse than this.*

Unfortunately, Turold would find out that he was wrong again.

A GREAT DAY FOR A BOAT TRIP

The revellers went to bed just after midnight and were woken at daybreak, since the tide was right. After a quick breakfast, they all made their way to the two boats that stood ready for the adventure ahead. The boats were of Viking design, with the head of a dragon at the front. One ship was larger than the other and was designed to take livestock. This was loaded with the horses. The longboats each had a large sail and many oars for power. The party waded out to their boats, pulling their tunics up to their waists and going barefoot, carrying various items including Harold's hawk and hunting dogs (well you never know when you might be able to sneak a bit of hunting into the schedule). Once on board, the men all started singing a Viking sea-shanty while raising the anchors, the masts, and sails, and then sat down to their task of rowing.

Ashore, a tall slender Norman wearing a black cloak with a red dragon embroidered on the back observed the ships as they headed out to sea. He muttered, 'Bon voyage,' and released his final homing pigeon, just as the boats left the inlet, rounded the headland, and joined the main estuary.

Aboard Harold's ship, the captain – known to many as Captain Reckless, being ever the optimist – yelled out to Harold, 'Should be a quiet crossing, but just as insurance, I strongly suggest you and your friends say a prayer or three!'

Turold had no idea what he should do, so he sat in a corner trying to look at the horizon as the boat bounced up and down on the waves. The wind had picked up and was getting stronger by the minute. He thought of jumping overboard, but that was not a solution since he could not swim.

Harold observed Turold's discomfort and laughed. 'Come on you sorry little man, I'm taking you home.'

Turold had not even reconciled himself to death by poisoning, and now there loomed another fate: death by drowning. The waves swept over the bow and soaked the occupants. As they left the shelter of the inlet, saying farewell to Hayling Island and the Witterings, they entered the Solent where the ships received the full force of the strong westerly wind. The men used their shields to defend themselves from the swell. The boats rocked and creaked. There was no turning back since the wind was too strong. It was blowing them off course from a southerly to a south-easterly direction and there was nothing that they could do to stop it. They looked anxiously at each other.

Harold tried to raise spirits by starting another song, but that was soon lost in the noise of the storm. 'Come on my stout men,' Harold exclaimed, 'let us not be scared, surely God is on our side and will deliver us from this hell!'

The boat sped past Selsey. They all looked at the land, hoping for a glimpse of Selsey Abbey and divine intervention. Even prayers to St Winifred did little to uplift their spirits. God had surely deserted them.

Hours passed as the rough sea continued to toss the ships.

Harold tried to improve morale. 'Men, let's all pray to God for protection. He will surely not abandon us in our time of need!'

Harold's men had by now concluded that Harold had a bit too much faith in God. Turold shivered as he lay in the bottom of the boat, making sure he kept a safe distance from the hunting dogs, which had already decided that he was to blame for their discomfort. *Why do I upset animals so?* But his question went unanswered. He sighed, and emptied the contents of his stomach over the side, forgetting that the wind direction meant that they came right back and hit him in the face. 'I don't remember eating that!' he exclaimed to the rower next to him, who looked as green as pea soup.

'No,' replied Rufus, 'I think that belongs to me, but you can keep it, there's plenty more where that came from!'

Turold sighed again. 'Well, that's something else to look forward to on this boat journey to unavoidable death.'

More hours passed, then Harold shouted, 'Put that French juggler on the dragon's head and get him to look for land.'

Turold shouted back, 'Norman not French!'

'Don't argue, let's not debate your place of birth, just get help to climb onto the back of the dragon and look out for rocks and such like. We must surely be near land.'

Harold, Turold thought, *remains annoyingly optimistic.* With some help from Rufus, Turold struggled onto the dragon, only to be hit by a sheet of water the height of Westminster Abbey. He nearly fell off, but clung on whilst praying. He scoured the horizon, looking for anything other than sea water. Eventually he thought he saw some shapes far off in the gloom but could not be sure.

One hour later, following the removal of a large crab, which had been trying to nibble his unprotected bits, he was sure he could see something, and he could hear something. Too late, he screamed, 'Possible land aaaaaahhhhoyyyy!' With those words, the ship crashed onto a sandy beach causing Turold to fall off the dragon's head into the water.

They had safely reached land, but where? Turold coughed and spluttered as he bounced up and down in the water. Rufus threw out one end of his oar and Turold grabbed it.

Rufus lifted Turold back into the boat exclaiming, 'Look men, what a strange fish I have caught!'

Everybody laughed except a very salty and wet Turold who wasn't amused at all.

One-eyed Gyrth threw out the anchor as if tossing an apple. He was called one-eyed not because of his lack of an eyeball but because that's how he tended to leave his enemies. It was said that he kept a collection of such parts in a large jar under his bed.

Harold jumped ashore. 'Thank you, God, for delivering us from the perils of the sea, by your will we have survived.'

Turold was convinced that God had merely saved them from one peril so as to inflict another on them. *No doubt something nasty is going to happen soon.* For once, he was right.

Harold turned to Turold. 'Keep your eyes open next time, you were too late with your warning, jester.'

Turold was starting to think that Harold didn't like him, but then the feeling was mutual.

LAND, SWEET LAND, BUT WHERE?

Once the occupants of the ships had disembarked, a fire was started and they all warmed and dried themselves by it. The next task was to find some food. Luckily the storm provided them with a great deal of stricken sea food that had washed up along the beach. Unfortunately for Harold, and fortunately for Captain Reckless and his fellow captain, the two captains knew exactly where they had landed but they weren't going to share their knowledge with the others. The captains had decided that they stood a much better chance of survival if they escaped as a small inconspicuous party of two scruffy salty seamen, so vanished unnoticed into the undergrowth.

Harold was unaware of this as he slapped Turold on the back. 'Happy to be back in Normandy, Turold?'

Turold looked around at the landscape. 'I'm not sure this is Normandy, it's too, um, French.'

Harold laughed. 'Don't be stupid. It's Normandy alright or I'll eat my helmet.' Unfortunately for all concerned, when a boy, Harold had also failed to grasp the basics of both navigation and geography.

Nearby, a French fisherman peered through the undergrowth and whispered to his dog, Chien, in French. 'Who are these Englishmen? Are we being invaded? No, I recognise that tall elegant man with the stupid moustache. I saw him at Dover castle a few weeks ago while I was taking brandy to a guard there. It's that Earl of Wessex, 'arold. I'll go to the count immediately and report this. There may well be a reward for us, Chien. I think it'll be meat on the table tonight rather than fish.'

Chien wagged his tail, but snarled at the diminutive Norman shivering by the fire some distance away. The man and his dog darted off towards the castle where Guy Count of Ponthieu resided. Harold and his companions had no knowledge of the danger they were in. If they had, they would have reloaded the ships quickly and sailed for a new shore, anywhere else but there, storm or no storm.

DUKE WILLIAM

Duke William was livid. He scratched his head and stroked his sword and then sharpened his long two-handed battle-axe. All these actions were bad signs, recognised by all who knew him, indeed many who observed these signs, were now under the lush green grass of Normandy.

'Where's that stupid Earl Harold Godwinson Wadard? my wife told me that he has set sail from Bosham, and so should have arrived on my shores hours ago. My men are strung out along the coast, dangling there like a vine of grapes but there has been no sighting. That's the last time I listen to her about important information that she and her agents have gathered from their contact at that London alehouse. Get my Knight Vital and my brother, Bishop Odo, immediately for a full report.'

Wadard corrected William without thinking which was often fatal when speaking to the duke. 'Your half-brother, Your Grace.'

William went as red as blood and gripped his long sword. 'What did you say?' he shouted.

'Eh, um, nothing, Your Grace,' Wadard replied, trying to get out of range. 'I'm sorry Your Grace, I'm suffering from horse riding fatigue after my long journey.'

Wadard practically ran for the door before William could decide on his next move. When the duke's battle-axe left his right hand, it was too late, and it merely imbedded itself in the closed wooden door.

Some two hours later, Odo and Vital entered the throne room. William was in no better mood, in fact, if possible, his demeanour was even worse. This was largely due to the performance of William's court jongleur, Dwarf Long Beard, whose impersonation of Edward offering the crown of England to a certain English royal exile had not gone down well. William had not been amused, and showed his displeasure in his normal way. The ex-jester was now in pieces and William was currently cleaning and sharpening his long sword. The moral is that one should never joke about such a matter in front of Duke William, especially considering his slender claim to the crown of England. There were many men ahead of him in the queue but as far as William was concerned whoever had the most strength and cunning had the most right, end of discussion.

Odo looked shifty as usual. Knight Vital looked anywhere but at the duke. He knew that William's eyes could kill at 100 paces, and he was well within range.

'What news, brother Bishop?' the duke asked.

Odo shrugged his shoulders, which was extremely difficult in his tight-fitting armour. 'Your Grace, he has probably drowned in the storm. We have had no sightings at all.'

William was irate. 'Look brother, you are in direct contact with God, so ask him.'

Vital tried to help calm the situation. 'Perhaps he's just late, delayed by bad weather.'

'If I have my way,' William shouted, 'he may well end up as late as his father!' This was as close to a joke that he could make, and all of his jokes contained more than a hint of harm and unnecessary violence.

Odo tried to distract William. 'What about a bit of light relief? Let's call for the jester, Dwarf Long Beard. Where is he?'

William laughed, pointing. 'He's here, there, under my throne, and on the walls.' This was another of his jokes.

Vital tried again. 'Your Grace, perhaps if we look at things logically, we may be able to determine Harold's location.'

'What do you mean?' William growled, continuing to sharpen his long sword with a stone.

Vital had to think quickly, which was not one of his best abilities. 'Well, we know he's left Bosham and given the direction of the winds, I can only conclude that the ships must have been blown off course, and that being the case, perhaps he ended up in Boulogne or Ponthieu.'

William charged towards him with his sword then at the last moment dropped it on the floor with an almighty clank. 'You know, Knight, I think you're correct, and you will be rewarded if you can locate him and his party within the next two days, so get some men and ride as hard as you can towards Guy, Count of Ponthieu. Insist on an audience with him as you're on my business and find out whether Earl Harold and his party have landed on his shores. If he says he has no information, then threaten him accordingly, and if necessary, suggest he will be entitled to a reward. That way you'll appeal to his worst nature. If you're sure he doesn't know anything, then carry on to the lands of Boulogne and do likewise. I want this Earl Godwinson handed over to me, preferably alive, but if this isn't possible, I require a dead body as proof of his demise. Either way I'll surely benefit in my quest to be the next

King of England, and as such you will be rewarded with lands taken from those Saxon pagans.'

Vital left quickly, knowing that the clock was ticking and his life was at stake.

Bishop Odo sat down next to William, making sure that he remained lower than his brother, who now sat on his throne again sharpening his blade (he found this very therapeutic). 'Is your plan on course dear brother?' Odo enquired.

'Yes,' replied William, 'I'm sure the pieces are going to fall into place one way or another. My will is greater than any man alive.' He was careful to say man rather than person given the dominating nature of his wife.

Bishop Odo had to admit that many a dead man would be able to testify to this if they had still been alive.

'It's a shame about Long Beard,' Odo observed.

William shrugged. 'I had grown tired of him anyway, and I hope that his replacement will be within my tight grasp within days. There is indeed someone who, according to my wife, will be more valuable to me than one hundred knights. As you know, she has divine Godly visions and is well informed!'

Odo didn't understand since he did not believe in God, so he asked permission to go to pray on William's behalf at the abbey in Bayeux, and prepare the funeral of Long Beard. William gave him leave to go, once he had found a servant, a bucket, and a shovel.

Odo smiled as he left. Within a few hours, he hoped to be in the arms of his latest conquest. It had been the duke that had made him Bishop. Being a bishop had proved extremely useful in his quest for the pleasures of the flesh and in becoming the second richest man in Normandy. If

William ever did succeed in becoming the King of England, Odo believed he could become the wealthiest man in the whole of Europe, by the grace and will of so-called God, if He did exist. Odo was a very cunning man and did indeed carry out his religious duties as required, and even commissioned the building of new abbeys and churches so as to pacify Matilda, who seemed to have a strange wish to purify all the peoples of Europe. As far as Odo was concerned, piety meant being boring and poor, and he wasn't in favour of either condition.

Matilda glided regally into the throne room. 'Well, my dear William, what have you been doing here?' She could see the servant clearing up the mess.

'I got upset, dearest,' he mumbled.

Matilda looked disapprovingly at her husband. 'We must be ready to receive our important guest.'

'If he arrives, and if he arrives alive,' William replied.

'Oh, he will arrive, God has spoken!' That said, Matilda swished out of the room, leaving William fiddling with his sword and mumbling to himself.

Despite her manner, Matilda was worried about the whereabouts of Earl Harold and God's first of the three who would carry out His will, but she trusted in God to have them delivered safely into her custody. God had told her in a vision that by his will and grace, her husband and family would rule England and would bring a proper respect for God to that country. This respect was lacking at present. She had sworn a solemn oath to carry out the will of God, and have magnificent churches and cathedrals built to hold the glory of God, and to inspire the English to be true believers. She had to concede that it would not be a bloodless endeavour, especially as William would be involved in the enterprise, but religious reformations never were. God would ensure the support of the Church of Rome in this venture. William was to be God's instrument and she was to steer him on his Christian crusade. So was the will of God, and nothing was going to stand in His way, including her brutish husband and that decrepit King Edward.

Matilda soon returned to her husband with another servant and bucket.

'How are the children?' William enquired. 'I am concerned about young Adeliza. We must find her a husband, otherwise we must send her to a nunnery.'

Matilda finished supervising the work of the servants then replied, 'She's only thirteen, dear, but I agree, and I hope I may have a suitable candidate. In fact, he is soon to be our guest!'

William screwed up his face. 'Surely not that wayward earl!'

Matilda concluded the discussion as usual, 'He will be more controllable as our son-in-law.'

William was now pondering. *What's my wife up to?*

'Now come William, its suppertime for you,' his wife declared.

'Yes dearest,' poor William replied, following her out into the corridor and wondering what was for supper. Hopefully wild boar, his favourite.

GUY THE RESCUER

If William was the Devil's son, then Count Guy was his
nephew. Count Guy danced around with gay abandon then
kissed his groom. He was so happy. *The wealthiest
nobleman in England has washed up on my shores. What
an opportunity to make some money! I will have Harold in
an iron grip, and if the dreaded Duke William did not find
out, things will turn out very well indeed!*

Count Guy was a middle-aged French noble with a
liking for the finer things in life. He was as cunning and
ruthless as William but preferred to be well behind his men
when there were sharp weapons about. He was a survivor,
and to be a survivor in that part of Europe, one had to be
capable of anything. His lands were between two powerful
rulers: William of course, and Count Eustace the Second of
Boulogne, one of William's relatives. Eustace was
descended from the great Charlemagne himself and had a
better right to the English crown than even William.
Eustace, however, was not as unscrupulous as William and
not as powerful. Power meant everything in the north of
France and William had it in abundance. Guy always had to
tread carefully with both rulers, which was on occasion
very confusing when they changed from being allies to
being foes. Guy had survived and meant to continue to
breathe. This was despite being imprisoned by Duke
William for two years following Guy's mistake of being on
the wrong side at the Battle of Mortemer in February 1053.

He soon learnt that if you lose against Duke William, you must pay a terrible price.

Guy shouted to his Captain of the Guard. 'Get twelve of your finest knights in shining armour along with twenty-four well-groomed horses ready as soon as possible, along with my hunting dogs and my falcon, Hugh. I'm going hunting and expect a large catch.'

The captain saluted and marched off in his bright pink tunic with matching boots. Captain Godfrey Long Shanks was meanwhile muttering under his breath. *Oh, God, please, not those colourful uniforms! They make us look so unmanly! The uncouth English are bound to laugh at us and not take our threats seriously!*

'Oh, and make sure their armour is well and truly polished and their faces and teeth are clean. Remind them that I will also be inspecting their fingernails.'

Godfrey shook his head and continued muttering as he left.

EDWARD THE WORRIED

Back in England, old Edward was worried. He had realised his stupid error almost as soon as Harold and Turold had left. Edward shook his head. *I've sent two sheep into the dragon's lair. I should have remained strong-willed and dealt with the Duke and Duchess of Normandy accordingly. Any consequences from this latest blunder will be the fault of no-one but myself. I should have commanded Harold not to go!* Edward coughed and spat in the royal privy bucket and thought, *that will give those damned doctors something to debate about when they examine the contents.* Edward was more worried about Duchess Matilda rather than Duke William. Edward had concluded within the last few years that she was even more dangerous than her husband, if that was possible. Matilda was both saintly and cunning. She had cast her spell on him when they had met for the first and last time all those years ago. However, he had since discovered that she was a Christian extremist, in fact no less than a fundamentalist, intent on purging England of all unbelievers and unrepentant sinners. She had written to him on several occasions and he knew her opinions only too well. She could not believe the state of the English Church and the take-it-or-leave-it attitude of the English people when it came to God. She had told Edward that the English Church needed reforming and that the excommunicated Archbishop of Canterbury, Stigand, should be removed from office. *Surely*, she argued, *if the Pope, as God's representative on earth, no longer recognises such a man as having any right to be part of the English Church, then any religious acts carried out by him in the name of God are basically blasphemous.* Edward wished he could get rid of Archbishop Stigand also, but that corrupt sinful cleric knew too many of his dirty secrets.

Edward sighed. *My hold on power has always been a weak one. There are now too many powerful wolves circling, ready to wear my crown.* Edward coughed again and he tried to find comfort in his bible, but somehow, he knew that God wasn't listening to his prayers and confessions. He sighed again and dozed off, initially dreaming of his new abbey, but later all he could dream about was his own tomb and a pack of wolves, one with the face of Duke William, commanded by Matilda, who was holding a blazing pitchfork and pointing an accusing finger at him.

GUY ON THE HUNT

Guy was in a good mood and was very excited about his wonderful stroke of luck. He had great expectations. However, as he led his men out of the castle, he knew he had to concentrate as he was being watched, so he shouted, 'Oh, tres Joyeux,' clapping his hands, 'now sing the song, men, as you ride.'

The men sang loudly as they left the castle. Guy looked back and waved, and two hands, one large and one small, waved back from the nursery window. As soon as they were out of sight, Guy told his men to relax and stop singing as the tune composed by his wife and daughter was driving him mad.

Now it was time for hunting. His dogs swept through the undergrowth and around the trees picking off any unsuspecting small wildlife like hares and rabbits, while Hugh circled above, managing to grab four pigeons and a squirrel. At the seashore they soon located poor Harold and his party. Harold saw their approach and knew from the colourful uniforms that this was no Norman welcoming committee. Those colours could mean only one thing. He had been wrong. This was the land of that French nobleman, Count Guy. Harold knew the name of the game in these parts. It was state hostage-taking with high stakes. He had just enough time to tell Turold and Rufus that they must escape and request help from Duke William and both were now observing proceedings from behind a bush, while waiting for the chance to escape.

Harold had said to Turold, 'Time to be a hero, and with your Norman haircut you may well stand the best chance of safely reaching Normandy.'

Turold would have preferred to take his chances with the colourful Frenchies rather than be in the presence of the notorious William the Bastard.

Harold offered his sword to Count Guy. He had met him some ten years ago when they had both attested to an important legal paper at the Count of Flanders' castle. Harold remembered Guy well and decided to keep his distance. Guy's men looked very embarrassed and the Englishmen thought perhaps they were being invited to a French version of a maypole dance.

'Bonjour Earl Harold, comment allez tu?'

'Very well given my unfortunate circumstances, sir,' Harold replied, and continued, 'You have me at a disadvantage sir, but I hope you will treat me and my party honourably.'

Guy laughed. 'Of course, although you are all, indeed, at a great disadvantage, and must pay the price. Now let us proceed to my castle at Beaurain, and there we can discuss matters at length. I hope I can rely on the good conduct of you and your fine brave but scruffy sailor friends.'

Guy looked them up and down with a twinkle in his eyes. One of Harold's party, Walter, an English sailor, seemed to have moved a bit too close to the count and he singled him out for special attention. He told Captain Godfrey to grab him by his scruffy neck and bind him. Guy offered each of the Englishmen a horse and the whole group of men, horses, dogs, birds of prey, and bags of dead wildlife, moved off towards the castle. Hugh gave Harold's bird a funny look, which made Alfonso very anxious, so Harold put the eye covering on its head.

It was the first time that Harold had seen a man ride side-saddle before. Guy was dressed in a brown leather hunting robe over a finely woven, colourful striped hose. Guy was very pleased with events, and hummed an old French song about making a fortune out of someone's bad luck. It was another song he had been made to learn which he wished he could forget. However, things were certainly looking up for him, and nothing was going to spoil the next few days as long as Duke William didn't find out.

TUROLD AND RUFUS RUSH FOR HELP

Turold and Rufus were running as fast as Turold's small legs could go, in basically a southerly direction. It was now a lovely day but neither could enjoy it. *Some plain English food and horn of ale would go down well at the moment,* they were both thinking, as their stomachs grumbled. They slipped through the towns of Abbeville and Eu, stealing some French bread and milk (they declined grabbing the frog legs dangling on a string outside the butchers), and continued along the coastal road towards the border with Normandy.

After a while, they saw a wooden fort. They entered the fort only to find twelve burley Normans armed to the teeth.

The Norman border post consisted of a wooden fort constructed on an earthen mound. Both Turold and Rufus were uneasy as two Normans approached. However, the Normans were smiling and laughing, and one was so happy that he came over to Turold and Rufus and gave both men a great big hug. Vital was extremely relieved. He'd journeyed as far as Abbeville, but he'd had to return to the fort before nightfall. William and Guy were supposed to be at peace but all of Normandy knew that you should never be alone in Count Guy's land at night in case you had the misfortune of meeting him or his men.

But just a moment, Vital thought, *where's the rest of the silly English?* 'Earl Harold Godwinson, where is he? Is he dead or alive? Tell me quick before I have time to get my dagger out.'

Rufus, being able to understand and speak some basic French, answered first as Turold pushed himself through the legs of his friend so he could stand behind him and pretended not to exist. 'He and the rest of the men are captives of that colourful French lord. I believe they have been taken to his castle.'

Vital considered his next move. He looked at his men. He decided to send two back to Duke William's castle with news of Earl Harold's whereabouts. But which of his men? Immediately he was able to make up his mind, as if God Himself had decided for him. 'Richard the First and Richard the Last, go immediately and report to Duke William and return with reinforcements. I'll need at least another twenty knights straight and true for this mission.'

As the two Richards turned to go, Vital had another inspired thought. 'Take these two as proof. Remember to be careful how you tell the duke of these events, you know how upset he can get. I need you to return with these Englishmen in one piece.'

The two soldiers and Rufus jumped on three large horses, then Rufus picked up Turold and placed the dwarf in front of him, and the group cantered off in a cloud of dust, with Richard the First thinking, *why do we always get the difficult jobs? Perhaps this time we'll not get into any trouble. However, he knew that, as usual, they would. I remember mother saying that we had been chosen by God to do great things, but so far, we have been dogged by bad luck and under-achievement. Perhaps our lives are about to change, God willing! Yes, we'll both become Norman heroes!*

BEAURAIN CASTLE, PONTHIEU

Meanwhile, Guy was getting things ready at the castle for his guests. He had organised a great feast for them. *Why not?* he thought, *I will soon have money coming out of my perfumed ears.*

His castle was a very impressive stone structure, one of the best and well-built fortifications in the north of France. Once within its confines, there was little chance of escape. *Zut Alors. I must be the luckiest count in the whole of France*, he thought. He called for his chef. In ran a tall elegant French man with a wonderful Norman haircut, shaved at the back but with locks of hair falling beautifully over his blue eyes, just like his master's. He looked so handsome in his apron, designed by Countess Agnes, pink in colour and white shorts. *But why so much pink?* thought Count Guy. Guy gave him the details of the menu for the night. The cook left for the hot kitchens. It was truly very hot in the kitchens, and Guy hated people sweating excessively so he'd come up with a wonderful solution as far as he was concerned. The wearing of just these items by the kitchen staff had proved a great success in many ways, including the inability of the staff to conceal a weapon or vials of poison. He'd also made a rule that no one should relieve themselves while in the kitchens. He was very much one for good hygiene. He told them to relieve themselves in the moat instead. This, of course resulted in all the fish dying, as well as a strong smell.

His new guests, except Walter who had disappeared, were all resting in a heavily guarded large room. They had been stripped and searched as a precaution and all weapons had been confiscated. Walter had been selected for special treatment. Count Guy had a reputation for torturing unfortunate guests. His brand of torture was more subtle than most. He was a great exponent of the art of psychological warfare. It made prisoners and enemies very compliant and gave him great satisfaction. Even he had to agree that his mind was particularly twisted, but that was Duchess Matilda and her men's fault. When the count had finished, Walter was not only a nervous wreck, but also dressed as one of the kitchen staff. Guy had really enjoyed the day so far, and there was even more entertainment to come. He went up to his bedchamber for a beauty sleep. As he entered, he found Agnes, his wife, sitting by the window, brushing her daughter's hair. Their daughter, young Agnes, was dressed in a beautiful pink dress with matching shoes, exactly like her mother's.

Agnes looked sternly at Guy. Guy looked down at his pink shoes as if there was something very interesting on them. She shook her head. 'I heard the screaming, husband. You've been up to your old tricks again!' she said accusingly.

Guy knew that when she said 'husband' she was not amused. 'I have a reputation to maintain dear. It's so difficult to play the part, but it has helped keep me alive over the years, and certain aspects give me great satisfaction.'

Agnes continued, 'Just don't overdo it. Duke William will be very displeased if you harm too many.'

Guy laughed. 'He'll have to find out first.'

Agnes knew better. 'I'm sure he knows already.'

Guy pondered, *Was that an observation or a threat?* Then he remembered that she was actually related to the duke. Guy felt forlorn. 'Don't spoil my mood please.'

Agnes sighed. 'Tonight only, tomorrow you treat them well or else. Oh, and how do my brave soldier boys like the uniforms I designed?'

Guy looked at his pink shoes and hose and sighed. 'Eh, yes, they are so pleased. Captain Godfrey remarked on their um, practicality, and smartness.'

Agnes smiled. 'And the song?'

'Oh, yes, wonderful.'

'That's splendid. Our young daughter has designed some more clothes for them, look at these drawings.'

Guy looked with wide eyes and mouth at the stick men dressed in colourful stripy costumes. 'Well, they are, eh, they are, wonderful.'

His wife looked disapprovingly at him, and elbowed him in the ribs.

Guy was forced to praise further. 'And so, um, so, colourful and stripy.'

Agnes junior clapped her hands and beamed from ear to ear. 'Thank you, Daddy! Here are a pair of hose and a cloak Mummy and I made for you, you must wear them tonight. And here's another song.'

Guy took the offending articles of clothing and sighed, then read the song and nearly fainted. If his men went into battle singing a song about beautiful flowers and frolicking lambs, the enemy would just laugh at them. 'Oh, thank you child.' He kissed her on the forehead, looking at his wife for approval. She smiled.

Guy left, just in time, as the two females started singing the La La song that their daughter had composed, while they brewed up a new batch of perfume. Agnes smiled at her child, thinking that they would have no smelly men in their castle. The young puppy, a gift from Duchess Matilda, whimpered as it hid under the chair in the corner, licking its bald patches. It tended to be the test subject for their brews. Guy closed the door quickly and with his fingers in his ears, trudged down the stairs to his study, wondering how he had become rightful owner of all he surveyed but the master of nothing. He also decided to have that over-cultured governess to both his wife and daughter shown the error of her teachings.

His guards then heard a loud scream inside their master's study. They rushed towards it, swords raised, and charged inside. Guy was sitting at his desk with his face in his hands, sobbing and moaning.

Godfrey went over to him, patted him on the back and whispered, 'Everything alright sir?' Then he saw the uniform drawings, the song, and the new clothes Guy was supposed to wear. 'Oh, I see. Your wife and daughter have been busy again, sir?'

Guy nodded, and wiped away his tears. 'Sorry Godfrey. I know, let's go and amuse ourselves with the guests, that'll cheer us up. Oh, and then I want to have words with that over-perfumed governess.'

Godfrey followed Guy, muttering under his breath. The men of the castle tended to do much muttering, but the pay and working conditions were excellent, as was their life expectancy.

Harold sat on his own, looking out of the barred window at the castle keep. Harold had always been very impressed with the stone-built castles of Europe. Nothing like them existed in England. He knew that the English were very backward when it came to warfare and in particular, strong defence. He had often wondered why. He eventually put it down to a lack of stability, which had meant that those in power were reluctant to build such structures only for them to fall into the enemy's clutches. Then there was the lack of money, and the lack of a skilled and willing workforce. *One day we English will have castles* he had concluded, *but not now.* The English could not even be bothered to maintain the city walls and forts left by the Romans over 500 years ago. Harold wished he was safe and secure at his manor house. *What an irresponsible idiot I've been, but regrets will get me nowhere. I must look forward and be positive.* His men on the other hand, although positive that their leader was an idiot, were definitely pessimistic about their chances. From experience they knew that there was usually collateral damage in such circumstances, and it was those at the bottom of the pile who tended to suffer the most, just like poor Walter.

THE FEAST

The feast had started. Guy was putting on a great performance. Harold enquired whether Guy had a spare drink and food taster available given the unfortunate regularity these days for guests to die at table. Guy looked around and thought for a while. 'Mais oui, I know just the homme for the job.' He placed his hand on Harold's knee and smiled a strange smile.

Harold felt very uncomfortable. He couldn't stand much more of this mental torture. This count was surely the evilest person in the whole of Europe. Torture of the mind, with all its subtleties, was definitely worse than any physical torture. Harold was starting to imagine all sorts of things that the count may have in store for him.

Walter the sailor was called over. 'Sit yourself down next to me mon petit, Harold and I have a task for you,' Guy commanded.

Walter seemed very happy now he was next to Harold, but there was plenty of time for a change in his demeanour.

Harold didn't like to ask Walter why he was now dressed so strangely and as Harold was no longer within reach of the count's slender fingers, he felt more relaxed, and had sufficient courage to ask his jailor, 'What is going to become of us?'

Guy replied, 'Ah, mais oui, that is a good question mon brave. I have not decided on the full details but much depends on you and your party's conduct.' Guy gave Walter a nudge and wink, 'and your generosity, monsieur.'

Ah well, thought Harold, *at least that seems straightforward, although very disturbing.*

Guy continued to speak. 'We will meet early tomorrow to discuss terms. In the meantime, eat, drink, and enjoy, you never know what lies around a castle's dark corners. I have some very interesting entertainment for us tonight

However, Harold found the entertainment very upsetting and had terrible nightmares that night.

Guy was exhausted by all his efforts as he slipped into bed next to his wife. It had been a long day but he had given the performance of a lifetime. He turned to Agnes, and nudging her in the back, enquired tenderly, 'Are you asleep dearest? Are you tired my flower petal?'

She turned over and smiled, and then kissed him on the lips, and he took her in his arms.

However, their intimacy was soon interrupted by a little voice enquiring, 'Daddy, can I have a drink of water?'

Guy sighed and got out of bed, thinking that it was time their little darling had her own room. The dog was in the wrong place at the wrong time and Guy tripped over it and fell heavily onto the floor. He got up, brushed down his pink nightdress, and sighed yet again. The dog, named Guy by young Agnes, now with more bald patches behind his ears, rushed for the relative safety of the damp spot next to the chamber pot under the bed, and whimpered.

The men in the castle tended to do much sighing, and even occasional whimpering, but most looked on the bright side. Alternatively, they could be in the dungeons at Duke William's castle. They were all aware that Countess Agnes was a distant relative of Duke William and was to be feared if crossed. However, if it were not for her their master would still be rotting in William's dungeon. Those two years had been terrible for both Guy (tortured by the duchess), and his men who were left with Countess Agnes in charge. However, Guy had learnt much from Duchess Matilda regarding subtle torture methods, and had returned to his castle a changed man. His men had welcomed him as if he were the next messiah, only to find out that Countess Agnes's grip on power continued.

WILLIAM IS RUDELY AWOKEN

The Captain of the Guard, Horace, rushed into William's bedchamber. 'Your Grace, I have great news. Two of your men from the border fort to the north have been sent by Vital, they have news about those stupid lost Englishmen, and they are without, with one and a half as proof.'

William stuck his head up above the bed sheets, wearing a colourful floral nightcap made by Matilda. 'Eh? Without what? It was not me, I was somewhere else at the time, so if he's without some bits, blame someone else.' His eyes were now focusing on Horace, and his brain moved into first gear. 'Oh, it's you Horace!' William exclaimed finally, coming round from his lovely dream about what he would do with the English if he ever got his backside on Edward's throne.

Horace quickly replied, 'Your Grace, there are two of your men outside with news, along with a lanky longhaired Englishman and a dwarf with a Norman-style haircut. You told me I could disturb you if there was something important to report, Your Graciousness, please don't kill me or start sharpening your sword or battle-axe.'

William was now ill tempered as well as awake. 'Show them in and I'll decide your fate after I hear what they have to say. You already have two strikes in my little black book for past misdemeanours and one more means you will have to suffer the consequences. You above all others know my rules.'

Horace bowed as low as possible, while retreating backwards towards the door, and after escaping the room, pushed the two messengers into the bedchamber and ran away as quickly as his clanking armour would allow. The two Richards bowed low towards their master.

'What?' exclaimed William, 'Am I seeing double? Fetch my physician.'

'No, Your Grace,' the soldiers replied in unison, 'we are Richard and we have great news.'

William was now even more confused – if that was possible – and looked around for his sword while his eyes focused on the targets.

'I am Richard the First, Your Grace,' said the soldier on the left, beginning to curse their parents for the name they shared.

'And I, Your Grace, am Richard the Last,' explained the other.

'Eh what who why when?' William babbled.

They continued as one, 'Your Grace, we have brought an Englishman and a jongleur as proof and they plead on behalf of Earl Harold for your help.'

The twins had been practising this little speech for hours while riding. It was short and sweet and surely couldn't be misinterpreted.

Richard the First dragged Rufus and one very dirty Turold into the room, and they both fell on their knees and started praying.

'Shut up English low life. I am still confused with these two, and now I've got one English quarterstaff and a small smelly ball of mud!' shouted William, pointing at the two Normans. He was now fully awake and angry. 'Listen carefully! Whoever I point my hand at will speak, you understand?'

'Yes, Your Grace,' the soldiers replied, again as one.

'And stop speaking together or your parents will be childless!' shouted William.

The men now knew the rules and stared at William's hand.

'Let's start, you on the left give the report.' William was pointing at Richard the Last. To add to the confusion, they had changed position.

'Your Grace, a dwarf and an English sailor came to us from Ponthieu and have requested your urgent assistance in rescuing Earl Harold and the rest of his men from the evil clutches of Count Guy. They are being held at Beaurain Castle. Unfortunately, the dwarf had a mishap with the horses and ended up in the castle dung heap.'

'Oh, not that strange man, Guy.' William sighed.

Richard continued, 'Your knight Vital has requested twenty knights to assist in their rescue.'

'I will send fifty. I do not trust that Guy one jot,' William replied.

Then Richard the First added (perhaps unwisely given William's mood and confusion), 'Your Grace, Vital has also kindly requested that they be straight and true.'

'What?' screamed William, hunting for his sharpening stone. 'There are no odd men in my army, and in any event, I didn't point my finger at you so keep quiet or else.'

Richard the First thought of offering a different opinion about some of William's knights, but looking at the way William was now busy with his sword, decided that silence was likely to extend his life by many years.

William looked back towards Richard the Last, pointed his index finger and said, 'Go and tell Captain Horace to make ready the men, and get to Beaurain as soon as possible. Take those two with you but clean them up first.'

'Now you,' continued William, and thrust the hand with the sword in it in the direction of Richard the First. He lost his grip and his sword hurtled like a javelin straight for the soldier's head. Richard the First ducked. The sword parted his short hair and vibrated noisily as it penetrated the wall. Richard the First wiped his damp forehead, then got hold of the sword by the hilt. Using the strength of both arms, he pulled it out.

He then ran over to William, handed him the sword and mumbled, 'Your Grace, sorry for talking but I think this belongs to you.' He then walked backwards to his allocated position, keeping his eyes focused on William's sword.

William tried to regain his composure. He was thinking that there was one too many Richards in the room. 'Stay and arrange some secure quarters for our soon-to-arrive guests.'

'Yes, Your Grace,' replied Richard the First.

Just as the knights were about to leave, dragging Rufus and Turold with them, Matilda's lady in waiting, Adelaide, burst in through another door. In her haste to get to William she was wearing only a nightdress.

'Vite, Your Grace, vite. My duchess has just had another vision!'

William turned quickly towards the maiden and on seeing her, dropped his sword since he didn't want any gossip about his poor ungodly attitude getting back to Duchess Matilda as that could result in severe consequences including being grounded and being denied certain privileges. He was now completely distracted by Adelaide's curves and her see-through nightdress.

The Richards meanwhile congratulated each other on surviving, shaking each other's hand and doing a little dance.

Luckily these actions were completed before William's hawk-like gaze hit them between the eyes like a thunderbolt. 'You on the right, in addition, get some plain English type food prepared for them. They don't eat proper food.'

The Richard on William's right was confused. 'Your Grace, you told me to go with the men to Beaurain, now you tell me to stay.'

'Eh? Are you arguing with me?' William enquired, retrieving his sword, despite the dangers of Matilda's wrath if he ever used it indoors again.

The careless Richards realised what they had done. They had changed places in their excitement and were now falling into a deep pit full of sharp spikes.

'Oh, sorry Your Grace,' Richard the Last apologised, lowly bowing his head, 'I am but a stupid soldier, I will carry out your orders immediately.'

All four ran for the open door, arriving as one, falling over and getting up quickly before a sharp sword could catch them. They left the room and dived to the left just in time as the sword swirled past them and embedded itself in a painting of William's father, Robert, slaying a large red-eyed bull that now had the point of a sword through its right eye socket.

Richard the First could not hold back his thought. 'Bullseye, Your Grace!' he exclaimed.

Richard the Last dusted himself down while his brother shook his head. 'He was very confused was he not, dear brother?'

'Yes, and so am I, so let's go over who is to do what.'

Richard the First decided he would be better suited to go to Beaurain as he was the older by one minute. He also decided that from now on they wouldn't dress the same way as it tended to create problems, the consequences of which were mounting daily.

William meanwhile studied the results of his tantrum, thinking, *this could be the basis of a great game, although swords would be a bit unwieldy, so perhaps daggers would be better.* Adelaide had been trying not to laugh at the two funny soldiers. They were unusual to say the least. She let out a small cough, which brought William out of his daydream.

William turned to Adelaide, dropping his retrieved sword and mumbled, 'Don't tell my wife, I just can't control myself sometimes.'

Adelaide replied calmly, 'Your secret is safe with me, Your Grace.'

William looked eagle-eyed at her, *it better be*, he thought, then lost concentration again, *um, she is a very beautiful young woman, I wonder if…* Then he stopped, realising the consequences if he strayed from the marriage bed with one of his wife's ladies in waiting. His wife might be small but she had a long reach, many eyes and ears, a great knowledge of poisons, and there was her closeness to God to consider. He looked at the maiden again, *perhaps she would like to…* He blushed. 'Eh, yes, Adelaide, isn't it?'

She nodded and smiled.

'Let me think, and stop distracting me with those lovely eyes of yours.' He added after a while, 'Tell my dear wife that I am on my way, I just need to dress and have a stiff drink, eh, for my nerves.'

Adelaide left, confused but relieved.

William thought to himself as he sat on his privy. *Luckily, I have already dealt with that Guy and as a result the count has sworn an oath to support me. He is bound to me like a dog. He knows he cannot break such a solemn oath to God; if he does, he will suffer both the wrath of God and the even worse wrath of Matilda and me.* He chuckled. He loved using oaths as a weapon. He did not believe in the might of God but most other men did. He only believed in his own, superior, might. He was the ultimate power in these parts. He left religious thinking to his dear wife, she understood such things. The pieces were indeed falling into place. *Now where's that straw?*

AT THE BORDER, AND ON TO BEAURAIN

The reinforcements and the English duo had ridden hard and arrived at the wooden fort at Eu just before daybreak. The fort had been prefabricated near Rouen at the main building yards and then transported in sections to the border. It was supposed to be a temporary structure while a permanent stone Norman keep was being built to replace it. It could then be dismantled and returned. However, relatively recent events had led to a truce between Duke William and Count Guy. Both hated each other but, from a political point of view, it was expedient to maintain good relations between the two lands, although William had shown Guy who was in charge, meaning Ponthieu was not much more than a client state of Normandy. This, together with the oath that William made Guy swear, bound Guy so strongly that he would never be able to break free unless he had the support of a strong neighbour. The Count of Boulogne, Eustace the Second's land shared a border with Guy but even together they would find it difficult to defeat Duke William. William was now just too strong and any ruler, including the French king, would be foolish to cross him. The future only seemed to hold one course of action for Guy and Eustace. They must become allies of Normandy and gain as much as they could from that. The neighbouring leaders always lived in hope that an unfortunate accident might befall Duke William.

Vital organised his men and after quick refreshments they sped away in a cloud of dust so huge that the locals thought it akin to a biblical sand storm; a plague had indeed come to Ponthieu. Turold had explained his problems with horses to Rufus, and his one true friend in France agreed that he could again ride the same horse, hoping that the horse would think it was just carrying one large man. After several hours of hard riding, they reached the castle gates. There was a terrible smell coming from the moat and they all had to cover their noses. The Captain of the Guard, Godfrey Long Shanks, approached them in his pink uniform, while the Normans sniggered.

'What do you want? The count is busy entertaining,' shouted Godfrey.

Vital replied, 'We are on the Duke of Normandy's urgent business and must see your lord immediately. You and your so-called count will surely not wish to upset my lord and master. He has sent us all to ensure compliance. Any disobedience will have dire consequences. You will all suffer if Count Guy dallies.'

Godfrey muttered, 'He's been dallying for years.'

Vital was getting hot under his helmet. 'What did you say, knave?'

'Eh, nothing. I shall go and tell Count Guy of your request, but he will not allow all of you in, armed to the teeth. Can we agree on just two of you seeing him?' Godfrey was pushing his luck, but sometimes one had to put one's pink boot down.

Luckily for Godfrey Vital was happy with this request, thinking it would save time as the sun was already high in the sky and he needed to get back to William with the wayward guests as soon as possible. He made it clear that William's wishes were not to be ignored. Godfrey turned and rushed off.

Vital jumped off his horse and called for Richard the First to follow. They had come for the stupid Englishmen and that was that, end of discussion. Vital left the reins of the horses in the hands of Turold who protested profusely, and followed in the direction of the pink uniform that was disappearing at a tremendous pace. In the castle, Godfrey breathed deeply, entered the antechamber and briefed Count Guy's squire. The squire scuttled off. Godfrey meanwhile waited for the two Normans and when they arrived, told them to wait.

Four hours before, daylight had come very slowly for Harold. He had endured a restless night, worrying about the futures of himself and his men. Walter had been escorted back, looking very tired, and unable to speak. In fact, he would never utter a word about his experiences. Two hours later, Guy had swept into the room looking very happy and singing a little French tune. *Blast it*, he thought, *another earworm I've got to thank dear little Agnes for*. Walter backed into a corner out of the way, his whole body shaking. Harold had stepped forward to meet the smiling count.

'Well, my English friends, let's have our petit dejeuner and get down to business,' said Guy, grinning broadly.

Guy and six of his solders took the Englishmen into the feasting hall where the table had been laid with a good spread of food and jugs of ale. The English ate a hearty breakfast as if it was their last, since for all they knew, it might be.

Following this, they were led into the receiving room where Guy was seated on his throne, wearing lovely flowing golden-threaded red robes and brightly coloured yellow and orange hose designed by his daughter. Guy looked like a court jester in his new clothes.

The Normans had just arrived at the castle when Guy was about to announce his demands. He was holding Harold's sword upside down as if it was a sceptre. He had made sure that he sat taller than any of his guests. Harold's men pushed the earl forward towards the count. Harold looked troubled and frowned, what did Guy have in store for them?

Guy pointed his finger at Harold and exclaimed, 'I have now settled on my demands. There will be no negotiations, these are my terms. Firstly, I req—'

This was when he was rudely interrupted by his squire.

'Sir, a whole army of Norman knights have arrived and insist on an audience, they look very hot and bothered and will not be trifled with. They are threatening all sorts if you don't comply. In addition, they say that if any harm has come to Earl Harold or his men, their lord, Duke William, has threatened dire consequences. Captain Godfrey has brought two Normans to speak with you.'

Guy looked uneasily at Walter. *Zut, quelle catastrophe*, he thought. 'I will come and speak to them outside.'

Outside, Turold was not happy. The two horses were not happy. Although their reins had been tied to a wooden post Turold was struggling to keep the horses under control. First, they tried to back into him, back legs flying, then when they missed, they pulled the other way, lifting poor Turold high off the ground. The post then broke and he was now flying. No one seemed to want to help him, they just all screamed with laughter, thinking how realistic this jongleur's performance was, acting like a flying man in deadly peril. Turold was now being pulled by the two horses across the grass towards the stagnant smelly moat. Rufus realised something was wrong as Turold's cries for help got louder and louder. Rufus rushed over to the horses and relieved the dwarf of his charges, but it was too late for poor Turold, the impetus of the gallop kept him sliding across the grass, and plop, he was in the moat. The horses settled after a few minutes although they kept a menacing eye or four on Turold, drowning in the swamp of despair. Rufus handed the horses over to one of the Normans (who was crying tears of laughter) and picking up the post, rushed over to the moat. Turold grabbed hold of the post and was dragged out by Rufus. The brown offending festering pile, that was Turold, staggered about like a drunken sailor, giving grateful thanks to God. God and Rufus had surely saved his life. The rest of the party weren't so thankful as they couldn't bear the smell. Even the horses were subdued, and kept out of range of the awful pong. The Normans hunted high and low for some water. Eventually they found some in a horse trough, and lifting Turold up, while covering their faces and swatting the flies, threw him in. Turold thought, *what's it with me and animals, and shit and horse troughs, God? Are these signs, or just you having a laugh?*

God could not reply since He was too busy wiping the tears of laughter from His eyes. *This hero of mine*, God thought, *is proving exceptionally entertaining, and his work has only just begun. I hope my other two heroes, those two Richards, are as amusing as this one!*

The unfolding drama outside was heard in the throne room. Count Guy thought they must be under attack and called the guards to investigate. Once he was told that there was nothing to worry about other than a very smelly Norman dwarf sitting in a horse trough, Guy ventured outside and greeted the two Normans, Vital and Richard.

'Bonjour, and what can I do for you fine looking men?'

'We have come for Harold and his men,' Vital said curtly, 'and Duke William knows you have them and he wants them taken to him immediately.'

'Harold who?' Count Guy innocently asked.

'Listen carefully, we know he is here. Don't give me and my men trouble; you must know the consequences.' Vital was losing patience and time.

'Alright, alright, my large well-built handsome irate close shaven Norman, I have him, and here is his great big English battle-sword to prove it (he was holding it behind his back, but its shaft still poked above his head), but I require recompensing,' Guy replied.

'I'm not here to negotiate, take such matters up with Duke William himself if you dare. All I can reward you with at present is keeping your head on your shoulders.' Vital twirled his lance menacingly.

'I will deliver the Englishmen personally, if you please. I shall meet Duke William at the border at Eu and conclude matters with him.' Guy was a gambler and the stakes were high.

Vital considered this solution. It was not ideal but better than risking harm to Harold. 'Agreed. I will go ahead with my colleague Richard, and advise Duke William accordingly. Hopefully as far as you are concerned, he will agree to ride to our border fort at Eu for the handover. Meanwhile, you will be responsible for the safe passage of Earl Godwinson and his men, and my knights outside will make sure you do not breach the agreement, on pain of your demise.'

Vital concluded the meeting by swirling his cloak and leaving. He and Richard would ride as fast as possible through the forests of Ponthieu and on to Rouen to confer with Duke William, and hopefully he would be in a good enough mood to meet the count at the Norman fort. Outside the castle he conveyed the details of the agreement to Knight Roland, who would be in charge in his absence. Roland was warned that William also needed the dwarf returning in an undamaged condition. Roland quickly got his men to wash Turold down, dry him off so he did not catch a chill, and provide him with brandy to help fight off any internal infections. *I will have to keep this precious cargo safe as if it were made of gold*, Sir Roland thought. The two Normans, Vital and Richard charged off in another cloud of dust. Turold coughed, having breathed in a lungful of dust, and got another nip of brandy. *Just as you think it's the blackest day of your life, the sun starts to shine again*! Turold thought. He coughed again and received some more warming liquid.

MATILDA'S VISION

Back at William's castle at Rouen, Matilda had related her latest vision to her husband, although as usual certain details had been withheld. She had made the decision to tell her husband so as to avoid any harm coming to the dwarf. As one of the instruments of God, that English jongleur was as precious as all the saint's bones in Normandy. She made it crystal clear that when the dwarf arrived, he must immediately be sent to her and be put under protective custody until the time was right. She suggested the two knights, Vital and Wadard should be put in charge of this task. William could only agree. She also scolded him for the way he had acted towards the two Richards. 'Both must be rewarded. They are the other two under the protection of God himself.'

'Yes dearest,' was all William could say before leaving her chamber. He knew there was no point arguing with her. He decided to immediately reward the one Richard still in the castle. *It will be so less confusing to deal with them one at a time*, he thought.

'Squire, go find that fathead Richard.'

After a short while, Richard the Last knocked, and entered William's throne room. 'Ah, it's you, I know who you are, you're Richard the First are you not?'

Richard the Last thought long and hard.

'Well, oaf, that's not a difficult question, is it?'

Richard considered carefully, and mumbled quietly, 'Yes.'

'What did you say?' William's face was going that bright red colour again.

Richard the Last replied loudly, 'Yes,' and added in case of any ambiguity, 'I am Richard the First.'

William calmed down, but thought how wrong he had been, since dealing with one was no easier than dealing with both. 'Well come here, I wish to make you my knight and honour you with arms.' With his sword, William beckoned Richard over to the throne. He added, 'Don't you worry, this is my blunt ceremonial sword,' sliding it across his hand to prove it. Blood gushed all over the place. He had picked up the wrong sword.

'Hell, damnation, and English peasants, that hurts!' William screamed.

Richard rushed over with a cleaning cloth that had been used for washing down the walls of the privy, and applied it to the wound, which looked better than it actually was. This would affect William's fighting prowess in future battles.

William sighed and continued, pointing to a corner of the room. 'Get me the other sword standing in the corner over there.'

Richard returned with the sword and enquired, 'You do just have two swords don't you Your Grace?'

'Of course, you idiot, I'm not going senile like King Edward.'

William quickly laid his sword on Richard's shoulders and announced, 'I now make you my knight, to be known as Knight Richard the First.'

Richard left. He was very pleased for his brother, who would be so excited to have been made a knight.

William studied his wound. It had nearly stopped bleeding but looked very angry. He hoped his next encounter with the other Richard would not be so painful. *Those two Richards are so confusing*, he thought, *I wonder what would happen if they both fought for me in the same battle. I'll probably die and one of them will become Duke of Normandy! Perhaps I should offer one to my enemy, Duke Conan of Brittany. Thinking about it, even better, perhaps I will send both as presents to King Edward. They'll inadvertently kill him within days and I'll be King of England by the end of the summer if not before!*

VITAL AND RICHARD THE FIRST AT ROUEN

The two hot riders with even hotter horses finally reached the castle at Rouen. Both men had been reflecting on their situations, as both wished to preserve their ability to breathe for as long as possible. Both horses were looking forward to a rest, a rub down, and some food and water. Vital carefully considered how he would convey the arrangements to Duke William so as not to offend or upset him. Meanwhile, Richard the First had met his brother and knew he had to be careful as he was supposed to be Richard the Last, and did not want to go down any cul-de-sac of absolute despair and despondency by correcting Duke William. Richard decided it would be best, and safer, to stay outside the room while Vital gave his report.

William was immediately told of their return, and although tucking into a second breakfast consisting of the unfortunate wildlife caught that morning during the hunt (for having the audacity of trying to live in his fields and forests), he was happy to see Vital as he entered. Vital closed his eyes and started his speech immediately so as not to be distracted by any quick actions by his master, or by looking at his countenance or his newly bandaged hand. He continued to keep his eyes firmly closed while giving his report.

'Your Grace, I have stupendous news. The count has agreed to bring the English miscreants to you under his personal protection, supervised by your knights. I have also taken additional precautions to ensure that the life of the dwarf known as Turold, son of the Norman jongleur Rollo, is fully protected. Count Guy has already set off with the party and in the circumstances, it seemed best for Count Guy to bring them all to your fort at Eu, so that he can hand them over to you personally.' Vital opened his eyes, and congratulated himself for a speech well delivered, then ducked just as a precaution.

William was not amused. He looked down at his roasted squirrel and sighed. He loved his second breakfast and he was sure that this conversation was going to spoil it. 'Why do I have to go to HIM, he should come to ME! I am his superior. I don't like these arrangements.' His face was going as bright red as the dragon on his shield. He shouted as vehemently as any human could while throwing his arms about. 'I will not go to the so-called count, he must come to me! He has languished in my dungeons as my guest for two years before at Bayeux, and by God he will suffer again!'

The squirrel he was holding inadvertently left William's right hand like a dagger, on course for Vital's heart, but having quick reflexes, Vital managed to catch it. 'Thank you, Your Grace. I have not eaten for hours, how very kind and I—'

Vital's words were cut short by the entrance of Duchess Matilda who had heard William's screaming from the other end of the castle and had rushed to prevent any unnecessary bloodletting. 'What's the matter dear?' she calmly enquired.

Vital closed his eyes, swallowed a piece of squirrel, and gave her the same speech.

She considered carefully his words, then advised her husband. 'Well dear, it seems to me that you must look at the greater picture and that is the safe receipt of both Earl

Godwinson and the dwarf. You know what a fool Count Guy is so I think it would be best if you ride with some fifty of your knights to Eu and show your strength to this Guy, threaten him a bit, but then give him a small present of some worthless land so he is not totally humiliated. I believe that the future goodwill and support of Count Guy and other French nobles will be central to your plan to become King of England. In any case, dear, you need some exercise, as you must lose some weight you know. Finally, that stupid Earl Harold can give Count Guy some reward for his release as well.'

William could say nothing except, 'Yes dear.'

The task well performed, Vital hoped to escape. 'By your leave, Your Grace,' and tried to slip out while William was gazing lovingly into his wife's stern eyes. William adored and admired her dominating personality. It made him all tingly. Unfortunately, as Vital turned to leave, he trod on Duchess Matilda's little dog, Foufou. The dog let out a yelp and then started limping round the room, whimpering loudly.

William's hawk-like gaze turned back to the disappearing knight. 'Stop there, you oeuf mollet. I have two items left on my agenda. Firstly, here's a blackbird for you as you are so hungry. The knight caught it in his other hand, suitably impressing William. Lastly, has that Richard returned to the castle?'

Vital, with both hands full, hoping that Duke William would not test his capabilities further by throwing a badger, replied, 'Your Grace, he waits without.'

'Well, send him in immediately, and give him this roasted blackbird if he's not had breakfast, we need to get to Eu as soon as possible.'

Vital left, juggling the three dead animals in his hands, found Richard and advised him, 'I hope your catching skills are up to scratch, Duke William wants you now.'

As Richard had already managed a brief conversation in the corridor, he was extremely excited about being made a knight but wished he had been present at the time.

Richard the First entered the room, munching on his blackbird. 'I'm here as requested, Your Grace.' Then after looking at Duke William, added, 'Oh dear, Your Grace, I see you've hurt your hand. Nothing nasty I hope.'

William looked him up and down. He could not believe how identical the two Richards were. *Perhaps*, he thought, *a scar or two would help tell them apart*, then again, his wife was still at his side. 'Your half-wit brot—, I mean,' he looked at his wife who was shaking her head. 'Your fine brother, was the cause of that. Now listen carefully, Richard the Last, my wife, I mean, I, wish to make you a full knight. Please come to me and kneel.'

Richard responded humbly, 'Your Grace, I am not worthy.'

Matilda held up her right hand and quickly interrupted saying, 'Just come here, brave unassuming knight, and say no more. Be mindful of the consequences.'

Richard stepped forward to kneel but trod on Foufou who was still whimpering and staggering around the room following its mishap with Vital. The dog dropped down dead, and to make matters worse, Richard lost his balance and fell forward headfirst onto Duke William, his helmet making harsh contact with William's groin. William screamed in distress, not having cared for that stupid yappy thing that his wife loved so much. Matilda screamed for her little darling dog, not overly worried about William's discomfort. Both then went for William's sharp sword. William got there first, having better reflexes.

Matilda was the first to calm down, just in time for Richard's sake, as William already had a tight grip on his weapon. 'STOP MY DEAR,' she commanded.

William was stunned by the loudness and magnificence of her voice and instantly dropped the weapon. He could never understand how such a masterful disposition could come from such a small female.

Matilda continued, 'No harm must come to this person, whatever personal animosity we feel towards him. He is necessary to your plan, William, by God's command. Once you have fulfilled your destiny, then we can dispose of him as we see fit.'

William could not wait until that day. Richard hoped that whatever this plan was, it would fail or take a lifetime.

'So be it, you, come here knight of few days, now kneel. You are now to be known as Knight Richard the Last, you will be my true and trustworthy knight until you die, which could be sooner than you would like, if I have my way. NOW BE GONE FROM MY SIGHT, and keep out of our way!'

Richard scurried out. He was delighted that his brother was now a knight as well, but wondered whether he should also tell him that his days were numbered.

Meanwhile, Harold's kin, Wulfnoth and Hakon were spending another endless day in the Rouen castle grounds. Yes, they were not imprisoned, but they were no better than prisoners. *When will we ever be rescued?* they wondered. They longed for freedom and to see Bosham again.

Wulfnoth turned to his son Hakon and tried to comfort the young lad by saying, 'Don't despair, I'm sure Harold will come soon!' But Wulfnoth knew that Harold would not be so rash and stupid as to attempt a rescue. He realised deep down that they would never see Bosham and England again, and that they would both die in Normandy, and their bodies would lie in unmarked graves forever.

THE HANDOVER AT EU

Matilda put some ointment on William's 'Richards' wounds as they would now be referred to, and then helped William to dress. With a large bandage on his hand, and another down his hose, he gingerly mounted his horse, known as 'The Beast of Bayeux', which was a fine large chestnut battle horse. William had to put padding in his hose to help subdue the pain. Together with his huge hawk and Vital and his men, he rode as fast as possible to the meeting place at Eu.

Both the Richards stayed behind at the insistence of Duchess Matilda, much to the relief of both William and the two new knights.

When William's party finally reached the fort, Guy had not arrived, so William insisted on some food, drink and ointment before meeting his guests. Shortly after he had finished with the ointment, Guy and the rest cantered into view. William and his knights rode out to meet them. William wore a regal red robe with gold embellishments and tassels. Guy rode a small sleek stallion covered with a large blue blanket made by his wife. He was dressed in velvet green robes and carried his hawk Hugh on his wrist. Harold sensed both fear and relief as did his hawk, hounds and men. Relief that they were to escape the clutches of Guy, but fearful as to what Duke William had planned to do with them.

Guy pointed to Harold and shouted, 'Dear Duke William, Your Grace! Here is the noble Englishman that you so wished to receive. I have brought him and his men to you as instructed.'

William wanted to conclude matters as quickly as possible, as he was in need of a good soak in a hot bath. 'So nice to see you, Guy, and thank you so much for escorting these shipwrecked Englishmen to me, and in seemingly such good condition. In appreciation of your co-operation in this important matter, I've decided to gift you some of my land near the river, where it borders yours; I'm sure the marshes can be of some use to you. It shall from now on be considered part of Ponthieu.'

Count Guy was amazed. William had never given him anything before except grief, and he was being so polite about it too. It was a little disturbing but he could see no reason not to accept the gift.

'In addition, in gratitude, I will make you one of my knights and shall give you arms in gratitude, thus binding us even closer together than ever. As such I will require your unfettered support in any future war I embark on. Finally, here is a fine battle sword for you to wield against my enemies.'

William had, metaphorically, caught the count with his colourful tights down. Guy was now more than ever William's man. Guy could only thank William for the honour.

William continued, looking directly at Harold, 'I'm sure that Earl Harold will also fully compensate you for the inconvenience.'

Harold sighed and nodded, handing over a purse full of gold coins, thinking, *it's only money*.

'Now that matters are concluded, you and your colourful men can rest and have some food and drink before returning to Beaurain. I, on the other hand, must set off straight away with my men and these poor wayward foreigners.'

With that, William turned his horse back in the direction of Rouen, gave his orders to his men, and the Normans and the Englishmen rode off in a cloud of dust, with Guy waving his pink hanky and shouting, 'Au revoir!'

Once the dust had settled, Guy singled out one of his men to act as food taster, thinking that only an idiot would not take precautions when it came to eating Norman food. He knew only too well that many Norman guests never left the feasting table alive. He had even been told by Bishop Odo, during a drinking session, that his half-brother Duke William always kept a large jar of leeches and a few coffins in a corner of his feasting hall in case of an unforeseen medical emergency.

Harold and his men were now completely at the mercy of the ruthless Duke of Normandy and his zealot wife. Harold would soon learn that he had made one serious mistake after another, ever since deciding to undertake this perilous mission of mercy.

HAROLD AT ROUEN PALACE AND CASTLE

Harold was deeply disturbed as he approached the grand palace and castle at Rouen. He was in an even worse mess than before. What had he been thinking, coming to Normandy in the first place? What could he have expected from William? Would William ever have agreed to release his brother and nephew without wanting something in return? And now that Duke William had him as well, perhaps he will use all three of them to put pressure on King Edward to name William as his successor. William was surely a dastardly, dangerous and diabolical man who could not be trusted any further than you could throw his huge horse. Harold was desolate.

Duchess Matilda greeted Harold and his men on their arrival at the castle. She was so gracious and friendly that everyone was immediately put at their ease. She was particularly kind to Turold and took a great personal interest in his well-being. Turold hoped this would lead to more brandy but none was forthcoming, even though he did a great deal of coughing. She also seemed extremely excited about his jester skills, although she warned him about ensuring his act was clean and pure. Turold thought, *that makes things difficult, I will hastily have to invent some new material. From what I understand from King Edward, the Normans will surely enjoy comic stories and songs about Duke Conan and the King of France.*

Matilda studied the exhausted men and her husband, who was in great discomfort after the ride, and so she announced to all present, 'In the circumstances I ask that you all retire early after you've had a light meal and have attended chapel to both confess your sins, and thank God for your deliverance by my kind husband. You will then be escorted to your quarters.'

The Englishmen were taken to an extremely secure part of the castle where they ate some food and rested. Turold started to consider his new acts. For once, he hoped his skills would be fully appreciated.

Meanwhile, William's medical needs required attending to. His squire suggested someone skilled in such matters, and soon a pretty English woman named Aedre Aelfgyva entered his bedchamber. She had been named after her English mother, but was known as Aedre by the Normans who had found it impossible to pronounce her real Saxon name. Young Aedre was a servant to the poor English hostages, Wulfnoth and Hakon, since she spoke excellent English as well as French. She had become a beautiful tall, slender, blond young woman. William sat back, closed his eyes and smiled, thinking, *this woman certainly has soft soothing hands*. Over the next few weeks, rumours would start to spread about their close relationship. Aedre Aelfgyva would often be seen in church confessing her sins and asking for absolution from the palace priest, who would place his hand on her head and pray fervently to God, as later depicted in the Bayeux Tapestry.

When Matilda heard about the affair, she experienced a kaleidoscope of emotions. She was naturally upset and angry, indeed angry enough to consider ordering the woman's death. However, she also experienced a feeling of tremendous relief. This was due to the overwhelming guilt she had carried for more than thirteen years. Her sin was a shared secret, known only to her and to her daughter Adeliza's father, King Edward. Their shared devotion to God had been their downfall, and their love had been more a merging of souls than anything sordid. She often daydreamed about how very different things might have been if she had been Edward's queen. With the help of her father and family, she could have created a true Christian empire comprising England, Wales, Scotland, Ireland, Normandy, and the whole of France. She decided to do nothing for now, since William's attention and energy would soon be made to fully focus on becoming the next King of England. In any event, she knew that when it came to pretty air-brained women, her husband had the attention span of a mussel. However, the woman's days on earth would certainly be numbered once her usefulness had come to an end.

MATILDA'S SPY NETWORK

At about the same time, the Richards were summoned to report to the chapel where a particularly curious-looking man in white robes met them. A red dragon was embroidered on the front of his white tunic, displaying its teeth.

The man spoke. 'Both of you have been brought here to swear a solemn oath to God. Kneel before the altar before Him and swear on this bible as follows, "We hereby swear that the secrets we are about to be told will not be discussed with anyone, on pain of death and eternal damnation so help us God." Do you understand?'

Richard the First asked, 'What if we do not swear so?'

'That is easy,' replied the man, 'You will be disposed of, and your remains fed to the dogs!'

Richard the Last quickly replied, 'That's fine, we just needed to clarify the situation.'

They both swore the oath to God while placing their right hands on the bible.

'I will now escort you to my master. Follow me.'

The white-robed man slipped out of the room in complete silence as if in stealth mode, and the two Richards scampered after him as quickly as they could. They finally reached a secret chamber under the dungeons. Their guide showed them in.

'Why, dear brother, has he left us all alone in this dark dank place?' Richard the Last, or First, enquired (it was too dark to determine which Richard had spoken).

'I do not know, but now that my eyes have grown accustomed to the gloom, I can make out several instruments of torture,' the other replied.

'Good evening gentlemen,' a disembodied voice boomed out, 'how nice of you to come. For some reason, Duchess Matilda believes that you have certain talents that make you useful to our organisation. From what I have heard and seen, I can see nothing that would make me select you for any of our missions, but by experience I know that Duchess Matilda is always right, especially as she seems to be guided by God. At least you are both tri-lingual because of your parents, so that will indeed be of use. It seems that Duchess Matilda sees you as being God's answer to her prayers and therefore critical to the success of her plans.'

As usual, the Richards did not really understand what was going on, but nodded their heads as if they had the mental capacity to comprehend. They had always found this the best approach.

The voice continued. 'Duchess Matilda has created a large spy network and I am the Grand Spy Master. You are to be trained in the dark arts of spying. You will be trained in covert operations, mayhem, and murder. Normally the training takes three months, but in your cases, probably six months. However, if necessary, your training will be cut short since the timing of your missions will be critical. At some time in the near future, one of you will be sent to Norway where one of our female agents will soon be working hard to gain the trust of that country's warlike but dim-witted King Harald Hardrada of Norway. This agent might be a woman, but she has more subtle ways of extracting information and killing people than any man alive. She lives under deep cover, especially at night. The other will be sent to England. Do you have any questions?'

The knights were now totally confused. Surely Harold was in Rouen not Norway, and he was definitely not a king, and why was his second name now Hardrada?

The voice concluded matters. 'Go back to your lodgings and rest, as you will be starting you training tomorrow.'

The two Richards were very excited about being Matilda's spies, they had never felt wanted before, since even their parents had seemed to dislike them. Their father was an English fisherman, smuggler, and part-time pirate, who like his sons, was very unlucky. This often led to problems when on board ships, and he became known as 'Jonah' although his actual name was Richard. In the end, men refused to sail with him, so he had to give up the sea in favour of life as a smuggler ashore. Their mother was Norwegian by birth. She could never have been considered caring, but there were three positive aspects to their harsh upbringing in Normandy. She had beaten Christianity into them from an early age which meant that God looked down on them favourably. She had constantly told them that they were blessed with a gift through their male line, which would eventually see their lineage become great kings (she was another strong Christian woman who believed she received visions direct from God). As they grew up, they developed a close bond of brotherhood which would last a lifetime. It's difficult to say whether they had also inherited their father's bad luck, or whether life was just full of coincidences. When they reached adulthood, their abilities started to manifest themselves with some disastrous consequences. After the strange destruction of their father's stock of brandy along with the family home and their neighbours' thatched cottages, their parents and the neighbours decided it was time for the twins to leave home and become soldiers. A few months later, while the Richards were at training camp, their parents took the opportunity to emigrate to Flanders, with no forwarding address.

The twins headed back to their lodgings via the alehouse, which also provided certain adult recreation. As they walked, they were unaware that they were being covertly followed by one of Matilda's agents.

Next morning at daybreak the Richards were rudely awoken by loud knocking on their door. It was someone from the agency. 'I am Master Perciville,' he announce. 'Come with me.'

They followed towards the cathedral, beside which stood a large house with small barred windows and a stout door. Above the door was a sign, which read, 'ENTREZ A VOUS RISQUES ET PERILS'. Master Perciville knocked three times, and a small door opened above the knocker.

'Do not eat mussels in June,' the small face behind the opening whispered.

Master Perciville replied, 'I know I was as sick as a dog.'

The front door opened with a loud creak. Inside, it was dark and dismal. They were taken to a room that was laid out as a classroom.

Master Perciville commanded, 'Asseyez vous.' They complied.

The master gave a speech, 'You will learn the basics in all the skills you require to carry out your tasks. We must improve both your physical and mental prowess. We will also improve your souls. You were followed last night and will be followed from now on. There will be no more excessive drinking or recreational activities with women unless required as part of your assignments and you will go to church daily. You will have lessons in surveillance and trailing, poisoning, murdering, rumour mongering, unrest, discontent, and rioting. You'll start immediately, with a break for food and light beer and short siesta at lunch time.'

The lessons began.

At the end of the day, Master Perciville counted the cost of the twins' lessons.

Master Jedick had been in charge of the surveillance lesson. The Richards were tasked with covertly following a target, and at the end to creep up and eliminate him. Richard the First managed to lose the subject and as a result attempted to murder a stranger. The poor unsuspecting man suffered a fatal heart attack. Richard the Last started arguing violently with his brother, and a large crowd soon gathered. Some people started stripping the dead body and some started betting on the winner of the fight. The spectacle escalated when Richard the First unintentionally hit the mayor, who at the time, was examining the body for signs of foul play. The mayor staggered back to his feet before an opportunist thief could complete his attempt to rob him of his purse and chain of office. The mayor shouted for his guards who had been distracted by their attempts to place bets. The guard of six heavily armed men tried to arrest the slippery thief, protect the body, and arrest the two Richards who were still wrestling on the ground. The crowd were not happy that the fight was going to end without a winner, since there was now a great deal of money at stake, so they started attacking the guards. Others then joined in, as they had nothing better to do and loved a good fight. At this stage a relief force arrived from the spy agency and, through stealth and sleight of hand and bribery, managed to extricate their trainees from the melee and return them back to the school.

Master Perciville looked through his small window and sighed. The riots were still going on, and he could see a red glow from the Hotel de Ville where the mayor and his guards were now hiding as the townspeople attacked with flaming torches.

The next lesson had been beginner's poisoning. The men were tasked with making a poisoned cake from a cupboard full of potions and chemicals. The teacher, Master Canobeck, thought that by giving the imbeciles such a task they would appreciate how difficult it was to achieve a good result. The Richards embraced the task with great enthusiasm. Unfortunately, they had not been concentrating on the master's instructions, and so didn't try reading the various labels. This, that, and the other were thrown into the bowl along with the dough and all mixed up using armoured gauntlets (Master Canobeck took health and safety issues very seriously). The despairing master stood in the corner wearing a battle helmet and just shook his head. As the Richards kneaded the dough before it went in the oven, there was a small explosion, but the Richards put this down to too little nitrous oxide (whatever that was), so they added some more and into the oven it went. Later, when Master Canobeck went to retrieve the result, the oven exploded with such intensity that it blew the door off its hinges, hitting the poor man in the chest. He flew backwards across the room and slammed into the reinforced wooden door with such force that its iron hinges buckled then broke. Both the door and Master Canobeck flew down the corridor until they hit three guards and then all five hit the far corridor wall and fell to the floor in a great heap of men and wood and iron. Unfortunately, it had been a supporting wall and there followed a great deal of trembling and rumbling before the wall collapsed on top of the luckless heap.

The Richards had definitely created a weapon of mass destruction, but it was not a poisoned cake. It took several hours to dig the survivors out. Strangely, the two Richards had survived unscathed, while the master had suffered life-changing injuries and the guards were mangled corpses. Canobeck was carefully put on a stretcher and taken away for medical treatment while being given the last rites. The Richards just had to be dusted down. Outside, it had been as if a localised but violent earthquake had struck. Any buildings next to the agency with weak foundations were now just piles of rubble. Another thirty people had been killed, fifty were injured, and twenty were unaccounted for.

In an act of respect, lessons were postponed for the rest of the day. *At least,* Master Perciville thought, *tomorrow can't go so badly.* He would be proved wrong.

The next day's lesson was beginner's murdering but this just resulted in the normally calm and saintly Master Jean Dubois trying to kill the twins and having to be pulled off them screaming and dribbling.

The basic murder lesson itself had gone well. Both Richards seemed very attentive and enthusiastic. The problems started when the master gave them the task of following and murdering a victim, a role to be played by Master Pinoid.

'There will be no mayhem in my class, do you understand you two? Ah, and don't look so innocent, you, monster in your red cloak, and you, moron in your green cloak. So, concentrate or else. Here is the knife you are to use. It has a retractable blade, so no one will get hurt. Follow Master Pinoid and once he has reached the cathedral, you may attack him, but beware, he is a slippery target and the best unarmed fighter alive.'

With that, Master Dubois gave Richard the Last the dagger.

'I think not, brother, I'm the oldest, give it here!' exclaimed his brother.

'No, I will not,' said Richard the Last, putting the dagger in his belt and ignoring his brother's demands.

The result was another fight, which ended when Richard the First snatched the dagger from his brother's belt before running after the disappearing victim, closely followed by the defeated brother. They followed the master at a discreet distance, still arguing. Eventually Richard the First promised that his brother could have second stab.

The three reached the cathedral just as a party of Welsh diplomats arrived to attend mass. They had been sent by King Bleddyn ap Cynfyn and the very influential recently widowed ex-Welsh queen, Ealdgyth, to negotiate a secret treaty with Duke William. The King of Wales wanted revenge for the death of King Gruffydd at the hands of Earl Harold and the English. The members of the delegation looked resplendent in their black coats with embroidered red dragons on the back. Master Pinoid, also wearing his black coat with a red dragon, took advantage of the situation and dived into the delegation. The Richards were now very confused.

Oh well, Richard the First thought, *I'll leave it up to God to help me choose the correct man, but just in case, to improve our chances…* 'Dear brother, I'll attack the third one on the right, then give you the dagger to attack the second on the right, then we'll run for our lives back to the school.'

Rhiwallen felt a sharp pain as the dagger's blade entered between his second and third ribs, which was followed by a scream from David as Richard the Last struck him in the back. The two men fell to the floor bleeding profusely, as their assailants sped away.

When they returned to the school, the Richards were both very confused and bemused with events.

The master enquired, 'Everything go to plan, men?'

Both Richards looked a bit sheepish. 'Well, I suppose so,' Richard the First replied, 'but the dagger's blade did seem difficult to push in.'

His brother nodded in agreement. 'Probably needed a bit of goose grease,' he added.

They both nodded and smiled meekly, just as Master Pinoid arrived. His face was as white as Duchess Matilda's underwear.

'What is wrong?' enquired Master Dubois.

'What is wrong? What is wrong? I'll tell you what's wrong, these two idiots have assassinated two high-ranking officials of the Welsh court, that's what's wrong. They have caused a major diplomatic incident. William's men are out in force looking for two identical men, one wearing a red cloak, one wearing a green cloak, and both matching the descriptions of the two who started yesterday's riots.'

Suddenly Richard the Last had an inspired thought. He looked down at his belt and pulled out the remaining knife. He pressed the blade and it retracted. 'Master, here's your knife. It's so funny, I'm sure you'll laugh when I tell you. It seems we used the wrong knife on our mission.'

Richard the First laughed, Master Dubois did not.

The Master studied the two men in front of him, one in red and one in green, and his face went scarlet. 'What have you two done?' he yelled. Those were his last words before he launched his attack. Master Dubois screamed as he grabbed Richard the First by the throat and stabbed him in the chest with his knife. Of course, no blood was spilt since the blade simply retracted into the handle. Richard the Last pulled the master off his brother and flung him round. Unfortunately, Master Dubois' head hit Master Pinoid in the chest, and Master Pinoid fell backwards, clattered into a wall, and finally collapsed on the floor in an unconscious heap.

Two of Master Dubois' servants entered the room and went to the aide of their master. Master Dubois was now a screaming babbling wreck.

The two servants got hold of their master and Richard the Last let go, saying, 'I think he needs a cold bath followed by a sleep!'

The servants took Master Dubois away, while he shouted, 'I'll be back, just give me some time to recover and find my sword. Then I'll show you both what's funny!'

Another two servants soon arrived with a stretcher and took Master Pinoid's body away.

The final lesson on unrest and rioting was considered unnecessary given the results of the other lessons. Instead, the Richards were given weapons training but this time each had their own teacher and room. The results were astounding: no fatal accidents, in fact, no accidents at all, no swearing, nothing untoward. Richard the Last was found to be a natural with the sword, and Richard the First was very adept with the battle-axe.

At the end of the day, Master Perciville looked at the two Richards. He shut his eyes, emptied his mind of malicious thoughts, and meditated a while. He had spent several years in the Holy Lands and beyond, and had learnt skills that most Europeans would never understand. As far as the mind was concerned, he had concluded that Europe was in the dark ages. He came to the only logical solution, if Duchess Matilda did not wish to sanction the twin's disposal, then they must be kept apart. Together they created chaos. In a very few situations, such doomsday devices would prove very useful to Normandy. However, he could not afford any more accidents leading to the deaths of teachers and the wider population, and the destruction of Norman towns and cities.

He eventually spoke. 'From now on you will be trained separately. In addition, given the turmoil outside and the fact that there are many looking for you with torture and pain in mind, you will both live in this house.'

Unfortunately, the master had not yet fully grasped the extent of their chaotic tendencies. As both the Duke and Duchess of Normandy could testify, and indeed Foufou if alive and capable of speech, merely their presence could cause great chaos, confusion, and catastrophe.

THE ENGLISH AT ROUEN CASTLE

Meanwhile back at the castle, the Englishmen were woken up mid-morning and given a hearty breakfast. Following their breakfast, Turold and Rufus were escorted to Duchess Matilda, and Harold and his men were told to relax in the castle keep.

Duchess Matilda looked at Turold, smiled, and spoke. 'I knew of your father. He was a great jongleur. I understand that King Edward thinks very highly of you as both his jester and advisor on certain matters. Strangely enough we need a jongleur. I believe someone with your various talents and knowledge of English matters would be very useful to us, and whilst you are our guest you will be well rewarded. As regards your sailor friend, here, he too will be very useful to us. In the circumstances, my husband and I have decided to keep you in protective custody. You are both too precious to be left unguarded. The Duke and I have many enemies, and there are currently many Normans who would cheerfully kill any foreigners following the recent riots. Our knights Vital and Wadard will attend to your needs and keep you safe. You will from now on be lodged closer to my rooms, and will both dine with me later so we can have a quiet discussion about the king and England, and then you can accompany me to chapel and light a candle for your elderly and fragile King Edward.' She smiled sweetly and gave them leave with a soft gesture of her hand.

Vital and Wadard escorted them to their new luxurious rooms and left them with a table stacked with food and wine. As far as Turold and Rufus were concerned, they had died and gone to heaven. The only drawback was that later that day they were both forced to have baths and be deloused, although the beauty of the young women in charge of these activities, Adelaide, Rose (short for Rosemary), and Daisy, provided some comfort and compensation. The result was two clean, externally parasite-free men, with full bellies, rosy cheeks, and large grins, and three giggling females.

William had spent most of the day trying to recover from recent events, so he decided not to see Harold. In any case, he thought, by making him wait, it would only make Earl Harold more unsettled and easier to manipulate. His wife had taught him well. This tactic was certainly working, since Harold was by now frantic. In the late afternoon the Englishmen were allowed a stroll around the battlements, more to impress on them how futile it would be to try and escape. They then had supper and were locked up in their rooms. It would be a long night for them, all worrying about their fates. They could cope with the cut and thrust of battle but not this mental torture.

ROUEN BECOMES A RUIN

Later that night, Duke William was awoken with news of more riots and fires in Rouen. He despatched most of his men to help restore order and fight the fires. By morning, half of Rouen had been burnt to the ground and was but a pile of smoking rubble and wood. Some seventy more people had been killed and another eighty seriously injured. It had been one of the worst events in the city's history. A substantial reward was offered for the capture of the two men responsible. The two culprits would never be caught and were eventually believed killed during the events. They were also thought to be English spies sent by King Edward. This was a convenient rumour spread by Matilda's spy network.

Some opportunists tried to claim the reward due upon the capture, dead or alive, of the two Englishmen, by dressing their recently deceased relatives or neighbours in red or green cloaks. All of these attempts failed.

Next day, William was too preoccupied with making decisions regarding the destruction of his capital, to be able to deal with the sensitive issue of Earl Harold, so again this left Harold in anguish. It had always been the intention of William to make Caen his capital, and he had recently completed his new castle there. It was strategically a better location, being further away from potential foes, and closer to the sea and England. Considering recent events, he decided it was now time to relocate.

While Harold and his men felt more like prisoners than guests, Turold was very happy with his present circumstances. He had had a lovely meal with Matilda, who was very attentive when it came to his stories about King Edward and England. She was so understanding, sympathetic, and otherworldly that he may have told her more than he should, but he did withhold certain important and sensitive details. She was one of those people who could immediately put anyone at ease. This was due to her upbringing and years of dealing with her husband, his friends, and his foes. Matilda actually seemed very well informed about the situation in England, and strangely, also about Turold's personal circumstances. Turold did wonder whether she might well have some contacts in London and throughout England. There were some facts that she seemed to know which only Turold and Edward shared, with the exception of his close friends at the alehouse of course. He was beginning to wonder whether there might be a spy in the alehouse he frequented, but dismissed this thought as ridiculous. He kept himself busy by spending the day practising his juggling and comical songs for a performance for Duchess Matilda. Rufus was learning French from Turold, and was to act as his assistant. Both were getting on very well with their Norman protectors, Vital and Wadard, who never seemed to leave their sides. The only worry for Turold was his family, so Duchess Matilda promised to get word to them that he was alive and well in Normandy. She also advised Turold that the messenger would give his wife some gold.

That night was generally uneventful. Another large explosion had been heard from the vicinity of the Cathedral but Duchess Matilda had personally instructed some men in black robes to investigate, and their report, censured by her, concluded that God had sent an earth tremor to warn sinners of the consequences of their actions. It seems that Richard the Last had been practising his baking skills again.

THE ENGLISH PRISONERS MEET THEIR JAILORS

Early next day Harold and his men were summoned to appear before Duke William and Duchess Matilda. Both William and Matilda were dressed in their finest red robes and sat on their thrones (Matilda always made sure hers was lower). The Englishmen were ushered in once all personnel and props had been put into position. Harold's men pushed him in first since they considered him responsible for their current misfortune.

William was first to speak. 'Earl Harold, we meet formally at last. I am sorry I have not been able to see you before,' he lied, 'but important matters of state have had to come first.' William had made the first move.

'Thank you, Your Grace, for your rescue and protection. I don't want to inconvenience you any more than I must. I've travelled across the channel on an important family matter. This delicate matter involves the protection you kindly offered to both my nephew and brother who were put into your tender care upon the instructions of the great King Edward as a guarantee of good conduct by my father and his family.' This was Harold's first move in this verbal game of chess.

'Oh yes sir, I had quite forgotten about them,' he lied. 'I'd thought that your visit would have been about my succession, considering the age of King Edward and the fact that he has no heir. I was hoping that King Edward was eventually fulfilling his promise to me through the provision of a formal letter. Now then, where are those two guests, dear?' William responded, looking at his wife. Both smiled broadly.

Harold had now to come up with a good defence. 'No, Your Grace, the question of the crown I leave to King Edward and the council of England, the Witan, and I have no influence or knowledge regarding it,' he lied. 'As I say, my matter is a personal one. I've made an oath before God that I would beseech you to release my kin, Wulfnoth and Hakon, and it is for that reason that I have come.'

'Oh, those two men. They are great knights in my army. I will command their presence immediately. I believe that they are at sword practice in the fields behind the castle.'

William's defensive move was followed by a quick attack. 'In the matter of the succession I am most disappointed. I thought considering past events and promises that King Edward had sent you here to confirm that I will be the next King of England. As regards your kin, I understand your position, no honourable and God-fearing man should ever break a sincere promise or an oath before God. Perhaps you can remind King Edward of this. In conclusion, in return for considering your request, I must ask you for your support in my ambition to become the rightful king of England upon the death of King Edward.' William looked at his wife for a sign, and she gave a sly wink.

She now spoke. 'Yes, my husband has a full and legitimate claim in his own right, but in addition, my eldest son too has a claim as I am descended from no less than King Alfred of England. You must surely agree therefore that there is no family in the known world that has a better claim. Indeed, God commands it.'

Harold realised that he was in a very weak position. He understood now that William definitely had decided that his claim to the English throne had great merit.

In the meantime, there was a clattering of metal and Wulfnoth was ushered in. He was dressed in his armour, carrying an English-style shield. He had an English-style haircut, moustache, and a big beard. He looked at his brother and rushed to greet him. They'd not laid eyes on each other for years. 'Brother, it is so wonderful to see you, but you shouldn't have come to Normandy.' Wulfnoth then broke down in tears.

Harold comforted his long-lost brother and wiped away his tears. 'I am here to obtain your release, along with your son. How is my nephew, dear little Hakon?'

'You can see for yourself, here he comes.'

The young man clanked in.

Harold hugged him. 'I don't believe it. You're now a fine man.'

'Uncle, I didn't believe it when they told me you were here! I assume you have brought an army with you?'

Harold shook his head. 'No, nephew, we are at peace with Normandy, and so I am sure Duke William will do the honourable thing.'

This distraction had given William another psychological advantage. The family reunion finally ended after more tears of joy, and after a pause to think and compose himself, Harold turned to William and spoke. 'Your Grace, I will do as you request, but as you know under English law the question of the succession is left to King Edward on his death bed and the English Council. May I add, King Edward is indeed old but I pray daily that he will live a great many more years.'

William made his final move. 'I understand what you say, but you must face facts. I'm reliably informed that King Edward is very unwell. I know that you are increasingly the power behind the throne. I'm therefore sure you can help my cause in this matter, and in return, I will return your kin to England. In addition, if you agree to marry one of my daughters, I will swear before God that you will become the second most powerful and wealthy man in England and all your family will benefit under my rule. I also swear before God that one way or another I will become King of England. It is up to you as to whether this can be done peaceably or with a great deal of death and destruction.' This was checkmate. William paused to allow Harold to assimilate the situation.

Harold was dumbfounded. How had he got into this mess and how could he get out of it?

William continued to speak. 'I think enough has been said, and we should retire to consider our positions. In the meantime, tonight you can have a celebratory feast with your kin and perhaps they can influence you in deciding upon your and their futures. Tomorrow we will all go hunting together and we will discuss matters further. You are all honoured guests and all your needs will be met while under my protection.' William gestured for all present to leave.

Once they had left, William turned to his wife and asked, 'How did I do dear?'

She replied, 'William, you were excellent, just as you, with my help, had planned. The final introduction of his kin unbalanced him and gave you victory. Indeed, all the pieces are in play and whichever way they go, you'll succeed, by the will of God.'

William respected his wife, and she was so confident about God being on their sides. He on the other hand knew of his misdemeanours, and also knew that if it came to a fight, he could well lose. The most pressing issue was how to get a large army across the sea to England. The Normans had tried and failed before, and currently had an insufficient number of ships. Yes, even his great father, Duke Robert, known as 'The Devil', had led an unsuccessful invasion, merely reaching the Isle of Jersey before storms and an invasion in Normandy forced him to return.

The feast that night went very well and all but Harold had a great time. They were well fed and entertained, with Turold being the star with his new acts, as vetted by his friend and benefactor, Duchess Matilda. Harold had long conversations with his brother and was overjoyed to find his nephew was in such good health and spirits. Wulfnoth was very careful what he said, but he made it clear to his brother that he'd indeed been very unwise in coming to Normandy, and that the prospect of him and his men returning to England was a distant one. Harold had to agree, and could only hope for God's intervention. He asked his brother and nephew to pray for God's deliverance. God would indeed intervene again and quite quickly, but this time through another.

TROUBLE BREWING TO THE WEST

Duke Conan of Brittany was flexing his muscles and threatening William's ally, Rivallon of Dol. Duke Conan controlled Brittany but aspired above his abilities. Certain advisors of his had been encouraging him to take advantage of the current problems in Rouen. These had not only diverted a lot of William's armed resources, but also his attention. He was told that it would be a good time for him to attack William's ally. These shadowy men were very convincing. Once he had made his mind up (with much encouragement) he made another bad decision by publicly announcing his intention to invade both Breton, and then Normandy itself. Duchess Matilda had spies in Brittany, one of whom had become a close advisor of Duke Conan. Matilda's plan was simple. Duke Conan had been a thorn in the side of Normandy for years and before her husband and his army could invade England, Brittany needed to be neutralised. She had decided that Duke Conan should die in battle or, if that failed, have an unfortunate accident, and that Brittany would then become an ally of Normandy.

WILLIAM'S PRE-EMPTIVE STRIKE

William and Harold had several days of enjoyable hunting. It had been a welcome diversion for Harold. Meanwhile, when Duchess Matilda received word of the intentions of Duke Conan, she was very pleased as it meant that her plan had worked. She immediately asked her agent, TuMoi, to dress suitably and seek an audience with her husband as his cover persona, the French emissary, Beaucoup de Champs. This he duly did. William was furious when he heard the news from de Champs. He decided, under the guidance of Matilda, to make the first move. He would use the opportunity to gain more power, deal with the upstart once and for all, show Harold what his army was capable of in battle, and see how Harold performed in combat. He would therefore make plans to go to the assistance of his ally at Dol. Once the plans had been finalised and everything was in place, he would spring the whole thing on Harold with no warning so as to keep him off guard. As a result, neither Wulfnoth nor Hakon were made aware of the forthcoming campaign.

MEANWHILE, BACK IN LONDON

Edgar was, as usual, enjoying a pie and ale in his gloomy corner of the alehouse.

Suddenly that dark robed Norman materialised and stood before him, 'Ah, bone jar, views eat bone moon amy?' he seemed to whisper.

'No, it's a meatless meat pie,' Edgar responded, wishing the Norman spoke better English.

'Well, my large pox-faced Englishman, I've a job for twos. I want you to take this bag of gold to Turold's wife and give her a message. You must tell her that her homme is eh how do you say, alive and kicking, and is very well. Also tell her that he's currently at the Duke of Normandy's palace, but will be delayed,' The shadow continued, 'I'll send further information to her when received.'

Edgar locked this message in his brain in proper plain English so it could be understood. He then asked, 'How's my mum?'

The spectre considered his reply, 'Ah yes, old Aelfgyva, she's no worse than before. As I told you before, she helped set up a school teaching the Norman women the art of English embroidery. It has become an important pastime of even the wealthy.'

Edgar was pleased, his mum was very good at embroidery, although losing one eye in a drunken brawl with a bishop had meant some of her work was a little uneven. Edgar re-focused his attention on his Norman ghost, but he'd already vanished. Edgar thought hard and long. He didn't get out much and he certainly wasn't used to thinking much. He'd met Turold's wife in the alehouse a few times when she'd had to carry her husband home after a heavy session of drinking and fighting. In the bag with the gold was a note of the address. He would have to ask the landlord for directions, or better still, find someone to take him. Before that however, he would need some more ale for courage.

When he returned to his corner with his ale, he sat down and tried to think by gazing blankly at the table. *Just a minute*, he thought, *where's my pie gone?* Then he looked under the table and could just make out two large rats dragging it off towards the hole in the wall. He sighed, felt inside his heavy overcoat and pulled out a large club. He hated cruelty but these rats were starting to take too many liberties. That was his fifth lost pie this week. It was time for them to learn a painful lesson.

THE DUCHESS MEETS RUFUS

A few more days passed, then Harold was summoned to meet William formally in the throne room. At the same time Duchess Matilda requested the pleasure of the company of Rufus. Turold was worried, but was told by Vital that Rufus was needed on a special mission and that he, Turold, was not required. The duchess gave Rufus a big hug and a blessing. Rufus had started attending chapel and learning French and this had been noticed.

She asked him to sit down, and then said, 'We require you to assist in safeguarding Earl Harold's person. We know that you saved Turold's life on at least two occasions and have therefore concluded that you will be well suited to this role. Also, being English, you will make Earl Harold feel less like a prisoner. You will go and say your goodbyes to Turold, attend chapel, and meet Earl Harold in the courtyard mid-morning. Now go, good fellow, and may God protect you.'

He was ushered out.

He firstly went to the chapel for quiet reflection and a prayer. He sat down in his favourite pew in front of a statue of Mary Mother of Jesus and considered his past life.

Rufus' life had been hard, harsh, and colourless. His ancestors were Kushites from the ancient capital of Meroe, in what is now Sudan. They moved to the Mediterranean port of Tanis, Egypt, many centuries ago. His grandfather was a well-respected seafaring captain. Unfortunately, Rufus' father, Arqamani, was a great disappointment to his grandfather and a terrible ship's captain. Arqamani's crew mutinied while docked at London and sailed without him. They had taken advantage of him being drunk and disorderly in an alehouse. Arqamani had to marry the alehouse keeper's daughter and she bore a son, who she named Rufus because of his skin colour. Over the years, in between bouts of drunkenness, Arqamani continued to crew merchant ships and enlarge his family. As happened with many sailors, Arqamani drowned. Unusually, he didn't drown at sea, he did so by falling head first into a muddy puddle outside the alehouse late at night while in a drunken stupor. Rufus' mother died one year later of the plague. So, whilst still children, Rufus and his siblings fled the infected alehouse like rats leaving a sinking ship but one month later, he'd been the only survivor. He'd wandered about England for a few years doing this and that, but mainly stealing. Then he'd decided to become a sailor like his father and grandfather before him. His life had been full of salt, bad smells, and just the colours blue and grey. He had salt in his veins, and his clothes normally stank of seaweed and fish. He would've been as handsome as he was tall if life would've let him. He had been lonely and rudderless. Then, one day he had gone on this fateful, frightful journey to Normandy and now had a best friend called Turold. Suddenly his life changed. There was purpose, adventure, colour, unsalted food and drink, washing, clean clothes, friends, respect, and recently, religion and learning.

On top of all that he'd met Marie who worked in the kitchens and served the food and drink. They'd immediately made a connection and were in love. It was the custom in the Middle Ages to act swiftly in such matters since life was short and definitely unpredictable.

She helped him with his French and he gave her English lessons, since at sometime soon they would have to decide where to live, subject to the agreement of Duchess Matilda. He'd never been happier. He loved Normandy and didn't care much about returning to England. He thought he must be the happiest man in Normandy (indeed, he was). What was there to return to? He knew that Duke William aspired to be the next King of England, but as far as the general population were concerned, did it really matter who was oppressing and abusing them? Whether it was the English or the Danes or the Vikings or a young exiled prince from Hungary or the Normans, did it matter? In any case, he had concluded, Duchess Matilda would make a fine Queen of England, and her ideas about the cleansing and improvement of the church in England seemed a good cause worth fighting for. Surely God was on her side and would look after all those who truly believed in the work of the next Queen of England, so as far as he was concerned, God save Queen Matilda. He did hope that the Norman succession to the throne would be a bloodless one, but from what he understood, this would depend on Earl Harold's actions. He prayed daily for Marie, Turold, Duchess Matilda, and Earl Harold. God was pleased with His new convert.

EDGAR DELIVERS

At last Edgar had found the courage to leave the alehouse
with his guide Ethelred the Eveready (a nick name given to
him by certain loose women in the area). He couldn't
believe how bright it was in the outside world, and oh so
smelly. He followed his guide to Turold's house, stopping
every few paces so Ethelred could acknowledge one
woman or another and give his regrets at not being able to
dally. At the house, Ethelred left him, saying some
important matters needed his urgent attention. He dashed
off in the direction he'd just come from, combing his beard
and moustache, and whistling a merry tune.

Edgar knocked loudly on the door. The door and Edgar
fell into a large room smelling of dog and pottage. He
picked himself and the door up and took a step forward, but
his eyes had not adjusted to the gloom, and he fell over a
furry toothy lump which turned out to be some sort of devil
wolf. Next, he was hit by a broom across the head.

Megan screamed. 'Who are you? Are you here for the
rent or to have your wicked way with me? I am armed with
a dog and broom and I'm not afraid to use either!'

Edgar replied, 'You must remember me, I'm Edgar,
Turold's friend from the alehouse. I have important news
about him. I don't want to interfere with you I assure you,
so kindly get your dog to release his teeth from my leg!'

Suddenly two small kicking, punching, and snarling
hurricanes grabbed him by the ankles.

Megan cried out, 'Off him you three, he's a friend.'

The dog and the twins obeyed reluctantly. It was the most fun and excitement they'd had since Turold had left.

She continued. 'In any case why don't you want to take advantage of me? What's wrong with me? What an insult!'

'I'm sorry if I offended you. I'm on important business and have no time for pleasantries.' He was not enjoying the outside world and wished to get back to his safe dank haven. In addition, it was the first time he'd spoken to a woman for fifteen years and that's if you count his mother. 'I have been reliably informed that your husband is alive and well and at the court of the Duke and Duchess of Normandy. Unfortunately delayed due to unforeseen circumstances. I've been asked to give you this bag which contains a note from Turold and gold.'

Megan took the bag and looked inside. There was a note, consisting of a picture of the family, crudely drawn like sticks, but she could clearly see herself, looking a bit like a pig, the twins, and a vicious animal consisting of mainly teeth with a small body and legs and tail. It was signed 'Turold'. Megan cried, she'd never had a note from him before. She would treasure it forever. Ah, and then the gold, that would come in handy and would last a year or more. She put the bag of gold in the most secure place she knew - down her bloomers.

Megan turned to Edgar who was being circled by the terrible three. 'I thank you from the bottom of my heart. Do you want some pottage and some ointment for your wounds? Please sit down here and hold out your hand and let the children smell and lick it. Once they have accepted you into the pack you should be fine, but don't make any sudden movements or the dog will go for you something horrible. We don't get much company you know.'

Edgar sat and replied, 'I'm sure you don't and if you did, they wouldn't stay long!'

They both laughed while the twins smelt and licked. Luckily Edgar had a bit of mouldy meat pie in his pocket that had attracted the dog's attention (it was currently ripping the pocket to pieces). He gave it to the dog and it calmed down, sitting down next to him in the hope that something else might materialise.

Edgar tried the pottage. It had an unusual taste and smell but was very good. He asked, 'What's in this delicious pottage?'

Megan whispered as if a secret, 'It's a special combination of vegetables and herbs as handed down through my family for generations. My mother and her mother before her were herbalists, although some called them witches. The females in my family have all been experts in understanding the beneficial nature of herbs, spices, and other plants. As they did before me, I add these to my cooking and I also sell potions.'

Edgar was starting to feel much better and relaxed now. It was incredible what the pottage had done to him both mentally and physically. He replied, 'No wonder Turold was so healthy and in good spirits.'

'Yes,' she replied, 'he often swore that it had put at least two inches on several bits of his body!'

He looked at her in a new light, no doubt influenced by the pottage. She was beginning to look very attractive now that his eyesight was going all hazy, with her long brown hair and full mouth of yellow teeth. He looked at the room and the beings in it. The dog was still next to him, but now on its back asking for its tummy to be tickled. Edgar wished it was Megan. Meanwhile the twins were gently chewing his shoes.

He finished the pottage and let the dog lick the bowl. 'I think, Megan, that the dog is a bad influence on the children, it's unnatural. I think they would be better off not having it as a role model.'

'I agree, but don't know what to do for the best,' she replied.

He had a think (the pottage had certainly improved his mind). 'I know that the dog and Turold don't get on. What if I take it to the alehouse? They can make good use of it there. And how about I arrange for the bar maid, who is fully trustworthy, although I would still suggest you hide anything valuable, to come to you a few days a week to help you with the children and the housework? Now that you have some money, you can easily afford it.'

Megan reflected on the proposal. 'Oh, I don't know, would they look after the dog?'

'Oh yes, they'll treat it very humanely.'

Megan replied, 'I'll have a think about it. In the meantime, please tell me how you knew about poor Turold.'

Edgar had a think, and sighed. He had never told anyone about his predicament. 'If you give me some more of the pottage, I'll tell you the whole sorry saga.'

And she did and he did.

Megan was a good listener and after the story was told, she considered things for a while and then spoke. 'What a difficult position you've been put in, but I fear that you may have been dreadfully misled and have relayed certain royal secrets to the Norman Duke William. You should consider the possibility that your dear mother may be in great danger or even worse. I'm thinking that your best way forward would be for you to sever your link with the shadowy figure and make your way to Normandy to find out the whereabouts of your mother. At the same time, you could also find my husband. I'm sure he'll be able to offer you some good advice.'

The pottage was certainly working because Edgar could for the first time see things clearly. 'You're correct. I must redeem myself and find both my mother and Turold and, if necessary, rescue both. I'll go to the nearest church to pray for forgiveness and ask for God's help. Can you please direct me to a church in the area.'

'Well, just follow the sounds of the bells. St. Mary's is nearby. Then you should return to the alehouse and seek help in finding a ship to take you to northern France. As regards my dog Lowell, please take him before I change my mind and while the twins are asleep, and ask that bar maid to visit me as soon as possible.' Megan gave him a vial of the herbal extract, adding, 'Only a maximum of four drops per meal, mind, or your brain will explode.'

Edgar laughed, but Megan was deadly serious. He looked at her again, and knew that if he didn't leave soon, things could get out of control, so he asked whether he could kiss her hand, which she allowed him to do, and he took the dog, which was now his best friend, and left, putting the door back in its frame. He was a completely new man. He was decisive and courageous. He would carry out his rescue plan, he thought, as he made his way towards the bells. After his visit to the church, he walked back to the alehouse (with the aid of someone's directions) where he left the dog and made arrangements for Betty the barmaid to visit Megan. He knew it was in the best interests of Turold's family, and particularly Turold, that the dog be removed. Turold hated the dog and the feeling was mutual, and at the end of the day, Turold was one of his best friends and so he should do the right thing for once in his life.

The next day the alehouse was selling meat pies with real meat, but it had all been quite humane, as Edgar had promised.

Edgar spent the next few days getting used to the sounds, smells, and peoples of London Town. This way, he built up his self-confidence and his fitness, ready for his mission. By the time he was ready to leave London, not only was his skin condition much improved, but he had also lost his fallen chest and could, for the first time in twelve years, see his waist. Mentally he was also so much better and he had regained his air of superiority. Overall, although older, he was once again the bold knight that he used to be when he had served as an officer in Edward's palace guards. He had left that employment following a disagreement with King Edward himself. As far as Edgar was concerned, he had done enough of Edward's dirty work over the years to last a lifetime.

TO WAR, BUT AVOID THE QUICKSAND

Earl Harold received a summons to meet Duke William. As
he entered the throne room and saw the duke sitting and
smiling regally on his beautifully carved chair, he knew
that whatever it was about he wasn't going to like it.
William beckoned Harold over and pointed to a simple
wooden chair in front of the red-curtained and carpeted
stage. Harold bowed, and sat on the uncomfortable chair,
feeling a splinter making its way into the flesh of his right
buttock. He was sure that it'd been put there deliberately,
which of course it had. It was another one of William's
strange jokes.

William smiled at Harold again, laughed as he thought
of Harold's discomfort, and then welcomed him. 'Good day
dear Harold, I've serious news. Normandy is about to be
attacked by an army from Brittany. I've decided to make a
pre-emptive strike before they launch a full-scale invasion.
I'm sure you would be only too pleased to offer your help
in my defence. As an honourable knight you will surely
join with me. Together we'll vanquish my enemy, Duke
Conan.'

William walked over and looked Harold straight in the
eyes, smiled yet again, then hugged him, laughed, and
declared, 'Come brother, let's teach him a painful lesson!'

He swept out of the throne room and Harold could do
nothing but follow.

William continued. 'My men are almost ready. I suggest
you and your men assemble in the courtyard, pick your

weapons and practise while the final preparations are made. I've sent your favourite battle-axe and sword to the courtyard for your use. Turold's friend, Rufus, will act as your personal bodyguard given his skills at protecting and saving people.'

Harold was astounded, and couldn't think what to say. His mind was in turmoil. He replied by announcing, 'I and my men will fight with honour, although my king should be the one who decides who I should ally myself with and who I should consider as being an enemy of England.'

William laughed. 'Well, he's not here, is he? I'm sure he would consider me a friend rather than a foe. Has he not promised me the crown of England upon his death? Surely as the commander of his armies you can make decisions in his absence, or are the English lacking in both initiative, spirit, and honour?'

Harold felt trapped and could only reply, 'We'll fight as hard as any of your own men.'

William showed him into the courtyard where the other Englishmen were already assembled.

William had already laid out his plans with his commanders. He would be taking a strong force, but he would minimise the number of mounted knights and archers in the army. He knew how the English fought. Their tactics were based upon those of the Vikings, and as such were vulnerable against a mobile enemy with heavily armoured horsemen with lances, protected by a strong force of bowmen. These perceived weaknesses, William concluded, he could exploit at a later time and place of his choosing, so he wouldn't alarm Harold regarding the damage that a well-trained European army could inflict upon a Viking-type shield wall, where the army consisted of a few rows of professional, heavily armed foot soldiers known as housecarls, backed up by several rows of lightly armed and untrained farmers and peasants.

Three hours later the army was assembled and ready to leave.

William gave a rousing speech to his men. 'We and our English brothers go to war to defeat this coward Duke Conan of Brittany. Our spies have informed us that he's about to move on our great friends and allies, the Bretons. We will defeat this dog before he has time to build up his forces. He means to defeat the Bretons and move on Normandy. His soldiers are violators of our Christian religion and our women. We must stop them now. We have the strength, and superior forces. We are Normans, descended from the Vikings, we will prevail since God is surely at our side.'

Bishop Odo blessed the men, and passed round a collection plate to help support the inevitable Norman widows. 'Your generosity will surely please God and protect you all.'

Odo was in a good mood when the plate was finally returned stacked with money. It would certainly pay for several days of his debauchery and feasting.

William looked quizzically at Harold as they left the castle. 'Are you sure you want to bring that hawk of yours with you? As you already know, the wildlife in my countryside can be very vicious. We have finches larger than that pathetic creature.'

Harold looked at his bird. 'He'll be fine. He's now fully recovered from his previous experience with one of

Normandy's demented squirrels and I can't leave him at the castle as he'll only pine for me.'

William shrugged his shoulders.

Out in the countryside, William offered Harold a challenge. 'How about a friendly wager? The one with the best bird wins, loser pays a forfeit. I suggest the bird with most species will be the victor but if a draw, then it'll be decided by the combined weight of their victims.'

Harold felt extremely confident. 'Agreed. Alfonso and I are the champions of England, but where's your bird?'

'Ah, yes Harold, I have my war bird today. I don't think you've met my darling Rouge yet, have you?'

William shouted. 'Bring me Red Claws!'

Two serfs wearing long leather gauntlets and leather masks came forward with a cart they had been pulling. It contained something covered in an embroidered sheet depicting many angry-looking red dragons. They pulled off the sheet, revealing a large cage in which some sort of feathered monster was glaring at all. Neither the Englishmen nor Harold's hunting dogs could believe their eyes. The dogs pulled so hard on their leashes that they managed to break free, and all of them ran off into the deep undergrowth never to be seen again. The two serfs carefully took a chunk of meat the size of a dinner plate out of a large leather bag and threw it into the cage. It was devoured in seconds. Next, they sang a soothing Viking song to the beast, and finally seeing that it'd calmed down sufficiently, removed it from its cage. On careful inspection, Harold decided that it must be some sort of cross between a golden eagle and a red dragon.

William put his hand on Harold's arm. 'Listen to me carefully. I highly recommend you do not look directly into his eyes since he doesn't like that. Best to look away and pretend he's not there. In fact, I suggest as you are going to be so close to him you should cover your eyes. He seems to have a liking for them, as one of his keepers can testify.'

Harold looked at one-eyed Francis. Harold quickly decided to comply. He was determined to retain both his eyes until his dying day.

William soke softly to the beast. 'Come to daddy, Robert Red Claws.'

The bird screeched loudly and obeyed. William was only just able to take its weight using both arms. 'I call him Robert after my dear father as he's got the same personality as him. Ready? Let the competition commence.'

The result of the competition was a tie as regards the number of species. Alfonso bagged a mouse, a rat, a vole, a starling, and a blackbird. Robert Red Claws returned with a piglet, a lamb, a cat, a puppy, and a baby. There followed a dispute as to whether the baby should count, but unfortunately for Harold, Norman rules applied and with the result being a tie, Robert won on weight.

'I think, dear Harold, that means you owe me a forfeit. We'll discuss details later.'

After compensating a young peasant woman for the loss of her youngest sister, dog, cat and livestock, the army marched on, leaving William with the fair maiden for a few brief moments. William looked at her and decided that he would also compensate her personally on his return, so he found out where she lived.

Aedre Aelfgyva, his current mistress, would surely find out that when it came to maidens, William had the attention span of a gnat. As with all charismatic and powerful leaders of the medieval period, it was the chase and the conquest that gave them the most satisfaction. It was just another form of sport as far as they were concerned. Unfortunately for the maidens, these men soon got bored with their conquests once caught. In this respect, Harold and King Edward were very unusual men indeed.

The large army passed into Breton at the mouth of the river Couesnon. A mile or so off-shore was the monastery of Mont Saint Michel, where William's family had established a colony of Benedictine monks. The monastery was a popular place of pilgrimage. William had chosen this as an apt place for more prayers and to receive God's blessings for his cause. Saint Michel was very important to many in the north of France, and hence a powerful aide to giving his men mental and spiritual strength. William, Harold, Harold's bodyguard Rufus, William's half-brother Count Robert of Mortain, and a few others were rowed out to the island where they were met by the monks and treated as royal visitors. With prayers and blessings said and a collection plate handed round, they all returned to the army on foot, as it was now low tide. William advised his men of his success in obtaining the support of Saint Michel and God.

One of the monks had accompanied them. He stood upon a wooden box he'd brought with him, said some prayers and gave a blessing, 'God bless you all and keep you safe. God make His face to shine on you.' He then took out a large gold plate saying, 'Your generosity will be rewarded by God!'

Once the monk had received his plate back filled with money, together with a set of toenails believed to be those of Saint Michel himself (as purchased by Vital from a market stallholder in Rouen), he snatched up his box and ran back towards the abbey before he was cut off by the quickly incoming tide.

The tide was now racing in, and as the army crossed the treacherous sands, they found that in places they had to wade through the waters with their shields and equipment held high. There was by now no way of turning back. They had to reach dry land soon or drown. Disaster was looming. William and Harold tried to rally the men. They were all getting exhausted and afraid, and many were getting stuck in the sand. Suddenly some of the men and horses fell into a submerged gully full of quicksand. Harold reacted first. He jumped off his horse, and plunged into the water, closely followed by Rufus, who was primarily concerned with the well-being of his impetuous charge. Harold managed to drag out several men, most of whom were Normans, while others helped pull out the frightened horses. Harold showed his great strength, determination, and selflessness as he dragged one Norman knight, Robert Count of Mortain, while carrying an Englishman on his back. Then back in he went, but this time he got into difficulty as he was now tiring. Rufus had to use all his strength to pull him and another Norman knight out of the sucking quicksand which was doing its utmost to devour them. After all the men had been rescued, they reached dry land and recovered. William pondered on the things he had witnessed. Harold was indeed strong and courageous, but he was also impetuous and cared too much for the safety of others. William considered that a leader putting his own life in danger for the sake of others was a character weakness that he could exploit.

The army marched southward and soon reached the old Church of Notre-Dame at Pontorson. Duke William commanded all present to give thanks to the Virgin for her deliverance from the quicksand. William, Harold, and other important men entered the church and said their prayers. Upon leaving the church, William vowed to have the church improved and enlarged, and that a large stain glassed window would be installed depicting the events of that day. Just as the army was about to march westward towards Brittany, one of Duchess' spies arrived on horseback. He informed William that Duke Conan and his army were now in the fort at Dol, just to the west of Pontorson. Before William could thank him, the agent had disappeared behind several large Norman soldiers, mounted his horse and was on his way back to Duchess Matilda.

Harold enquired. 'Duke William, who was that black-cloaked stranger?'

William scratched his closely shaven head and laughed. 'I don't know, but I know a duchess who does!'

It seems Matilda was not the only one with a spy and intelligence gathering network. Without his, William would have been dead years ago, but perhaps more importantly he would never have known what his wife was up to.

THE EUROPEAN TRUCE OF GOD

As regards fighting in Europe, I believe that this needs
explaining. Certain traditions, rules and strategies had been
established over the years. Unlike England, where at this
time there was a strong central government and therefore
no large standing army or castles or fortified towns and
cities, countries like Normandy were fully fortified and full
of men not only willing to fight, but brought up purely to
fight. These aristocratic men had been chosen at the early
age of seven or eight to follow the cult of chivalry and
become chevaliers, also known as knights. Most could
neither read nor write, since they did not need to. They only
understood riding, hunting, and fighting. They were violent
men, following a code regarding their own kind, but they
had no sensitivities as regards peasants, tradesmen, or the
lower classes. When there were no local wars, they became
mercenaries fighting for glory, pay and plunder. This is
what made an army like William's so different from one in
England, which would be composed of a core of
professional soldiers, the rest being farmers who took no
joy in fighting or being away from their lands and loved
ones.

As the European knights increased in numbers and
violence, they soon got out of control and in the end the
Church in Rome had to step in and lay down some rules.
The Pope reconciled himself to the concept that men would
always fight, but these knights took great pleasure in
rampaging all over the countryside carrying out atrocities

against any Christian peasants they came across. As a result, the economy of Europe was being affected. The Church of Rome introduced rules known as 'The Truce of God'. These rules were updated on a regular basis. Originally no fighting was allowed at Lent, on saint days, and from Saturday evening until Monday morning. This was later extended to cover the period from Wednesday evening to Monday morning, although some feudal lords ignored this extension when it suited them. This meant that peasants and the low classes were relatively safe to work at least three days a week, and have a pleasant rest on Sunday. After church on Sunday, they would increasingly worry about Monday and the fact that from daybreak they were fair game. Anyone breaking the rules, unless agreed beforehand by the Church of Rome would be damned. Normandy adopted the code in 1042, subject to the discretion of the Duke of Normandy.

As regards strategy in war, because every European nobleman had a fortified castle (otherwise he would not last longer than the lifespan of an ant) and because of the lack of heavy armaments, the first phase of any attack was to surprise the defenders. If this did not work, then the attackers were left with the alternatives of starving, or bribing, or frightening the defenders.

LET BATTLE COMMENCE

Firstly, William let loose his knights for some healthy rampaging and pillaging throughout Brittany, making sure they were fully compliant within the rules as set out in The Truce of God, as amended by Duke William. Then having frightened the population, his army advanced quickly to the town of Dol. William's army arrived suddenly at the fort and took Duke Conan by surprise, forcing him to escape by climbing down a rope at the back. Duke Conan then fled in the direction of his capital, Rennes, with the Normans in hot pursuit. At Rennes, Duke Conan joined up with the rest of his army and marched on to his wooden fort at Dinan. William reached that fort and planned the assault. He sent his main force out to attack the front of the fort while some of his men snuck around to the back and started fires. This eventually created an inferno, followed by a lot of coughing and panic from those within. Duke Conan had no alternative. He offered the Normans the keys to the fort by putting them on the end of a lance. Sir Robert took them triumphantly, bowed and handed them to William. The battle was over. William was victorious and the Norman casualties minimal.

William was extremely pleased with the way things had gone. *And now for the piece de resistance*, he thought. He called over Harold and Rufus. He extolled their bravery and courage, both before and during the battle. He also thanked them for saving his brother's life. 'You must both be awarded, especially you, Harold, who I will now call my brother.' He asked them both to bow down to him, which they did. 'I honour you both. You are true knights of Normandy. As my knights, I give you these arms as a token of my gratitude. Brother Harold, these magnificent arms are my gift to you. It is an honour to have such a fine leader and soldier fight for me and Normandy.'

Rufus was overcome with joy. In England he had been a low-life salty smelly sailor, but in Normandy he was a man of some standing, respected by all who knew him. Conversely, Harold was devastated as he was now officially, as far as the Normans were concerned, William's man.

RUFUS RECEIVES HIS REWARD

When the army returned to Caen Castle, Duchess Matilda called for Rufus. At their meeting, Marie helped with the translation.

'I hear that you have been brave yet again, and probably saved the lives of Earl Harold and my husband's brother, Robert. You must be rewarded. I understand that you are an English sailor and know the south coast of England well, including its harbours, tides and currents, sand bars and other dangers, am I right?'

'Yes, Your Grace, I am and do,' he replied, 'I have been a sailor since a young boy.'

'Good, I want you to help my shipbuilders and pilots. As you probably know, we have few naval ships, and therefore lack knowledge in this area. However, Duke William and I wish closer links with England and want to increase trade with other countries. I'm sure that with your knowledge, you can help us build a small fleet of ships, both for trade and defence. In addition, we want some accurate information about the tides, currents, and sand banks and rocks along the south coast of England, and in particular the counties of Sussex and Kent, including information on the ports and beaches. For your advice, you will be well rewarded. Also, I understand that you have become friends with one of our servants,' she pointed towards Marie. 'We will put nothing in your way if you wish to marry her, and we even offer you Norman citizenship, together with land. Finally, if you do wish to wed, we can arrange this at the partially completed cathedral at Bayeux. Unfortunately, given the recent riots, we do not consider it safe at this time for any foreigner to visit Rouen or its cathedral. They are still looking for someone to blame. I do therefore suggest you seriously consider looking more like a Norman by dealing with your hairstyle, oh, poor Walter can become your assistant. He needs a mental distraction and should be of some help to you.'

This was a lot for Rufus to take in, but it still seemed like a dream come true, and he could see no reason why he should not become their advisor given the help that the Normans had previously given the king of England, and the current peace that existed between the two powers. He therefore accepted Matilda's proposal, and he and Marie left swiftly.

They were both very happy and immediately started to make plans for their wedding.

THE TWINS' FIELD ASSIGNMENT-PART 1

The two Richards had advanced very well in their studies and were considered ready for their field test. Richard the First and his brother sat in front of Master Perciville. Just in case of any accident he was wearing a full set of armour and had a quick exit strategy.

'Listen carefully, you two. You have completed your foundation course and must now successfully complete a field test in order that you may progress to the next level. You have mastered some of your so-called powers but still lack the ability to fully control them. Your mission, if you are prepared to accept it, will be to go to the City of Lyon. There you will find many sinners, including the ruler, who dared to make rude comments about Duke William and our glorious Duchess Matilda. He called our great William a bastard who had ideas above his common lowly lineage. There are those in Lyon who laughed and agreed that our fine Duke William was the devil incarnate and not fit to rule a pigsty, let alone a country like England, and that our saintly Duchess Matilda was a dangerous religious fanatic who should be burnt as a witch. These people must be punished. Now listen very carefully. They have an annual dance festival on their bridge. You will disrupt this event and cause a level three destruction. Remember, level three only and not four!'

The twins looked at their agent's handbooks, and determined what that meant. They were surprised how harsh the punishment would be, but orders were orders especially if they were doing Duchess Matilda's divine work.

The master continued, 'Here are the details of your assignment. Please report to Master Quelle for your equipment.'

When they entered Quelle's quarters, they found him in the middle of testing a new weapon consisting of a long metal barrel with a wooden handle attached. Where they joined was some sort of trigger mechanism.

'Ah, men, just in time, watch this.' He gave the signal to his new assistant to hold the weapon to his cheek and pull the trigger. There was a loud explosion, and much smoke, followed by a great deal of gore and blood. When the air cleared, the three could see both the remains of the weapon and those of the assistant.

Quelle sighed. 'Too much black Chinese powder. Sir Perciville had acquired some from his contacts in the Far East, but so far, I have found no safe practical uses. Still, you can't make an omelette without cracking a few assistants, that's what I say.'

The master went to his desk, opened a drawer and pulled out a sign to display on the front door. It read in French, 'Man needed for stimulating work, no experience necessary. Would suit a single man with no family commitments.'

'To business, men. Here is your equipment.' Quelle gave them the basic agent kit, plus several disguises, many with large moustaches and floppy hats, hooked noses, false scars and even a peg leg. The twins had a great time trying them all on, but then things got out of hand. Quelle ended up with a broken leg and knife wound when Richard the

First managed to trip over while playing with the false leg and wearing two eye patches and juggling two daggers.

They were later severely reprimanded by Master Perciville and told in no uncertain words that their days would be numbered if such an event happened again. They were then both escorted to a back room by Master O'Really, a Viking from the Irish town of Duiblinn (Now known as Dublin).

'Welcome! You two sit down and don't do anything unless I tell you to. Good. Now look at the blackboard. You need to learn this simple Irish tune.'

Both scratched their heads. Richard the Last was first to ask, 'What's those black lines and those black dots and things?'

The master sighed, thinking it was going to be a long day. Indeed, it was.

By midnight the next day the two could whistle the tune like choral experts.

Master O'Really was exhausted but still in one piece, which was more than could be said for the glass in the two windows which had suffered from the twins' loud synchronised whistling.

'Go and eat, go to church, then go directly to bed with no dallying. Tomorrow, go to Lyon, enter the dance contest, and give them this routine. I'll give you someone to guide you as far as Limoges. Then it'll be down to you to head across the mountains to Lyon. Those mountains are full of dangers including gorges and wild animals and even wild ungodly humans. Your progress will be monitored at a safe distance throughout by several shady characters and you'll be assessed accordingly.'

The Richards took the manuscript and left, whistling. The master collapsed on the floor, hoping that he would never hear another whistle as long as he lived. Two shadowy characters entered and he gave them their instructions from a horizontal position. Duchess Matilda needed to know whether her blunt instruments would be of use on their forthcoming live assignments. The master could not understand why she thought the future of the crown of England could depend on these two buffoons if Earl Harold dared to double cross Duke William.

Early the next morning the two Richards rode towards Lyon with their guide, stopping overnight at various places on the way. At Limoges the guide reminded them of their assignment and then disappeared into the nearest eating house, searching for refreshments and soothing company after being with them for several days.

The twins rested in Limoges that night and after discussions with the innkeeper as to the best route east, and after a last flagon of beer and some fish stew, set off towards the mountains. Eventually they arrived at an eatery situated in a lovely village. The establishment was perched half way up the side of a gorge on the site of a natural water source. The original owner saw the economic benefit of building the village well in the courtyard, making it the focal point of the local population. The building was stoutly built, as were the current owner and his wife. They gave the knights a generous welcome and their horses were well fed and watered while the two Richards were well wined and dined. They slept well in their soft cushioned beds and awoke as new men.

'What an idyllic place!' Richard the First exclaimed to his brother.

'It is like I've died and gone to heaven,' replied Richard the Last, as he stroked a very well-fed black cat that had crept in during the night. It had no real visual appearance of any legs, just four paws emerging from a furry black ball.

They both agreed that this would make an ideal retirement location and marked it as such.

After a hearty breakfast for all four strangers (two men and two horses) and the even stranger black round cat, the two men and their horses were ready for the last part of the journey. Richard the First thanked the owner profusely, swore that they would return, and now as brothers, they embraced. Then Richard the Last gave him a final great big hug and slapped the rotund man on the back, tickled the purring cat, jumped on his horse and they both galloped off towards Lyon, leaving the poor man choking and staggering as the slap had made him swallow his wooden teeth. He was now going blue and waving his hands furiously. The Richards turned as one and waved back at him, and rode on, oblivious of his discomfort.

'What a wonderful man that Roland is. We must return on our way back and cement our friendship.'

Richard the other agreed with his brother, 'Yes, brother we will, and we will look at property in the village with a view to our retirement.'

Roland was now in mortal danger of choking, but luckily wouldn't meet his maker that way. He staggered forward, fell over the black cat, bumped into the wall of the well, and then toppled head first down into its dark dank interior. The cat looked on, purred as if happy with events, and made his way back to his mistress for his reward. His owner was the local witch and she had a score to settle with the villagers. The cat had been her instrument of revenge.

There was no escape for Roland. There was a plop, a gurgle, a glug, and a final, 'I'll kill those two when I ...' Then total peace. He had not choked to death. Unluckily, he had drowned.

No one knew he was down there. His wife thought he'd gone off on one of his occasional sulks in the woods since village life can be very claustrophobic. Next day it became clear that he'd just disappeared. Search parties found no signs of him. That moment of joy and friendship at the time of departure had caused a chain reaction, and the consequences had been dire for poor Roland and would soon be deadly for the rest of the community. The witch's plan had succeeded.

THE TWINS' FIELD ASSIGNMENT-PART 2

Later that day, the two riders arrived at Lyon. They put on their disguises. Wigs to hide their Norman haircuts, large floppy moustaches, and finally long beards. They both looked at each other and laughed. Then they entered the city. It was all very festive with colourful streamers of ribbons hung up and festooned everywhere, and there were containers full of flowers in front of the lovely painted houses. It looked unreal and the twins had never seen anything like it. As for the people, many of them seemed similarly embellished and some also had small ribbons and bells tied to their legs. They seemed to be in distinctive costumes, as if in teams. Most were just there for a good time and they meant to enjoy themselves to the full whether they won or not. Attendances at church masses had certainly fallen since the beginning of the week, although the number of people attending confession had increased enormously.

The Normans felt underdressed and awkward, and everyone was staring and pointing at them. They stood out like sparrows in a flock of blue tits. *Oh well, too late now,* they agreed, and moved on into the centre of town. There they found a pretty square, and the Hotel de Ville, with a sign stating in French, 'Sign up here for the dance competition'. This would be where the twins should enter their routine. There were two competition categories. One line was for the dance teams, and one for the dance creators. The two joined the latter.

When they reached the desk, the colourfully dressed man looked them up and down and exclaimed, 'This is not an undertakers' convention you know!'

The twins took a deep breath and counted to ten so as not to lose control, before Richard the First replied, 'We have a dance routine that we wish to enter. It was offered to Duke William of Normandy, that devilish despot, who refused to have it performed saying that it would need a braver man than him to do so.'

Someone large and with an air of superiority, dressed in red and yellow robes, sprang forward, and pushed his minion to one side, who consequently fell off his chair, hit his head on a table and was knocked out.

'Quelle dit vous?' he shouted, 'I am the Count Artaud of Forez, and I hate that evil so-called Duke William.'

Count Artaud had become very powerful in Lyon following a power vacuum after the incorporation of the region into the Holy Roman Empire. He had taken advantage of weak remote governance.

Richard the Last replied, 'If you are indeed brave enough to allow us to present our dance, you'll be able to prove your superiority over him.'

'I agree to the challenge. I am no snivelling coward. Have these two enter the competition and get them to teach the music and steps to our best groups. I'll show that William who is the bravest ruler in all of France!'

Count Artaud pointed his chubby fingers this way and that while talking to his underlings, and then the boys were ushered into a large empty room which soon filled up with a band of pipers, trumpeters, strange stringed instruments, and drummers. The Normans got to work relaying the tune, which had been written down on parchment by their master. They were also able to convey the tune by whistling it. It was a simple tune, with much repetition. The twins emphasised that it must be played quietly and relatively slowly at first and then progressively loud and fast. The name of the tune would be 'Danse de la Rivier' (translated from the Irish Gaelic, Rince Abhainn, or in English, River Dance). This was very apt, as it would be performed on the ancient wooden bridge of Lyon. This bridge spanned the wide river Rhone, which was now a raging torrent due to recent localised thunderstorms upstream in the mountains. These storms had been previously created by no less than the two Richards, through the will of God. The old Pont du Change was soon to be replaced by a new stone bridge, which would not only be much lower, but also would have houses and shops built on it. The dance competition would be the last event before the bridge was demolished.

It was an Irish sailor known as 'Mick the Sailor' who had possessed the manuscript detailing the ancient Irish dance. He was a trader in curiosities and was always looking for a pot of gold at the end of a rainbow. On the dockside at Caen, he'd traded a cargo of peat and Irish Whisky for a donkey and a map showing the location of the Ark of the Covenant. Master O'Really had met this Mick the Sailor in a den of ill repute in Caen. Mick had been asking anyone he met for directions to the Land of Kush and the upper reaches of the river Nile. Mick had offered the score and details of the dance to the master for the price of five gold pieces, four bottles of wine and three large garlic sausages. The master had immediately recognised the hypnotic qualities of the dance, and the power of it in the wrong hands. He had therefore acquired it on behalf of the agency.

Incidentally, the adventure of Mick commenced in 1063 when he and his now beloved donkey, Bryan, departed on a merchant ship bound for Constantinople. Many of his drinking companions had waived him off, whilst laughing. They all believed that he was either mad or simple-minded. Either way, they believed he would be dead within the year. However, Mick would have the last laugh. Three years later, he would return to Normandy from Africa, via Rome, were he sold his prize to Pope Alexander II. He was now a very rich man and ready to undertake another expedition on behalf of the Roman Catholic Church. He was in Normandy in order to obtain a document on behalf of Pope Alexander, held at the Norman Priory of St. Arnoul. He had received a great deal of information from Pope Alexander, and together with this document, believed that, God willing, he would find that most revered Christian relic, the Holy Grail. At the same time, he took the opportunity to hide certain objects and documents within the walls of the Priory of St. Arnoul. One of the monks would accompany him on his quest, which would last nearly four years. All of this would have important consequences for Richard Henry.

Once the musicians had learnt the tune, the twins showed three professional dance troupes the basics of the actual dance. This was based upon traditional Irish group line dancing. By the end of the day, they were all doing the synchronised dance perfectly, and as it got faster and faster, they all seemed to go into a trance. Count Artaud came and viewed the dance and it soon had his feet tapping. The Richards praised his footwork and prowess and he was easily persuaded to be the chairman of the judges.

Job well done, the twins were given a passable supper and plenty of wine, and shown to their sleeping quarters. They discussed the day's activities. It all seemed a bit convoluted, but the agency had decided that there should be no path of blame that could lead to Normandy, so normal brutish methods were out of the question. Duchess Matilda did not want to upset the Church of Rome and in particular the Pope, as Normandy may need his future support. In addition, the Richards had been told that this field test and study should fully determine their abilities and powers since their actual live assignments were so crucial and complicated.

As the morning broke, so did the twins' bed, since Richard the Last, desperate to relieve himself, tripped over the chamber pot and landed on his twin who was fast asleep. After some wrestling, which Richard the First won by one fall and a submission, they got dressed and had breakfast. Their room would remain uninhabitable for days.

After breakfast they made their way to the ancient bridge. At the bridge they supervised the setting up of the furniture ready for the performance. The bridge comprised a high single long wooden span connected to each side of the gorge by grey stone parapets and arches. It was known as the Devil's Bridge, partly due to it costing the lives of thirteen men in its construction, and partly due to the number of unexplained deaths associated with it. A recent event had worsened its reputation. A local powerful pagan known as Witch Hazel had stood in the centre of the bridge accompanied by her black legless cat and cursed the bridge and all those who walked on it. This followed a heated dispute with Count Artaud over an outstanding payment relating to the supply of spells and pagan rituals designed to harm his foes and improve his virility.

The Richards set up the judges' long table on the edge of the centre section of the wooden span, putting Count Artaud's plush red chair in the centre with three chairs either side. Jugs of wine and goblets were place on the table, along with scorecards. Once everything was in place, there was a procession consisting of Count Artaud and his assistant judges, followed by most of the townspeople. The spectators stood along the sides of the river Rhone to watch. The judges made themselves comfortable and with the drinks poured, the performances could commence.

The twins watched from a safe distance. They'd decided on the sequence of the teams. The various local towns' clog dancing teams would begin, and they consisted of seven teams of eight. They were led in one group at a time, with their mascot carrying their town flag. Eventually they were all in place. Each team was lined up before the judges in two rows of four, creating two lines of twenty-eight dancers. The teams had to perform in unison, so all had to start together and finish together, and all had to do the same sequence of figures at the same time, thus allowing the judges to more easily mark them for timing, accuracy of their footwork, and artistic expression. Finally, the band took their place on the stone section of the town side of the bridge.

Count Artaud stood up and raised his right hand, then dropped it to his side and sat down. The band commenced the tune 'River Dance', with a drum introduction, then a flag was lowered to start the dancers. Off they went with great flourish and gusto. To begin with they were all in sequence, but after a while one team started to falter. Some of the team's dancers had been too expressive so lost their clogs, which then flew off in all directions, causing several injuries to the performers and even one judge. All the dancers continued, clogs or no clogs. The wooden structure was now beginning to sway and flex as the clogs crashed down on the timbers after the various jumps and figures. The twins shut their eyes, prayed to God, and concentrated their minds on the bridge. Clouds of dust started to rise around the dancers like a fog. Small bits of timber fell from the bridge like confetti. The dancers continued, the crowds swayed and clapped. Everything was shaking, like a small earthquake. The dance was getting faster and faster and eventually the swaying seemed to reach a certain frequency of pitch that made the structure fail. The whole wooden section seemed to bounce up and down and then detach itself from the stone supports. It temporarily hovered unsupported, before finally falling horizontally as one piece into the gorge. The teams were oblivious to the end as they were concentrating on their dancing. The judges, coughing and wiping their eyes because of the dust, were unaware of the danger. There was a loud crash as the bridge hit the water, and for a moment it looked like a flat wooden ferry with accompanying dusty passengers, dancing, coughing, and wheezing. Suddenly the wooden structure disintegrated into the torrent that was the river. The passengers screamed for several minutes before disappearing under the water. All that was left were a few planks of wood and some clogs.

That was the fate of Count Artaud, his colleagues, and the dancers. God looked down, thinking, *job well done*. There would always be collateral damage on any religious quest, but the sinners of Lyon had been taught a lesson about the consequences of performing lewd and pagan dances strictly against His will.

The lesson had indeed been learnt and once the new stone bridge had been built, notices were put up on both sides of the new stone bridge stating, 'No dancing, on pain of death'. A memorial was also erected below the bridge. 'Here died Count Artaud, his nobles, and his dancers, who were all judged by God to be sinners'.

THE TWINS' FIELD ASSIGNMENT-PART 3

Job done, the twins quickly disappeared into the distraught crowds and set off back to the oasis they'd recently found. *Great food and plenty of wine would cheer them up,* they thought. Unfortunately, when they arrived, they found the whole village in turmoil.

The wife of Roland saw them coming and rushed out to meet them. 'Sacre blue, my husband, he has disappeared without trace leaving just this one shoe next to the well.'

Richard the Last was the first to reply. 'We left him two days ago in good spirits and waving energetically while we galloped away.'

'Oh, zut alors, what has happened? We are going to launch another search party!' she shouted.

Richard the Last was about to offer to help, but Richard the First grabbed him by the arm and shook his head. He jumped off his horse and went over to the well and peered into the gloom. He could just make out a bloated body floating in the water.

Richard the First frowned, realising what had happened, walked back, and mounted his horse. 'We would love to help, but we have very important business to attend to. I'm sure Roland will be found!' He then whispered something in his brother's ear.

The two men looked at each other, and their two horses, which could smell something putrid, also looked at each other. All four came to the same conclusion, time to go. The twins said their goodbyes, offered some comforting words, and slowly trotted off. Once out of sight the twins breathed a sigh of relief. Richard the First spoke, saying, 'Dear brother, we seem to have killed poor Roland! I think in the circumstances, we should never return to this place!'

Soon they passed a large rock monolith. It seemed to be a place of pagan ritual. There were offerings laid out before it, and certain symbols and crude pictures had been painted on it. Now turning their heads to the other side of the road, they saw a small, uncared for church in need of renovation and repair, with a likewise priest hunched on a chair in front of it.

He looked up, shrugged his shoulders, and said to them, 'I keep warning them that their sins will condemn them all, but they will not listen.'

After a few miles of climbing, they came to a bleak, dark dense forest. There were warning signs stating, 'Beware of the Wolves'. At the edge of the forest, in a small clearing, was a dull-looking small wooden house advertising food and wine for sale. The travellers stopped and Richard the First dismounted and knocked on the front door. He could hear footsteps that got louder and eventually a small gloomy woman all in black, holding a black round cat with no legs, opened the door letting out some very strange pungent smells.

She cackled and said, 'Why hello, you lovely well-nourished young things, can I help? I do not get many visitors you know.'

The cat looked at them strangely.

Richard the Last thought he recognised the cat, but decided just to order. 'A bottle of wine and some bread and cheese please. We will sit on your veranda.'

'Straight away young sir. I know not to cross you or your friend, I can feel that your God is with you both.'

'Some hay for our companions as well if you please.'

The twins sat down. The old woman, Witch Hazel, bought them two goblets, an open bottle of very red wine and a plate with unusual-looking bread and cheese. Everything tasted and smelt very odd. The twins looked at each other and then at the cat that was busy spraying Richard the First's left boot, and wondered, as a foul musty smell filled their nostrils, whether the cat was to blame. Later, the horses were given their water and musty smelling hay, and they too looked at each other and came to the same conclusion.

The Richards were depressed. They put their heads in their hands and meditated. The day had started off so well, but somehow, they could not celebrate their success. Their most favourite of places was in turmoil and to top it all, they had found the most depressing and decrepit eatery in the whole of France. Their mood seemed to influence the weather. Suddenly the wind picked up and a tremendous thunderstorm descended from the mountains. The rain came down in sheets. The twins were too deep in dark meditation to take notice. By now there was a stream running down the road, and after a while, this became a torrent. Next there was some creaking and cracking sounds and the building behind them suddenly parted from the veranda and floated off down the road. It failed to turn round a sharp bend and so plummeted over the cliff into the gorge below. As it fell, the cat had its stomach flat against the side window with its paws outstretched while the witch was spreadeagled over the cat trying to complete a cursing spell against the men, but failing as the dwelling hit a group of pagans below, just as they were removing their clothes.

The leader had been looking skyward for a sign from the god of the sky a few seconds before the building, its contents, and the water hit him. 'Oh, dragons' teeth! Thanks a lot sky god!' he screamed.

The twins were oblivious to all of this.

After a fair period Richard the Last came back to the real world. 'Brother, we must cheer up, since we're getting drowned here even though we are under this porch.'

Richard the First looked up at the porch, only to see the clouds.

He shrugged his shoulders and frowned. 'I hate to worry you brother, but the porch is gone. I shall get some more wine and see if the witch has any other food that is edible.'

He turned to walk through the door only to find it was also missing along with the inn and its occupants. 'Brother, you know the eatery, the old woman, and the cat, well they have all gone.'

'Eh?' Richard the Last exclaimed, and turned to look. 'Our fault no doubt. I think it best if we move on. Tell you what brother, tell me one of your jokes to make me laugh.'

Richard the First was looking sharply behind his brother at that moment and replied, 'What has a hundred legs and a thousand teeth?'

Richard the Last thought a while and shrugged, 'That's not a joke, it's a riddle, and I have no idea. You know I'm no good at riddles.'

His twin shouted as he ran for his horse, 'A pack of twenty-five hungry wolves, just look behind you!'

Richard the Last shouted at the receding back of his brother, 'That's not funny.'

Then he heard howling behind him. He turned and saw the fast-approaching snarling grey pack, and sprinted after his brother. Both jumped on their horses and all four sped away. The pack howled and ran after them.

God looked down. *That will teach that witch to work her magic*, he thought, *let alone the pagans below. Those twins also saved my holy priest. Shame about the cat though. Perhaps I'll give it another life.*

Luckily the wolves smelt blood from the gorge below and lost interest in their high-speed quarry. *Dead meat is easy pickings so why waste energy?* they all thought.

A plaque can be seen to this day amongst the few remaining bits of wood. It reads in French, 'Here lies the remains of a witch and thirteen sinners killed by act of God in the year of our Lord 1064. May their souls rot in hell.'

It is said that at night when the moon is full you can often see a ghostly black cat sitting on the pagan rock caterwauling, as if waiting for his mistress to come back from the dead.

The horses moved like the wind. It must have been something the old witch had put in their hay. Three days later, the twins were at the Normandy border and in the late afternoon, they were back at the agency. The horses were exhausted. They neighed their last neigh, collapsed and died on the spot. The twins were pulled off and carried inside to their beds where they slept for four days and nights.

When they awoke, they were given a big breakfast and escorted by Master Perciville to meet the Grand Master.

Richard the First said to his brother, 'I don't think we did too badly, considering. We may have lost points here and there but all in all we should have passed.'

Master Perciville was tight lipped, and they could see he wasn't in a good mood. He left them in the dungeon.

A disembodied voice boomed out of the darkness, 'You are here for your debriefing and assessment. Do you want to hear the bad news first or last?'

Richard the Last replied, 'That does not seem much of a choice.'

'I'll deal with your set assignment first,' continued the voice.

The boys looked puzzled. What could he mean?

'Your task was completed satisfactorily although we assessed the damage at level four rather than three. We have, however, decided to pass you at foundation stage mainly due to your ingenuity. Now as regards the other matters—'

'What other matters, master?' interjected Richard the First, totally confused.

'The collateral damage you both caused. Firstly, that idyllic village nestling on the side of the hill is now completely deserted. It has had to be evacuated because the water supply was contaminated, and will remain so for many years. So far there have been over forty cases of the plague.'

Richard the Last asked, looking as confused as ever, 'Was the landlord ever found?'

'Yes, eventually. He was the cause of the plague, having fallen down the well as a result of your energetic farewells.'

The twin asked further, 'What about his wife?'

The voice continued. 'She has the plague and by giving the search parties contaminated water, helped spread the disease throughout the valley.'

The twins shifted their feet, thinking it could only happen to them.

The Grand Master went on with his assessment. 'Then there is the question of the witch and cat, swept away in the localised thunderstorm and flood presumably caused by you two again.'

Richard the First quickly spoke up. 'Well, at least that's limited to those two beings.'

The Grand Master sighed. 'If only her house had not fallen on worshipers at a pagan sacrificial ritual in the valley below. The resulting death toll is fourteen humans. Luckily for you, as heretics, they all deserved to die.'

The twins lowered their heads in shame.

The Grand Master made his final summing up by saying, 'I cannot put all the blame on you two. We underestimated your God-sent powers. By your actions you have passed your intermediate field tests as well, but both of you require more intensive mind training by Master Perciville and Master Canobeck. Together they will succeed or all four of you will suffer the consequences. Duchess Matilda believes it is the will of God that you are used as His instruments, but we must bend and meld your minds to minimise unnecessary casualties. Now be gone and start your training. You must be ready for your intended field assignments.'

Master Perciville was summoned, and he led them away. The master was not a happy man. *These two will be the death of me,* he thought. He was probably correct.

EDGAR TO THE RESCUE

After two days at sea, Edgar finally reached Eu. He then made his way overland towards Rouen. On the outskirts of the city, he could see two men walking towards him who seemed in a terrible way, being covered in cuts and bruises, and with one limping badly. As they met Edgar the men recognised him as English from his clothes and his haircut and moustache.

One of the men spoke in English, and Edgar immediately realised that they were fellow countrymen. 'Don't go to THAT city mate. The locals are out for blood following the terrible fire, and are attacking anyone with a foreign accent or haircut or a moustache like yours.'

Edgar was shocked by their appearance and what fate may await him but he remained resolute. 'I must go. I am searching for my mother and my jester friend.'

'Well, if you must, I suggest you enter by the west gate as the buildings on that side of the city largely survived due to the westerly wind blowing at the time of the fire. Then you should see if you can find a moneylender, as they tend to know what is going on and speak English. However, firstly I suggest you get a haircut in the Norman fashion and have your fine moustache removed and pretend to be mute when meeting any strangers. I'll make you look more Norman for the price of two ales, a terrific offer considering that I could be saving your life.'

Half an hour later it was done, and Edgar looked like a true clean-shaven Norman.

'God be with you, gentlemen,' he said, and started to walk away.

'Stop sir, there is still one detail to address. Your English clothes give you away. Now coincidentally I have in my bag a woman's dress, hat, and cloak that I had bought for my wife. I think with these and some luck you may get away with being a mute Norman woman. For the price of four ales, they are yours.'

Edgar thought long and hard.

'Come please sir, make your mind up, we must get going as we have a boat to catch!'

Edgar decided he had nothing to lose other than his reputation. 'Very well, it's a deal!'

The Englishmen helped him dress and with the hat and hood of the cloak down over his head and part of his face, he could be mistaken for a tall shapeless woman.

Edgar said his farewells yet again, and was about to depart when one of the men grabbed his arm and said, 'Not so fast sir; you'll need a moneylender's address. For the price of two ales, I'll write it down for you plus a note in French. Just give the piece of paper to one of the guards at the west gate. Your dress should do the rest!' He then laughed.

Edgar was starting to wonder whether he was being taken advantage of but decided to accept, replying, 'As long as that's all I'll need!'

The other Englishman laughed and took out a large parchment. 'Well, it so happens that I have here a map showing the location of King Solomon's mines. I obtained it from a certain Irish sailor called Mick. Now, I can let you have it for the much-reduced price of —'

Edgar interrupted. 'No thank you. At this rate I'll have no money left!'

The two men grinned. Edgar took the piece of paper with the address and swiftly left the two men, who were both still grinning from ear to ear.

One of the Englishmen looked at Edgar's back as it receded, pointed at it with his bloodied finger, and said to his friend, 'Oh well, he was not as stupid as he looked. I must say however that I do not rate his chances of seeing tomorrow.'

They both started laughing as they continued their way to the nearest port.

Edgar would never know that the map that he was offered was genuine.

Edgar took out the vial of potion that Megan had given him and took a sip for courage. He had to circle around the city from the east to the west, eventually reaching the west gate at dusk.

There he was challenged by one of six large soldiers on gate duty. 'Bonjour madame, qui est somme nous?'

Edgar did not reply. He pointed to his mouth and shook his head.

'Ah tu ne peux pas parler.'

Edgar nodded. They looked him up and down. 'Ou allez vous madame?'

Edgar gave one of the guards the piece of paper.

'Ah un preteur d'argent.'

Edgar nodded his head; at least he seemed to be getting somewhere.

One of the men took him by the hand and led him down the streets, chatting away in French. Edgar's understanding of French was quite basic, but he could understand from the hand gestures that it was something to do with an explosion and fire and what bits they would cut off if they ever caught the culprits. Edgar just tried to nod and shake his head at the right moments. After a few minutes they were outside a grubby shop. The Norman spoke some more French, kissed him on the cheek, and left him on the doorstep. Edgar had the distinct impression that he had a date with the Norman soldier, and that he was to meet him at the eating house opposite at nightfall.

Edgar knocked on the door, and an old bent man in long robes opened it. 'Ah, entrée silver plate,' he seemed to say.

Edgar replied, 'Thank you sir, I need some information about the whereabouts of my mother and a jester called Turold.'

The old man quickly grabbed Edgar, pulled him in and locked the door.

'Don't speak English around here my good woman; it's dangerous to my health,' and added, 'in any case information for an Englishwoman these days doesn't come cheap.'

Edgar replied, 'I have plenty of money.'

Edgar had said the magic words.

'Ah,' the Frenchman hissed, 'luckily for you I am doing a two-for-the-price-of-one offer today. I am Dubois Junior by the way.'

'Where is Dubois Senior?' enquired Edgar, trying to break the ice.

'Counting the stock down in the cellar. He started just over a year ago, but for some reason hasn't finished yet. I'll get him if you want but he is a bit old, deaf, crusty, and dusty, and would probably take a week or so to get up the stairs, that's if he's still alive.'

Edgar decided not to pursue that line of enquiry. 'I want two pieces of information. Firstly, I want to know where my poor mum is. Duke William had her kidnapped. Her name is Aelfgyva. She is an English embroiderer by trade. Secondly, the whereabouts of a jester called Turold who was travelling with Earl Harold Godwinson.'

Junior scratched his head and a few other parts, then realised what was worrying him. 'You are a man not a woman! I'm afraid the price is more for an Englishman.'

Junior continued, 'Number two is easy, number one is more difficult. Pass over one, no, two, pieces of silver, and I will give you my answers.'

Edgar put the silver coins in the palm of Junior's spindly right hand.

'I believe the answer to one lies in Bayeux. You should go to the part-built cathedral and search out a certain Priest called Pierre the Pius. There is a monastery next to the cathedral. Ask someone there where you can find this Priest Pierre. He will know where your mother is. I knew her when she set up her business under the patronage of Bishop Odo. She borrowed some money from me, and thinking about it, she still owes some interest, but in the circumstances, I will write it off. We only hound lenders to the grave and not beyond, our policy is firm but fair. She set up the Taunt Aelfgyva Ecole de Embroidery, and it was very profitable, gaining the support of many of the nobility, including Duchess Matilda. Your mother was well known in embroidery circles and Duchess Matilda continues to run the school in your mother's name, although I understand that not all their activities relate to the needle and thread

Even today one of Duchess Matilda's daughters has a regular embroidery circle meeting at which they sing your mother's special sewing song. So go and see the priest and he'll bring you to her. As regards the jester, Turold, he's now jongleur to Duke William, and currently resides at the castle and palace of Caen under his protective custody. I suggest you deal with your mother first, before tackling the second quest. Turold is as secure as a gold coin in a moneylender's cellar!' He laughed again.

Edgar thanked Dubois Junior and left.

Junior went to the cellar trap door and shouted down, 'Do you want any supper, brother?' There was no reply. 'Alright, I'll take that for a no!'

The cost of food and drink has certainly gone down this last year, he thought. He did not want to go down into the cellar just in case it would result in additional expenditure on a coffin, funeral and so forth.

RUFUS AND TUROLD AT CAEN

Rufus was of extreme help to the Norman shipbuilders and pilots, and they were soon busy completing the plans for the various types of ships required by Duke William. These plans not only included craft to take men but also larger boats to take horses and even larger ships still to take provisions, including prefabricated wooden forts. The pilots were particularly interested in Dover and Pevensey, and Rufus was able to provide them with a great deal of information. He was happy in his work since it was so nice to be appreciated for a change.

Turold was also in a great frame of mind. Yes, he missed his wife and twins, but his work kept him busy. He was forever thinking up new entertainment, as vetted by Duchess Matilda. She had reassured Turold about his family, saying that they had been visited by no less than his friend Edgar, and were now well provided for. Turold was, however, a bit concerned about Rufus, who had gone completely native and no longer seemed to care about England. Turold did understand Rufus's point of view considering the way he had been treated in England, but he seemed to have no respect for English nobility or for the royal family. Turold was beginning to think that Duchess Matilda was a bad influence on his friend. She did seem a lovely and saintly person, but there was something more sinister behind this exterior show of kindness, he could feel it. He also saw the way she could subtly manipulate the will of her husband, and he was starting to wonder who was really in charge of Normandy. He decided that he would have to be more on his guard from now on, and warn Rufus accordingly. Turold still had a sense of loyalty to Edward and to Edward's wishes regarding the succession.

It was a gloomy morning in early June. Turold woke up with a start. His head was pounding, and his body felt as if a horse had kicked it. He couldn't open his eyes at first, worried about what he would see. He tried to remember the previous night but it was all a fog. He kept still for a few minutes and assessed the damage in his mind. He felt about the bed. He could feel two bumps on his left side and two on his right. He felt again, yes there were several lumps and bumps. He remembered that Vital and Wadard had decided on a man's night off in celebration of the advancement of Rufus. They had taken Rufus and him out to a place they knew, known as the Duke's Revenge (La Vengeance du Duc), and plied them with red wine, Camembert, and what resembled horse's unmentionables (being long round packets of meat product and herbs that made your mouth tingle), leading to yet more wine. He opened his eyes, and could make out another lump and two dark dangly feet poking out from under the sheet.

Turold looked under the sheet and enquired, 'Hello, and who are you?'

The lump groaned and stirred. It had a face and red eyes and once it had found its mouth and tongue it replied, 'It's me, Turold you daft jester, it's Rufus.'

'Oh, sorry my old friend, I didn't recognise you without any clothes on. I must say you look a lot larger in the flesh so to speak.'

The chamber door opened and in walked Vital and Wadard.

Vital laughed. 'Time to get up. I must say you were both very entertaining last night!'

Turold and Rufus both yawned stretched, and once the bedchamber and its floor had stabilised, they fell out of bed, stood up, fell down again, stood up and slowly dressed. Once their legs were fully obeying their brains, they were helped downstairs by Wadard and Vital and out into the cold fresh air. Through the courtyard, through the gates, and down the main road they staggered.

Wadard announced on the way, 'Time for breakfast and some hair of the dog!'

Turold collapsed onto his knees. 'Please leave me here to die, you can pick up my body on the way back!'

Vital shook his head and wagged his finger in the direction of Turold's red half-shut eyes. 'It's for your own good as well as ours! You'll both thank us for our help afterwards!'

Rufus was not too sure, but helped Turold get up. In through a large damaged wooden door they went, and Vital and Wadard helped their patients sit at a large table in the corner. Both Turold and Rufus collapsed on the benches.

Wadard ordered breakfast that consisted of bread, eggs, and milk containing a little something to help after all that wine. After a while, Turold and Rufus looked at their surroundings, now that their eyes could focus. It was a large eating house, with a great deal of broken furniture. The owner was looking at them while shaking his head and speaking some vile French under his breath. He then continued to sweep smaller parts of tables and chairs into a corner, only looking up now and again in the direction of

Turold and Rufus so he could quietly utter some more curses. With the knights present, he could not take matters further, but if they were ever left alone, he thought, he could take his revenge. His two daughters were still recovering upstairs and had a great deal of explaining to do, along with one of his serving wenches who currently had a huge grin on her face as she looked at Rufus and waved.

In another corner was a young woman of about Turold's age. She was a gift from Vital to Turold. Vital had investigated Turold's ancestry to establish his remaining family in Normandy. It seemed she was one of his cousins and her name was Jeanne. She looked like a female version of Turold. She even had the same large ears.

Through conversations and interpretations between the four men and Jeanne it became clear that the woman had certain gifts, which ran through the female side of Turold's family. She had the gift of prediction and used it to make a meagre living. Vital had asked her to come and meet her cousin and give him a prophecy. Turold and she had a lovely discussion about his father and the family, and then she agreed to investigate Turold's and Rufus' future, which seemed to be done through a mixture of palm reading and the holding of their heads with her hands. When she had completed her procedures, she looked up, amazed, glanced and pointed at the boys, gabbled a lot of quick French to Vital, and then through him declared the predictions, which were almost identical. The men, it seemed, had two futures. One path led to their destruction, one led to the destruction of others but to the glory of the unlikely pair. Other information was given, none of it particularly precise, but food for thought for the two of them. Turold had a good long think and asked Vital whether it would be at all possible for his cousin to meet Earl Harold for a prediction.

The Norman rubbed his face and played with the hilt of his sword for a while, then decided. 'I see no harm in it but it must be done discreetly. I will make the arrangements. Eh, do you two remember what happened last night?' He looked apologetic.

Rufus, being more anxious than Turold given his recent engagement, was the first to reply, 'No, I remember absolutely nothing!'

Vital thought for a while. 'Best if I don't but I can say that Wadard and I learnt a new fighting move off Turold, and you, Rufus, are an excellent chair wielder and thrower, as several Normans can testify. It will go down in the Norman chronicles as one of the best drunken brawls in history. As regards the rest, I will just suggest you both ask God for forgiveness.'

Rufus sighed, 'Oh God.'

'That would definitely be a good start,' laughed Wadard,

'Now we must get back before we are missed as Duchess Matilda has eyes everywhere.'

Upon their return Turold and Rufus immediately went to chapel and asked for divine guidance and forgiveness, although they did not know exactly what their recent sins were.

HAROLD AND THE FUTURE

The arrangements made, four guards led Earl Harold to the palace gardens on the pretext of having sword practice. There he met Vital and Wadard, Turold and his cousin, Jeanne. Vital dismissed the guards.

Harold was bemused. 'What in heaven's name is going on?'

Turold came forward and replied, 'I know that we do not see eye to eye, and not just because of the difference in our heights, but I thought I might be of assistance to you regarding your current predicament. I believe that you need some enlightenment as regards your possible future so that you may choose the correct path that you must walk. These two Norman knights have at great personal risk brought you here to meet this talented soothsayer. Now I know you may not believe in such things, but I beseech you, sir, to let them help you, especially considering the danger that all five of us have put ourselves in. No doubt you know by now what will happen if Duke William does not become the next King of England.'

Harold was completely taken aback. He had to acknowledge that Turold spoke the truth. He was beginning to wonder whether he should have sought Turold's help and advice as soon as he had got into trouble. Perhaps if he had, he would not have been in this situation.

Harold therefore agreed to the proceedings and the lady looked into his future by holding his hand. She could see how important Harold was to the future of both England

and Normandy, and possibly the surrounding French-speaking lands, especially the county of Anjou. She could see two possible futures. If Earl Harold agreed to ally himself with Duke William, then together they would make England one of the most powerful countries in Europe. If he did not, but stood in the way of Duke William becoming the next King of England, then this would lead to war and several battles. She also saw that Turold, two twins called Richard, and others could also influence the future depending which path Earl Harold took. Finally, she could also see that as a result of decisions already made and deeds already done, Earl Harold's options and outcomes were extremely limited. He had a binary choice to make.

She thought for a few moments before deciding what to say to Harold. 'You have two futures. You can either follow the wishes of King Edward or the determined wills of Duke William and Duchess Matilda. Both will lead to bloodshed and death. Whose death and whose blood, depends upon the choice you must make. Finally, I warn you not to defy God since this will lead to death, destruction, and great suffering both to you, your family, and the English people.'

Harold did not really believe in such prophesies, but decided to be kind to the woman considering the risks everyone had taken. But then again, she was correct, he had an important decision to make. He thanked the woman and gave her a gold coin. She was very grateful, but at the same time, troubled. She had this feeling that Earl Harold was not strong willed enough to make the difficult decisions he must make. Deep down, she believed, he was too nice a man to do the right thing at the right time. She was led away by Wadard, and then the guards were recalled to escort Harold back to his quarters. Turold and his Norman friends returned to the eatery for a good goblet of wine and further discussions.

Later that afternoon, Harold considered his terrible dilemma while he was exercising within the castle bailey. *To defy Duke William while still in Normandy would be suicide and leave my kin and my men to rot in Normandy for the rest of their lives. Also, I'm needed in England to ensure the safety of the realm. There are threats from Scotland, Denmark, and Norway. My priority must be to escape with my brother, nephew, and men, back to England. No, if I stand up to William now, this will not help England. The best plan is for me to do and say anything so that we may return to England. Once there, I'll try and persuade King Edward and the English Council, The Witan, to support my suggestion that Duke William should succeed King Edward. If I ally myself with William, I can see the positives. I have no real aspiration to be king. I'll survive if Duchess Matilda allows me to breathe. She is the ultimate power in Normandy. I've met regularly with her in the evening while William amused himself elsewhere. As a result, I believe we have become friends. I must agree with her, what England needs now is a strong king on the English throne, and William would be the right candidate. Together me, William, Matilda, and her father would make England too powerful to be invaded by anyone. Yes, Harold thought, my family and I could well have a comfortable and long life under Norman rule.* Another thought came to his mind. *But what if King Edward and the Witan reject my suggestion? What if they insist on me being King Harold of England? No, I must not be negative!*

'Oh, God!' he shouted, 'Give me a sign!'

Harold fell to his knees, put his hands together, and looked up to heaven.

The sun was strong and the sky blue and cloudless.

'Please God, give me a miracle like you did when I was young, when you cured me at Waltham Abbey of my paralysis. Show me what I should do!'

After a short while, he could make out the outline of, of, YES it was an angel no less! He could see the pure white feathers of the outstretched wings as the angel descended from heaven. The angel now seemed to hover directly above him, and then dropped something. The beautiful white package fell towards him. *Soon all will be revealed*, he thought. A few seconds later he was hit in the eye with a large blob of white chalky faeces, and then the angel gave out a loud squawk as it flew overhead. Harold was now blind in his right eye. He wiped the substance out, realising that it had merely been a very large seagull. *Typical, although on reflection*, he thought, *perhaps it is some sort of heaven-sent sign. All I need now is for Duchess Matilda to spring some unwelcomed gift or surprise on me.*

God looked down and chuckled. *Your wish is my command! I didn't realise that Harold could predict the future so well! I'll not disappoint him!*

HAROLD, YOU'RE ENGAGED

Harold received a request to meet Duchess Matilda after his evening meal as usual. Matilda sat waiting nervously for his arrival. She and her family had come to like Harold a great deal. There was nothing sexual in her desire to be with him. It was just that Harold was everything dear William was not. Unfortunately, William had recently found out about these assignations and had become jealous and suspicious. This had led to a sharp increase in injuries amongst the servants and soldiers due to his sulks. In the circumstances, she felt it best to end these enjoyable meetings, and conclude her agenda. Things had taken a strange turn, but perhaps one that would save Harold's life. There was a knock on the door and Harold was ushered in by her most loyal and discreet lady in waiting, Adelaide. Adelaide left giggling.

Yes, these meetings must cease, Matilda thought, as the door closed and the giggling continued. 'Ah, sit down dear Harold, I have some serious matters to discuss.'

Harold sat down uneasily.

She continued. 'William seems to have got it into his head that there is something going on between us.'

Harold laughed.

'It is no laughing matter. He's deeply distrustful and as you know that is not a good emotion for him to have. He seems to like and admire you greatly, but I am worried that your life is now hanging but by a thread.'

Harold tried to clear his head of all the possible deaths William was contemplating.

'However, there is another complication that has come to my attention.'

Oh, dear, Harold thought, *what's next?*

'You seem to have made an impression on one of my children.'

She called out, 'Come here, Adel.'

A young, dark-haired girl with beautiful brown shining eyes, just like her mother's, entered from another door. She curtsied and sat on a stool beside her mother. She was only in her early teens but anyone could see that she had the makings of a fine-looking intelligent lady. Harold was amazed. He had spent much time with Adeliza, known as Adel, mainly trying to teach her English and the English customs. She had been a good student, but he had not thought of her in any other way. This was a total surprise, or was it a nightmare?

'Adel has, it seems, taken quite a liking for you, and would make a fine wife for someone like yourself. In addition, such a match would not only bind our two families together but also stop these malicious rumours, since such a topic of conversation would reasonably take up a lot of our time. You must see the benefits of this proposed match. I know that deep down you would be happy to accept my husband as your king and would work with the two of us to bring strength and stability to both England and Normandy. In practice, you would be able to rule England on behalf of us, since I in particular will spend all of my time in Normandy.'

Harold looked at Matilda, and then at Adel. Both were smiling from ear to ear

After what seemed like hours but was probably just a few moments, he spoke. 'It certainly seems a practical solution to both my predicament and that of England.'

'Then it's agreed.' Matilda stood up to her full height of four feet two inches and held out her hand.

Harold could do nothing but bow and kiss it, then Adel held out her hand and Harold kissed that as well.

Adel looked concerned. 'Sir, your right eye is so red and inflamed, does it hurt?'

Harold had not really noticed, merely perhaps a slight discomfort.

Matilda was naturally concerned and so rushed over and looked. 'Did anything unusual happen that could have caused this?' she enquired.

Harold nodded. 'Actually, yes, today in fact. I was hit in the eye by seagull droppings.'

Matilda took command of the situation. 'Adel dear, go and fetch some salt and some of our special clean fresh holy water.'

Adel rushed off, and soon returned with a soft clean linen cloth and a towel, a small jug of water and a cup with some salt. Matilda mixed up a saline solution, and then added a small quantity of something she kept safely locked up in her personal medical cupboard. Harold was able to see some of its contents, some small bottles with French writing on them, several with the word 'Poison' on their labels. *No doubt,* he thought, *the source of many a death.*

'Adel, you know what to do; I'll leave you to attend to Harold. I must now leave and seek the Lord's help.'

With these words Matilda left the room.

Adel smiled at Harold as she bathed his eye. At first the liquid stung, but soon began to give him some relief.

At the end of the treatment, she kissed Harold on the forehead, then spoke. 'Sir, you will need further care to avoid any possibility of blindness. I will see you after breakfast tomorrow.'

She helped him get up from the chair.

Harold kissed her hand again and said, 'Thank you and good night eh, dear.'

He turned and staggered out of the room as if on a ship in a gale. *Congratulations*, he thought, *you're engaged.*

Over the next week, Harold concluded that his new young fiancée had all the mental characteristics of her mother and a fervent Christian. Although her body was still maturing, her mind was already fully developed and as sharp as the blade of a dagger. Beneath that shy exterior was a woman born to be a queen. The words that she had said to him at the last session were seared into his mind.

'Harold dearest, what if we marry as my parents wish, but rather than you support my diabolical father in becoming king of England, you yourself take the crown once the old King Edward dies! What could my parents do to stop us ruling England? Or, what if we allow my father to become king and then soon after he has a very unfortunate hunting accident and we take the throne before my eldest brother has time to even leave Normandy!'

Harold was stunned. After several minutes in thought, he had had to agree that if he did marry Adel there would be various ways of neutralising the Norman threat.

'My dear, you are as devious as your parents!' he had told her.

Adel had smiled. 'Perhaps even more so!'

WILLIAM'S TERMS

The next day Harold was taken to see Duke William. William sat on his throne looking every inch a king. 'Ah, my knight in shining armour, and my son, since you're now betrothed to my daughter Adel, and my brother since that's who you are, after saving my brother from the quicksand. It is time we strike a formal agreement.'

Harold replied, 'I agree, sir, I'm happy to conclude matters so that I, my kin, and my men can return to England. It is in neither of our interests to leave England's armed forces so poorly commanded. As you know there are several knaves waiting for just such an opportunity to attack the country. So, what pray are your terms, sir?'

William was taken aback by Harold's resolute reply. He and Matilda had discussed the day's proceedings but hadn't counted on this. Harold seemed strong, and unconfused, and his body language had changed.

'Oh, eh....' William spluttered, wiggling his sceptre. Regaining his composure, he continued. 'These, brother, are my terms. You will support my claim to the English throne. You must make ready the castle at Dover for me, and my army, to be initially used by us upon the death of King Edward. Upon the death of the king, we will join our two families together by the marriage of you, brother Harold, to my beloved daughter, Adel. You will support me in becoming the next king of England. As a show of good faith, once I have your agreement, I will immediately ready ships to take you, your nephew, and your men back to England. You will be escorted to ensure your safety. As regards two of your party, namely Turold and Rufus, they will be allowed to remain here if they so decide, but your brother will be held as security and released once all matters are concluded. As regards your reward, I will make you the second most powerful man in England and we will rule England as brothers.'

Harold considered the proposals. Most were as he expected, except for Dover. As regards Dover, yes that was possible, but could be awkward. As regards marriage, he and Adel had already agreed upon her plan to make him and her king and queen of England. As regards those left behind in Normandy, if they had to be sacrificed for the greater good, then so be it.

'I agree,' announced Harold.

William was again wrong-footed, expecting at least some resistance, especially as regards Harold's brother, and began to question whether Harold was taking his agreement seriously or just playing along so he could get back to England. He pondered for a few minutes and suddenly he had a miraculous idea, as if from God. Perhaps Matilda's visions were rubbing off on him.

'Then let's seal our agreement and bind ourselves before God. We will meet in the field close to the cathedral under construction at Bayeux and swear our agreement in front of the sacred bones of our Norman saints. This will make the agreement both secular and religious,' said William, rushing over to Harold and hugging him.

Harold thought, *oh well, let's just get it done and we can all get back to England.* However, he knew deep down that things would never be the same again and he would be walking a tightrope until the William situation was resolved. He had decided that he had two choices. Either persuade King Edward to choose William as his successor, or obtain King Edward's agreement to him marrying Adel, and following the marriage, get Edward to formally declare him as Edward's successor with Adel to be the next Queen of England.

Harold broke from the hug, and slapping William on the back (which nearly caused William to unsheathe his sword) said, 'Now let's have some food and wine.'

The new best friends walked off together. Matilda and Adel, who had been hiding behind a screen, smiled, and hugged before heading off to church. Adel would pray to God and Jesus. They would surely help her become Queen Adeliza of England. She was determined to be the power behind the man, just like her mother. She would make Harold the greatest ruler in Europe, and perhaps even the next Holy Roman Emperor. Her ambition was indeed boundless.

THE DAY OF CONVERGENCE: PART 1 - EARLY MORNING

The swearing of the oaths was to be held on Easter Saturday to make the spectacle even more religiously significant. Matilda was determined to have her husband's claim to the throne sanctified by God. It would be seen by all present that the will of God had decided that England needed to be purified and that Duke William was the man to do it, supported by the most powerful Englishman alive. Matilda would carefully choreograph the event and nothing would go wrong. Her agents and the army would see to that. All dissidents or potential ones were rounded up and the two Richards were escorted by armed guard to a secret location at least two days' ride from Normandy. The twins were considered too dangerous to be anywhere near the most important event so far in Normandy's history.

The day of convergence was upon the various players of the drama. Firstly, that morning, Rufus was to wed his beloved at a small church in Bayeux, with Turold as best man, and Vital and Wadard as escorts. Duchess Matilda had insisted on a simple service so as to not upstage the main event.

Edgar meanwhile had stayed overnight at an eatery in Bayeux, and had plans to visit the monastery with the intent of locating Priest Pierre the Pius.

That afternoon, Harold and William were to swear their oaths at a field beside the part-completed cathedral at Bayeux, in front of a great multitude. God was in command of events and the players merely his sheep, and one was being led like a lamb to its slaughter. Many did not realise that they were no longer in control of their destiny.

Rufus was up early as it was his wedding day and he was very excited. Soon he and his one true love would be wed. He had made Turold best man, which had made Turold cry with happiness.

Rufus had said to him, 'That's not the English way. Be steadfast.'

Turold had replied, 'I am not English, and in any case, you are to become a Norman soon, so start crying immediately. We Normans know how to be emotional.'

They had both cried with joy.

Vital and Wadard had a wedding breakfast prepared by the kitchen staff as their gift to Rufus. After breakfast Rufus was made to have a bath and dress smartly for once. Vital and Wadard then escorted Turold and Rufus to the small church at Bayeux along with twenty horsemen who, with some prodding with their lances, cleared the way through the throng heading in the other direction towards the cathedral. Marie had already left and would meet them at the church.

Edgar had also risen early and was on his way to the monastery. He could not believe how busy the town was getting, but understood from a man, who had started celebrating early, that there was to be a great event in the field next to the cathedral. Edgar eventually found the monastery down a small lane next to the cathedral. He knocked on the stout ornamental wooden door with a carving of a large cross on it. There was a sign on the door in French, 'Welcome all true Christians' and another smaller one under it, 'By invitation only'.

After what seemed ages, he heard footsteps far away that got louder and louder, and then a small wooden slat at eye level (for most people of a certain height) opened and a round white large-eyed head commanded, 'Qu'est-ce que vous voulez?'

Edgar replied, 'I seek the location of a priest called Priest Pierre who I believe resides in this town.'

'Ah, you are the English. That's indeed a dangerous language to speak. You must either be stupid or reckless.' The head turned around and shouted, 'I've a silly Englishman here! Well, I think his face is that of an Englishman but his clothes are those of a woman. He or she is looking for a local priest called Pierre. Does anyone know him?'

Various voices replied, 'I know a Priest Pierre the Pusillanimous.' 'I know a Priest Pierre the Penitent.' 'I Know a Priest Pierre the Plump.' 'I know a Priest Pierre the Sacrificed, oh just a moment I believe he's dead, burnt at the stake by pagans near Lyon.' 'I know a Priest Frere Jacques but, as usual, I don't suppose anyone is interested in who I know.' 'I know a Priest Patrick—'

Edgar interjected, 'My God shut up! I'm a man in a hurry. I just need to know the whereabouts of Priest Pierre the Pius.'

The head turned and glared at him. 'Did you just blaspheme?' The head turned back and shouted, 'Did you hear that, brothers? This person just called the name of our maker in vain.'

'Yes,' they all cried aloud, 'Blasphemer!'

The head turned to him again. 'You must repent or be punished by God. We don't normally allow guests, but if you have gold then in this emergency you can enter and we'll go to chapel so you can repent before God.'

Edgar gave up and said, 'Yes, I have gold.'

The man grinned and started to unlock the door, which seemed to have several locks and innumerable bolts.

Someone in the background cried out, 'It's nearly time for prayers. He cannot come in.'

The man scratched himself and said, 'Oh damn, I mean oh dear, eh, I know, promise to come back at daybreak tomorrow and we will sort this all out. Now going back to your question—'

'Yes, yes,' cried Edgar.

'You want to know about Priest Pierre the Pius.' The head turned again. 'He wants to know where he can find Priest Pierre the Pius, brothers.'

'Finally!' Edgar exclaimed.

There was total silence behind the door, so the head turned and said, 'Sorry, we've never heard of him.'

Then he closed the cover, locked and bolted the door and walked away saying to the others, 'People these days are so impatient.'

Edgar slid down the door and collapsed onto his knees. The sun was shining down on him but he was gloomy, exasperated, and exhausted. He meditated for a while, thinking of God, and then a cloud came over the sun and he felt a refreshing breeze. Someone tapped him lightly on the shoulder.

A voice gently spoke. 'Can I help you, madam?'

Edgar looked up and saw a tall stout white-bearded man in a shiny white swirling robe with a hood, holding a crook in his right hand.

Edgar thought he must be God.

Edgar replied, 'Lord, I am just looking for a Priest Pierre. Oh, and I'm so sorry about blaspheming, please forgive me Lord! I do truly repent!'

The heavenly apparition spoke again. 'I'm the priest whom you seek.'

Edgar was raised to his feet by two white arms, and then the man laid his lily-white hands on his shoulders and blessed him.

Edgar felt pure energy flowing through his body, as if he was drinking a glass of rich ruby wine. He seemed fully restored and invigorated.

He managed to utter, 'Are you Priest Pierre the Pius?'

The man replied softly, 'Well I'm no shepherd that's for sure,' as he pointed to his cloak and crook. He continued, 'Yes I am he, also known as Priest Peter, and these days as Priest Pierre the Sacrificed.'

'But you're dead!' exclaimed Edgar.

Pierre looked up to heaven and said, 'I know, but God had other plans.'

Edgar could not comprehend. 'I don't understand.'

'I don't either, but we must never question the will of God. Now, sir, we must get going, we can't afford to be late. God has His timetable. Walk with me to my church and I will help you seek answers to your questions.'

They walked together arm in arm, which was difficult given the crowds, but most seemed to immediately recognise the priest and let them through, some touching the white robe and asking for him to place his hands on them. It seemed many considered him a saint on earth and the holiest man in Normandy.

'I was told by God at prayer yesterday to come to the monastery where I would find a distressed Englishman in need. I was further told to take you to my church, where I am today entrusted to perform a very important marriage, and where certain people are destined to come together in the same place at the same time by the will of God.'

Edgar repeated, 'But you're dead!'

Pierre thought for a while, trying to make sense of it as well, then told his tale. 'I was commanded by God to visit two villages in France which had become bastions of pagan worship. I was to bring them back to God. My first stop was at a small rundown village church with an even more rundown village priest. He warned me not to go to the village, as it was full of pagans who would gladly sacrifice any stranger, especially a Christian one. I replied that I was on a mission from God and had to go. He shook his head and blessed me, more in hope than in the certainty of deliverance. I went to the first village, but they were not only unrepentant but also decided to tie me up and sacrifice me to their pagan god. They took me out to a pagan site at the bottom of a gorge. I could hear wolves howling above like devils. They tied me to a stake and surrounded me with firewood. They then started their diabolical ritual, led by a dark master. At the climax of the ritual, they all started to disrobe and the master lit a torch and looked skyward, his arms outstretched. He set fire to the firewood and the flames started to lick around my feet. The master looked up again towards the sky, when suddenly a torrent of water and a building came tumbling down towards us all. I was immediately knocked out. When I awoke, I found total devastation. No one seemed to stir. Somehow, I had survived. The water had extinguished the flames and it seems only the front of the building had collapsed on me, and with the front door open, I had only received superficial wounds. Yes, a miracle indeed. I stepped out of the door and walked around. All had perished. Then I heard some scratching and saw a large black longhaired cat squeeze out from underneath some old woman's body. It cried, 'Meow', came over to me, and rubbed against my legs. I decided then and there to keep it and call it 'Beelzebub' in recognition of the events. I managed to stagger away from the scene, and the cat led me across a small wooden bridge to the other side of the river, and then up the cliff to a cave where I rested awhile and recovered. As I sat looking out, I could see the pack of wolves feeding on the corpses. I closed my eyes and prayed. Later that day, we left the cave and again I started to stagger, then I collapsed, hit my head and was unconscious. I was rescued a day later by a search party looking for a man called Roland who had disappeared in unusual circumstances. When I told the authorities my tale, they gave me the name 'Priest Pierre the Sacrificed'. Once I was fully recovered, I went on to the next village, but found it totally abandoned and was told that most had perished through disease and plague by the wrath of God and I had been too late. As a result of these events, I seemed to have become someone who God raised from the dead, and therefore a divine being and living saint!'

'Incredible!' Edgar exclaimed.

Pierre continued, 'Now we must hurry; God doesn't like His sheep to be late.'

THE DAY OF CONVERGENCE: PART 2 - THE MARRIAGE

Priest Pierre opened the door to the small ancient church and ushered Edgar into the vestry and sat him down. 'Now, we have but a short span of time to conclude the matters you have come to me about. Please concisely lay out your requests. I feel God's breath on my neck.'

Edgar replied, 'Firstly, I'm looking for my mother, Aelfgyva. She's very special to me. I've travelled a long way to find her.'

Pierre showed extreme interest. 'Please provide some more detail.'

Edgar replied, 'I understand she has set up an embroidery school in this town and teaches both to the poor and the rich.'

Pierre looked shocked. He rose and pointed to the fine embroidery on the wall. It showed scenes from the New Testament, following the life of Christ from his birth to his death and resurrection. It was large enough to cover two walls. It contained wonderfully sewn figures and scenes with some Latin inscriptions. A small border ran along the top and bottom, with beautifully stitched birds, animals, fish, trees, and flowers pertinent to the main scenes. Some of it was not quite in line, but that just added to the quaintness of the work.

Pointing, he said, 'That is the work of her school. She supervised its completion as a present to me personally and to this church. She held a weekly sewing circle here for the poor women to learn a trade, and her patron, Duchess Matilda, financed the project, and once complete she was here at its dedication. Would you like me to take you to your mother? She is in this church!'

Edgar was overjoyed. 'Yes please! I've so much to say to her and I need her forgiveness. I have been so naïve!'

Pierre led the way and Edgar followed, confused as they descended into the crypt. *What a strange place to live*, he thought. Pierre walked towards a wonderfully ornate tomb. Edgar was suddenly so cold, as if covered by large icy hands. He shivered and his feet seemed stuck to the floor. He had to use all his strength to reach the tomb. Pierre pointed to the inscription with his delicate white hand.

Edgar read aloud, 'Here lieth the body of Aunt Aelfgyva, our beloved teacher, died this day on 2 September 1061, God rest her soul.' This was then repeated in French.

Edgar sobbed. He was overwhelmed with a sense of sadness and betrayal. Not only had he lost his mother, but he had been lied to, and as a result he had been a traitor to King Edward and England. He was distraught.

Priest Pierre had no time to console him since God was pressing His heavy hand on his shoulder. 'Please, we must move on, I must conduct a marriage now and I need you as a witness. You'll have time enough to talk with your dear departed mother, and I promise to relate to you all the details of her life and death later, although I can say that she did die in suspicious circumstances. Tonight, you'll eat, drink and board with me. Now come, the time of the convergence is nigh.'

Pierre dragged Edgar away from his mother's tomb, and ascended into the light that was cascading through the large stained-glass windows and from some skylights in the small dome in the roof. It was a stout, simple type of church, which upon entering gave a person an immediate feeling of spiritual well-being, a sanctuary whatever the cold cruel unforgiving and sharp world threw at you. This sort of pure religious Christianity was so lacking in the new dominating buildings that the cruel, despotic, powerful leaders were building from money wrongfully gained through their insatiable greed. Those were political statements of strength and riches, not of humble obedience to God. When the two men's eyes grew accustomed to the bright pure light of God, they could make out six shapes, one small, the others not so. Then Edgar saw that the little man, well-groomed in his best clothes, was his friend Turold. He ran to him, swept him off his feet and gave him the biggest hug that Turold could bear before yelping, and Edgar then broke down in tears.

Turold exclaimed, 'Who is this woman? I deny everything and if I did do something, it was because I was drunk at the time and not in possession of my faculties!' Then looking the person up and down, realised it was a man not a woman, and not only that but his old drinking companion. 'What are you doing here and what's with that Norman haircut, cloak, and dress? And why the tears?'

Edgar lowered his head and confessed, 'I have betrayed you, King Edward, and England, and on top of that, my mum's dead, probably killed by one of Duchess Matilda's men.'

Turold took a pace backwards, and fell down the steps behind him. Luckily, he'd learnt the art of acrobatics, and turned the whole affair into a backward flip and somersault, finally landing on his feet.

Priest Pierre chastised him, 'None of that sort of thing in the house of God please, say ten Hail Mary's and one Glory Be and let's get on with the wedding.'

Turold apologised to God, and everyone regained some level of composure although Marie had to lend Edgar her lace hanky. Her mother and father stood beside her, and Turold and Edgar likewise beside Rufus. Marie's parents were not happy with her choice of husband, him being a foreigner and all, but Duchess Matilda had convinced them that it would be in everyone's best interests for the marriage to take place without a hitch. There was more than a hint of violence and that, together with a purse of money, had sealed the deal. The simple marriage did indeed take place without any problems, other than the usual one of the best man, Turold, losing the rings when trying to perform one of his sleights of hand to try and cheer everyone up. Luckily the parents offered theirs quickly enough, although there was initially talk of some surgery to remove the mother's wedding ring, but Edgar came to the rescue by finding some leftover grease from a meatless meat pie in his bag of provisions. This lifted everyone's spirits and by the end of the service, all were smiling happily except for the mother and Edgar who both broke down, Edgar with tears of joy, as his hormones and emotions were all out of balance, and Marie's mother with tears because, well just because. The two hugged each other for what seemed ages, until Marie's father broke the holds. The register was signed, and then strangely the original rings were found in a glass of holy water that had mysteriously appeared on the altar.

Priest Pierre went to the glass, pulled out the rings and gave them to the wedded couple, then poured the holy water into a vial. He put a stopper in the end, then blessed it in front of the altar, said a prayer, and gave it to Turold saying, 'This holy water is for King Edward, make sure he gets it before the month is out.'

Turold took it in disbelief. 'Will it make him well again?'

The priest turned to him and replied, 'No, nothing can stop the ravages of time, but I can assure you that it'll do him no harm and at least a little good.'

Priest Pierre touched Turold on the shoulder, and immediately the priest could see Turold's future and Turold could feel the holy man's power. Pierre smiled at Turold and said, 'You will live long and prosper.'

Oh yes, thought Turold, *and pigeons grow on gooseberry trees.*

Before leaving, Turold advised Edgar to pretend he was Marie's sister since their security team was waiting outside to escort them all to a field next to the part-built cathedral. They were all to attend an important event that afternoon.

Turold further advised Edgar not to speak. Edgar replied, 'Oh I'm good at being mute. I had a great deal of experience in Rouen.'

Priest Pierre had a final talk with God, and he had the feeling that God was pleased with events. Pierre asked all present to give thanks to God and to ask for guidance in certain decisions that must be made. All this done, they left the sanctuary to face the cruel and chaotic world outside.

Vital and Wadard were very edgy and looked quizzically at Edgar. 'Who is this odd-looking woman?' Vital enquired.

Rufus, still confused about what was going on, and in any case still getting used to being married, just squeezed his wife's hand, and looked down at his shiny clean boots.

Turold took command. 'This is Marie's sister Maud the Mute. She acted as one of the witnesses.'

The two guards thought for a while, then Vital replied, 'Alright then, let's all get going. Duke William doesn't like to be kept waiting.'

Priest Pierre thought, *and nor does God.*

On the way to the field, Vital tried to strike up a conversation with Maud, but found it extremely difficult and exasperating. However, he thought that the rewards could make his efforts worthwhile. For some reason he was oddly attracted to the woman, and there were great advantages in having a wife who did not answer back or nag all day.

THE DAY OF CONVERGENCE: PART 3 - THE PROCESSIONS

The wedding party and full escort made their way towards the field, and to all those watching it looked like a regal procession. They all soon lined the road cheering and waving, then seeing their saintly priest who'd recently even cheated death, went down on one knee as he passed, while holding their hands together and praying. Some tried to touch him, but were dealt with harshly by the guards. Pierre rebuked the guards and held the hands of the injured faithful, making their short-lived pain vanish, being now full of God's spirit. When they reached the field, the wedding party were led to a small raised stage next to a very large one, and were escorted to their seats. Priest Pierre sat in the centre on a larger higher chair than the others. They were given refreshments, as it would be a long, warm afternoon. Next to them the large platform had been laid with a royal red carpet, on which was a smaller stage where Duke William's impressive throne was placed. Harold was to sit on a small chair to the left of William. Seating for William's family was placed on either side of the two men, with William's daughter, Adel, next to Harold. There was a canopy over the whole structure. There were other pavilions for the knights and other nobles and dignitaries, together with stable lines and feed for their horses, and blacksmiths ready to re-shoe the horses as required. Duchess Matilda was going to make sure that it would be a day to remember, not only for Harold but also for all those others present, including those counts, dukes, and other leaders that William would have to seek help from if he ever had to fight for the English throne.

In front of William's stage was another raised area, this time covered with religious textiles showing various biblical scenes, on which would be placed the two boxes containing the bones of the saints. There was sufficient space between the two stages for suitable entertainment to take place. Everywhere was festooned with banners and flags, most with William's red dragon displayed on them, and many with religious connotations. The crowds were kept entertained by choirs singing hymns. There was also an archery contest, with the winner taking a purse of money, and a lance throwing competition, where the prize was a whole barrel of wine. Both activities had drawn large crowds and were nearing the end, with the prizes to be given by William himself. This was also proving a great opportunity for William's commanders to assess the prowess of Norman manhood, with an eye to the future inevitability of war with some foe or other. Several men had already been marked for new positions as trainers in a new military facility that was being built in a secret location outside Rouen. Some clever Normans were selling souvenirs including hand puppets of a large Duke William and a small Earl Harold, while others sold various religious jewellery and the remains of saints. Duchess Matilda, on pain of something horrible, had banned the selling of these so-called relics since such items were fake and unholy. The army and spy agents tried to clamp down on these hawkers, but most were too sly and slippery for them. Any caught would become unwilling conscripts in William's army. There were also several authorised stalls selling food, drink and under the stall table, essentials for a good and safe night out.

With everything ready the ceremony began. Priest Pierre was led by Count Robert to the podium where the two large embellished wooden boxes would be placed, and told to stand behind them and be ready to pray to the saints. As the crowds saw this, a hush descended. They all loved and revered this recently reborn holy man.

Duke William led Earl Harold by the hand, closely followed by Duchess Matilda and the rest of the family. Finally came the retinue. The trumpets sounded as the parade walked into the field, making its regal-like way to the red carpet and then onto the stage. They were then served drinks.

Again, the trumpets sounded, and the religious procession entered the field. Bishop Odo had led it all the way from the cathedral. Clothed in his finest white and gold silk bishop's robe with his golden bishop's crook, and holding a golden cross before him, he looked almost holy. Next in the procession were the other bishops, again all in fine robes, followed by priests swaying incense burners. Then came other priests chanting psalms and holding religious banners, followed by four monks carrying a square, canopied, gold-leafed wooden plinth on which was placed a statue of the Virgin Mary with robes painted in blues and white, holding the newly born Jesus, representing his birth. Next in line was one tall muscular monk carrying a large, pure gold cross, representing the death and resurrection of Christ, and finally came chanting Benedictine monks from the monastery of Mont Saint Michel with the two large reliquaries containing the bones and clothing and other holy relics relating to the most important saints of Normandy. The procession had taken over an hour to reach the field because of the crowds. The onlookers had never seen such an event before and were in awe of the saints' remains. Some of the crowd had travelled great distances to be there, many with afflictions, hoping to be able to touch or at least be near these powerful relics. Some managed to touch the boxes as they passed; all fell to their knees as it progressed, prayed, and gave the sign of the cross. Several people swore that touching the box had cured them of various ailments including the pox, lameness, blindness, and flatulence.

Now, as the trumpets sounded again, the procession entered the field. Matilda looked on and smiled as tears fell down her cheeks. The outpouring of so much Christian faith had overwhelmed her. Bishop Odo was enjoying himself. He strutted up to William and Matilda, bowed low to them and then turned around to kneel before the boxes as they were put in place. William looked as regal as any man could be who was not a king, and to add to the effect, held his jewel-encrusted ceremonial sword heavenward. After saying a prayer, Odo stood up and walked over to the boxes, gave the sign of the cross over each, and stood in front of them as the other bishops joined him. The monks sang a glorious psalm, and were then led to one of the pavilions. Bishop Odo went over to Priest Pierre and offered his hand to him, which he kissed dutifully, with little relish. The priest was the closest that Normandy had to a living saint, and Matilda, realising this, had reluctantly included him in the proceedings. The bishop accompanied the priest across the field towards William, bowed to his brother, and then to Harold.

Bishop Odo looked directly at Priest Pierre and said, 'Now take Earl Godwinson to the boxes. It is time for his oath.'

Priest Pierre looked long and hard at Earl Godwinson. He had a great personal reason to loathe Harold and the rest of his family, but he could only love and pity the man who sat in front of him. He was his father's son in looks, but there was no sign of the family's evil traits. The priest could not blank out the memory of that terrible day in 1035. That was the day when he met Harold's father, Earl Godwin, and his thugs. It had been a nightmare for him as a twelve-year-old boy, but it had led to him finding God and Jesus and his future life as a priest in Normandy.

PRIEST PIERRE'S ORIGINS

That day in 1035 had started as any normal day. Peter's father, Edmund, was a wine and beer merchant. He had a house and store right on the bank of the river Wey, just outside the town of Guildford in the county of Surrey. On that fateful morning the family's routine was rudely interrupted when four surly and battle-scared men rode into the courtyard. They jumped off their horses and stomped into the house.

A giant of a man, and strong as an ox, banged on the table and announced in a thick accent (originating from the English region of Mercia which supported the new Danish King of England, Harold Harefoot), 'My master, Earl Godwin of Wessex, wants a supply of wine and beer for a feast tonight in honour of Prince Alfred, son of the dead King Ethelred. He's returned to England and arrives this evening in Guildford Town.'

Peter's father was stunned by this news. He had always hated the Danes and had supported the claim of Edward, brother of Alfred, as the true heir to the throne of England. *Why were Alfred's enemies giving him a feast? It makes no sense.* He engaged in conversation with the giant, who he discovered was called Thor, agreed to deliver the order to Guildford's Great Hall that afternoon. Edmund asked his son, young Peter, to supply the four men with samples to taste, which he duly did.

Edmund continued the conversation with Thor, as the ruffian gulped down his ale. 'And how's the fine prince and his men?'

Thor replied laughing, 'Ah very well at present! Earl Godwin, leads them like lambs to the slaughter. You, boy, be quick and give me more ale, or you'll feel the leather of my boot up your backside!' Peter scampered off as Thor's men laughed.

Edmund could now piece together a trap that Earl Godwin and the Danish king were laying for the unsuspecting prince, who thought Earl Godwin to be his ally but was to find out that he was his Judas.

When the men had finally departed, Edmund turned to Peter and discussed the matter. Since the age of ten his father had treated him as a man, especially since his intelligence and spiritual nature were well above normal. His father had recognised early on that his special son was born to perform some important tasks for God.

Well, this may be the time, Edmund thought. 'Son, as you know, our family supports Prince Edward as the rightful King of England, and his mother in Winchester, and his brother Alfred, as our royal family. We don't believe God wishes the Danes to rule England. Therefore, we must warn Alfred of the plot to kill him and his men. I can't go, as I must make the delivery, so I am asking you to go on this dangerous errand. Will you do this for me and England, my son?'

Peter replied immediately, 'Yes father, of course.'

'Then take Black Bess and the message I will give you and find Prince Alfred. Follow the road south from Guildford and you should come across them. Be careful to hand the note to Prince Alfred alone. I will give you this likeness of him but you should be able to recognise him from the royal clothes he will be wearing. Hopefully, the enemy won't be suspicious of a young boy. If they do query why you're wishing to see Prince Alfred, say you have an important message from his mother Emma. I know I put you in grave danger, but it's the only way of saving Prince Alfred. Once he reaches Guildford, it'll be too late.'

His father wrote the note, gave it to Peter, blessed him and wished him Godspeed. He said goodbye to his father, then ran into the kitchen, and kissed his mother goodbye, and jumped on the horse and galloped off.

His mother rushed outside, stood next to her husband, and enquired, 'Where is Peter going in such a hurry?'

'To save a prince.'

That would be the last time that Peter would ever see his father or his mother alive.

THE DAY OF CONVERGENCE: PART 4 - HAROLD'S OATH

Bishop Odo shouted to Priest Pierre yet again, 'Take the earl to the two boxes NOW '

Duke William had his sword pointing towards God, and his other arm outstretched with his finger pointing towards Harold and then at the boxes, as if commanding Harold to go. His arms were tiring and he was beginning to look foolish. The priest came back to the present and, under his breath, prayed to God for strength, then led Harold to the boxes, placing him between the two.

He said quietly to Harold so no one could hear, 'You still have time to stop this, and I implore you to think very hard before proceeding. If you do swear this oath before God and then break it, I assure you that you'll incur the wrath of God. Don't make the same mistakes that your father made. You will be punished by God if you do. Your father burns in hell, and you may too unless you are extremely careful.'

Bishop Odo followed them over. 'What's going on?'

Priest Pierre answered, 'I was merely informing Earl Harold that God was with us all at this time.'

'Well, let's not keep Him waiting then,' the bishop exclaimed, and handed Harold a scroll which had the oath written on it.

Priest Pierre came over to Harold, took one of his hands in turn, and placed each one on a casket. Harold noticed a mark on each of the priest's hands. Then Pierre lifted his arms up to the heavens and requested God to bless the bones of the saints and to accept the oath to be made before Him. The crowd gasped as they could see the wounds on the priest's hands. They were identical to those that Jesus suffered, and these stigmata were a powerful symbol of Priest Pierre's spiritual greatness. It was as if the crowd expected some sort of sign or miracle there and then, and seemed disappointed when nothing happened.

The priest turned to Harold and commanded, 'If you're of free will, willing to swear this oath before God, then please read the scroll while touching our holy boxes containing our glorious saints of old.'

Harold hesitated, considering Pierre's warning, then took a deep breath and with an unemotional face, read the oath out loud with a strong commanding voice. While he did so, Pierre continued to think of his past.

PRIEST PIERRE'S MUSING CONTINUES

When Peter found many armed men, just to the south of Guildford, he was challenged by a Mercian soldier, 'Halt. State your business.'

Peter tried to be brave and replied, 'I have a message for Prince Alfred from his mother. I was told to deliver it to him personally.'

The man laughed. 'What, they're sending boys to do a man's job now? I will seek out my commander, and he'll escort you. I assume you are not armed.'

Before the Mercian could mount his horse, an old nobleman came up on his pure white stallion, looked at Peter and briskly said, 'What's going on, who is this squab?'

Peter looked at the man's face. Behind the jet-black eyes, he could sense pure evil, as of the Devil himself. Even at his tender inexperienced age, Peter knew there was absolutely no spark of goodness in this man.

'Earl Godwin sir, this boy has a message for Prince Alfred from his mother, that old Norman witch, Emma.'

'Well, take him to one side and deal with him. Get the Ox, he'll know what to do.'

So, off the soldier went and after a while returned with a giant of a man. It was no less than Thor. 'Ah, it's the little shrimp who served me ale at that merchant's house.'

'But Captain, he says he's from Winchester delivering a letter from that old devil woman, Emma.'

Thor grabbed Peter right off his horse and dropped him to the ground like a sack of seed, breaking his left leg in the process. Peter yelled in pain. Thor jumped off his horse, picked the boy up as if a feather, and carried him off into the undergrowth, where he searched his clothes and crevices for any papers. Peter tried to fight back, gripping this or that, but to no avail, and although he tightened his hold on the paper, Thor the Ox pulled his fingers away one by one, breaking several, until he had the letter in his grasp. He read it.

'I think your foolish father will soon have uninvited angry visitors. As for you, I think those hands grasped that treasonable message too tightly and need to be taught a lesson.'

With that, he took out his dagger and ran each hand through with it.

'Now, I don't kill children, but just teach them a lesson, so I'll leave you to your fate. God will save you if He wants to.'

With that, he left the poor sobbing boy, jumped back on his horse, and with another nine men, went to call on Peter's father.

Peter passed out with pain and remined unconscious for several hours. Eventually, Peter stirred and a voice seemed to whisper in his ear. 'I will endure your pain and injuries as you would mine. These marks on your hands will mirror mine, and help you remember the sacrifices we all must make in the name of God. You have been chosen to do God's work. You will bury your mother and father and offer up their good souls to my Father, and then make your way to Normandy, and there you will go to the abbey at Bayeux, and seek out Abbott Louis. He will be your family and will teach you the true straight path and you will do great things. Now get up and go to your home.'

Peter was alone and fully awake. Somehow his injuries had been healed, although he still had the marks of the dagger and his legs and fingers were badly swollen. It had been a miracle. It was as if he'd been reborn. He found Black Bess and slowly made his way back to his home, where a horrific scene of destruction and violation awaited him, the images of which would remain with him until his dying day.

THE DAY OF CONVERGENCE: PART 5 - WILLIAM'S OATH

Bishop Odo interrupted Priest Pierre's thoughts again. 'Come on priest, Earl Harold has said the oath. Let my brother say his and then close proceedings so that we can return to the palace for a well-deserved feast.'

Priest Pierre went back to the main pavilion, bowed to Duke William, saying, 'Your Grace, it is time for your oath.' He walked behind Duke William as they went to the boxes.

William put his hands on the two boxes and said in a clear and loud voice, 'God has decreed that I should be the next King of England. I swear that once king, I will purify the English Church and stamp out all paganism. If the English defy God, then I will wage a holy war and take what should be mine by right, by the will of God.'

The priest turned to Harold, who was looking somewhat forlorn, fragile and vulnerable, shook his head, then with head, arms and crook pointing to the sky, declared to all present, 'These solemn oaths before God must not be broken by any mere mortal. God will punish these men without mercy if they break their oaths. Praise be to God and his Son. Amen.'

The whole crowd responded, 'Amen.'

Everybody returned to their seats.

William and Matilda looked at each other and both gave a little smile. They believed that the crown of England was nearly theirs.

Priest Pierre managed to whisper to Harold as they walked, 'Your soul is in extreme peril. Do not defy God's will. Your actions will determine the fate of many.'

Harold was about to collapse, so Pierre quickly took his arm and helped him to his chair. Harold could feel the energy flowing through him. It was a clear, perfect, white energy that seemed to fill his spirit. It was very disturbing, he had just been warned by a great spiritual man, with an undeniable connection to God. He felt like the condemned man who would die soon whatever happened or whatever he did. However, he thought, since he was mortal in any case, he must do as the priest had said. He must carefully look after his soul. He decided that he would only break the oath if forced to do so by others. He must hope that God would look upon him favourably since he'd no alternative but to make the oath in the first place. Surely God and Pope Alexander would understand that the oath was made under duress. However, he could not help but think that he'd already reached a crossroads in his life and that he had made the wrong choice as to his future path.

William turned to Harold, rose, and took him by the hand. 'Come brother, why so glum, it's now time to celebrate our allegiance, and your forthcoming safe return to England.'

Priest Pierre looked at William. Unlike his father, Robert the Devil, he was not totally evil, just a man convinced it was his destiny to be King William of England. Pierre then looked at Matilda, and she at him. They both had the power of insight and both were committed Christians, but his was a pure belief in the love of God and in particular his Son, whereas she believed in a cruel Old Testament God, easy to anger and slow to forgive. They both knew these and other things without having to speak to each other.

The priest bowed low, stood, and gave the sign of the cross, and walked back to the marriage party. He looked at Rufus and Marie. 'Come, it's time for you to celebrate your marriage. As for me, it's been a long day, and I must still carry out my duties as priest and hear confessions. Finally, I must speak to God and Jesus and ask for their help. These are dangerous times.'

He gave all those in the wedding party his blessing and swirled off as if carried by his angels, with those impatient to see him coming up to him and touching his robe and asking for his blessing. There was an aura of light around his head from the setting sun, and those who managed to touch him felt his love and grace.

The marriage party was escorted by Vital and Wadard to the palace where they joined the feast. Turold was asked to provide some of the entertainment, but he could not put his heart into it. He was worried. He needed to speak openly and frankly with his friends Rufus and Edgar.

Edgar, as Maud, felt very uncomfortable, and could not wait to get out of the palace. He was getting too much attention from Vital. When Adelaide told Vital and Wadard that Duchess Matilda wished to speak to them, Edgar managed to tell Turold that his family were well and that Duchess Matilda had been generous and given Megan a great deal of money, but that the dog was dead. He also advised Turold that Megan now had domestic help and that the twins were gradually being made more human and less canine. Turold was extremely happy and relieved about all the news he had been told. At least he would never have to face that dog again. At the end of the feast, the mute, Maud, was escorted out of the castle along with Rufus, Marie, and her parents. Since Edgar had nowhere to stay, Marie's mother insisted he stay with them that night. She had decided that he was so sensitive and lovely and vulnerable and would surely fall foul of any marauding miscreants if left alone. She believed that what he needed was a mother's shoulder to cry on and a mother's guidance. Her husband had other ideas but was outvoted by Marie and his wife

WILLIAM AND MATILDA

William held Matilda in his arms. The night was cool and cloudless and through the large window they could see the stars and the full moon shining brightly, casting its light on their embroidered bedspread. Matilda looked down at the embroidery that showed scenes from the Old Testament, including Adam and Eve, the burning of the bush, Sodom and Gomorrah, Noah and his ark, Moses and the plagues, the parting of the waters, the Ark of the Covenant, and other important events. The embroidery had been made by that lovely old English lady, Aelfgyva. Matilda believed that Aelfgyva had been sent to her by God to help her minimise the influence of her husband on their children. She had in return looked after the English lady until her untimely death. It was she who introduced old Aelfgyva to Priest Pierre, and together they had done such good Christian acts in helping the poor by teaching Norman women a trade and giving them a safe place to meet. The closeness of that pair often caused Matilda concern, but as far as she and her agents were aware, their love was a spiritual one not a physical one, especially following the marriage of Aelfgyva to a Norman merchant. Matilda sighed, thinking, *In the end I had to take drastic action as a result of her continuing to criticise the actions of both William and me. I did warn her! It was such a shame, but necessary. Now I'm left with just that priest to deal with. He's not only too popular but, again, criticising us. He's just too liberal in his Christian views and a threat to the status quo. He'll just have to go! But since he's so close to God and Jesus, I'll have to get someone else to do the deed! Yes, it's a problem for which I have yet to find a solution. Then there's old Aelfgyva's daughter. Her time on earth needs to come to an end! Oh well, time to give my husband some attention!*

Matilda turned to her husband and caressed his short hair. 'You've done extremely well my dear. You've Harold at a great disadvantage, and hopefully he'll support you. However, if he doesn't, but instead betrays you, then not only is he damned, but also, we've the plans and pieces in place to take England by force. Your fleet grows bigger daily as do the size and skills of your army. Edward is weak both physically and politically and he or his successor would have difficulty uniting England and raising an army of sufficient size to defeat the combined army of Normandy and northern France. Also, as I've suggested and as you agreed, we have an additional surprise to inflict on the English, when required. At this moment, I have those two men that wreaked havoc on you, Rouen, Lyon, and the surrounds, and who murdered poor Foufou, being trained for their missions.'

William immediately removed his hands from her body, and with one movement dived them under his pillow, removed his great sword and waved it above his head. Matilda looked disapprovingly at him.

William looked sheepish. 'Sorry, my angel, it's just a reflex action whenever I think of those two. As soon as you have had them do whatever they have to do, wherever they have to do it, and with whatever they have to do it with, I want a private audience with those Richard idiots.'

Matilda shook her head. 'No, you can't. They are our most powerful weapons and unpalatable as it may seem, they must be preserved. In addition, they're much more powerful than before, and I'm scared that if they did manage to meet you, the consequences would be dire.'

William did not understand much of what Matilda said, but understood the basics. He had convinced himself early in their marriage that he was the ideas man driven by his strong will, and the one to do all the fun things like hunting, fishing, feasting, fighting, torturing, and abusing anyone who upset him, while Matilda was more practical and dealt with the boring details and any messes he left in his wake. He knew she had her spy organisation and agents, and if they were useful to him in achieving his sole overall ambition of becoming King William of England, he would let her have her spies. Unbeknown to her (or so he thought) he too had his spies, who kept watch on her and her organisation's activities. Unfortunately, he was wrong. Her agents had infiltrated his spy network a long time ago. William put away his sword and held Matilda again.

Matilda sighed. 'I wish you didn't have to sleep with that sword every night. I do believe you love it more than me.'

He thought for several minutes. He did love that sword so, it was his father's and it was so beautiful and comforting, but thought he best reply, 'Of course I don't dear.'

EDYTH SWANNECK'S VISION

It was a windy, rainy, dank, dismal autumn day in Little Walsingham, north of the large city of Norwich. Edyth Swanneck, known to many as Rychold, meaning 'fair and rich', was kneeling before a shrine and praying. Not only was she one of the richest women in England, she was also considered locally as being blessed by God and known for her good works in caring for the poor. In 1061 she had a vision on that very spot. In her vision she was taken by Mary, mother of Jesus, to the house in Nazareth where archangel Gabriel had foretold the birth of Christ. Mary had commanded her to have a simple wooden structure built in the form of that Holy House. This subsequently became a holy shrine and a place of pilgrimage, to be later known as The Shrine of Our Lady of Walsingham.

She cried allowed, 'Oh, blessed Mary, hear my prayers, please tell me when I can expect my husband, Harold, to return to the safe shores of England. I know he has his faults, but his heart is true. He may not believe in anything that he can not grasp with both hands, but he does believe in God. You have told me that he lives, but I miss him so, and worry about his soul. I beg you to answer my prayer.'

Edyth closed her eyes and waited, and received a vision as if from Mary herself. She stood up and rushed back to her manor house, passing several people in need of a blessing from her. Eventually she reached Walsingham Manor and opened the door.

She entered the house and shouted, 'Cynewise and Brona, pack our possessions and get everyone ready for a journey. We leave immediately for Bosham.'

She gathered up her children and as they all sat in front of the fire, said, 'Children, we go on a long journey. Your father returns. For the next two years we must all be strong. We will pray to God daily for His protection. Now, we must eat and get ready for the journey.'

She had recently been given several disturbing visions but she had decided that she would remain positive for Harold's and the children's sakes. It was true that occasionally some of her visions did not come true. In any event she knew that Harold did not like her telling him about such matters. She would ensure that his family would be ready to support him when required whatever happened.

THE ENGLISH MAKE READY

It was a windy, rainy, dank, dismal day in the autumn of 1064, and Harold and his men needed to leave Normandy before the inevitable storms of winter set in. Mid-morning William announced that the English would be departing in three days and everything should be made ready. The Normans had previously secured Harold's ships and brought them around to the sheltered port of Caen where they were repaired. William agreed to supply an escort that would travel with the ships as far as the Isle of Wight.

Two days later, Harold's nephew, Hakon, said his goodbyes to his father, and was led to where Harold was resting. His nephew was reluctant to leave his father all alone, and said to Harold, 'Uncle, I don't want to leave my father in Normandy. Can I please remain with him? Not only will we miss each other terribly but I also fear that I will never see him again. I can't see how you can uphold your side of the agreement. You must realise that you'll never be able to convince either the King Edward or the Witan to accept Duke William as our next king.'

Harold looked sorrowfully at his young nephew. 'I've decided to do my best to persuade those in England to agree to it. Having thought long and hard about the problem of succession, I've concluded that it would be best for England to come to a peaceable arrangement with this most determined and powerful man. For now, my priority must be to return to England as soon as possible. England is vulnerable without me to lead the army. For all I know, the Danish king may be landing on the shores of Kent as I speak. Your father might just have to become a sacrifice in this game for the English throne. There is however one glimmer of hope, in the form of my fiancée, but it's best we don't discuss this any further, since as you told me, walls have ears!'

His nephew was deeply unhappy. 'You should never have come to Normandy.'

Harold replied, 'I know. I misunderstood the situation and underestimated Duke William and Duchess Matilda. All I can do now is get you, my men and me back to England and try and sort things out the best I can. Let us go and have a hearty evening meal with our fellow Englishmen, drink some fine French wine, and visit the chapel so we may pray to God for good weather ahead of our journey tomorrow. Who knows what God has planned for us!'

His nephew followed him and his Norman escort to the grand hall where all the others were assembled.

Duchess Matilda allowed Turold to give a full and frank performance of his art, much to the enjoyment of most present. While this was taking place, she and Harold left and had a private discussion about religion in England and the need for reform. Harold was in full agreement with her on the necessity of this, and promised to discuss the topic with King Edward on his return, although he had to warn her that Edward seemed more interested in his own salvation, rather than that of his people.

During the festivities, Rufus was able to say his farewells to his sailor acquaintances while keeping a watchful eye on his wonderful wife. Turold had a discussion with Rufus after his third and final encore, and suggested a meeting with Edgar and one other person at the little church where hopefully they could speak with Priest Pierre. He thought that they needed to decide finally where their allegiances lay as regards possible future events, and what they should do. Rufus would get word of the meeting to Edgar through Marie, but the question remained as to how they could get permission to see Priest Pierre. In the end it was decided that Turold would ask the Duchess Matilda for permission to see the priest in order that he might be properly baptised, which he believed his parents had failed to do. He would tell her that he felt that his soul was at risk, and that this needed to be resolved. Rufus was not convinced and shrugged his large shoulders, but Turold decided to put the plan into effect.

Turold managed to speak to Duchess Matilda at the end of the feast and she seemed delighted that he was so concerned about his standing with God, and agreed to make the arrangements. Later, she organised the meeting but ensured that one of her agents would observe from a distance.

Turold also managed to speak to Earl Harold. 'Sir, that holy man Priest Pierre told me that this vial containing holy water should be given to our dear King Edward immediately upon your return. As you know, I am to stay here, so I must leave it in your capable hands.'

Harold looked at Turold. 'Did the priest speak to you too and did you feel his Godly power?'

'Yes, I did,' Turold replied, 'he seems to have direct contact with our Lord and I believe he can be trusted.'

Harold concluded the conversation, 'And so do I,' and he took the vial and concealed it on his person.

HAROLD'S RETURN TO BOSHAM

The next morning all the English were ready at dawn. They could not wait to get back to their loved ones and England. The weather seemed set fair and there was optimism in the air. William, Matilda, and Adeliza were there to see them depart, and William gave Harold a hug and allowed him to kiss his ring and his daughter. Harold mounted his horse, and carrying his hawk, led his men, also on horseback, followed by an escort of fully armoured knights with their long lances and swords. Both Turold and Rufus were also present, with Turold doing some double somersaults and jumps, then attempting a back somersault and twist, failing to get it right, falling headlong into the ornamental fountain, and coming to the surface with weed all over his head. Rufus was there to rescue him in seconds. The whole column of men, including Harold and his nephew, laughed as they left.

They eventually reached the port of Caen, and after refreshments and a prayer, embarked on their ships. The Norman escort ship was already manned. As the tide started to ebb the order was given to make oars, the mooring ropes were released, and the ships glided off towards the sea. The waters were calm and the sky blue. There were many onlookers waving and cheering. On one side of the crowd was a priest in white robes with his crook, looking hard at Harold and praying to God. Finally, he gave the sign of the cross and walked away. Some of the crowd recognised him and diverted their attention to the slowly disappearing figure as he blessed and gently touched their heads. Harold never looked back, but resolutely forward towards England.

Once the ships had left the harbour the sails were raised and the oars stowed.

The ships made good speed since the wind was from the southwest. After about half a day of sailing they could see the white cliffs of the Isle of Wight. Once near, the escort turned and gradually disappeared back towards Normandy. Men in watch towers on the island could now see Harold's ships and word was sent to Bosham. On they sailed towards the Solent, where they changed course and steered east towards Bosham Harbour. Other watchers along the English coast could identify the ships as Harold's and soon the word was put out that Harold was returning. Just before sunset the sails were lowered and the oarsmen started rowing towards the entrance of Bosham harbour.

Once the ships entered the estuary at Bosham many soldiers on horseback could be seen shadowing them and cheering. The sun glinted off their armour and shields. On the ships went. Some men started to do a Viking ritual of running the oars, which inevitably ended with them falling in the water. They did not mind. They were so happy. One sailor had to be saved from a watery grave when it was realised that he could not swim. Harold stood on the prow of his ship looking forward in heroic fashion. Suddenly he saw Edyth and his children. He waved frantically, and wept with joy. When they reached the beach, the oars were lifted skywards and then stored, and Harold's sailors, helped by some of his servants, pulled the ships up the gravel and onto the shore. A crowd of well-wishers and Harold's servants, were all cheering as Harold and Hakon walked up the beach. The rest of the wayward Englishmen followed them, kissing the soil first and then laughing and crying and thanking God. There were many hugs, kisses and handshakes as the long-lost Englishmen met their families and friends. Most of the returning men could not believe their luck, and many made an oath to God that they would never set foot on a ship again, especially if it meant sailing with Earl Harold. The first destination for all was the small church of Bosham where a service of thanksgiving was held, followed by a feast at Bosham Manor.

Harold stayed alone in the church for an hour or so, first talking to the priest, and then talking to God. He was relieved to be back in England but he could not celebrate his return with the others. He was deeply concerned and looked for some comfort. He went over to the tomb of Sigyn, Cnute's dead daughter, knelt in front of it and started crying. He felt a small hand being placed on his shoulder, but he was too scared to look around to see its owner.

'Harold, do not cry for me, I am with my mother and father. Do not regret the past. You must look forward and carry out God's will. I will be waiting to greet you when you leave your cruel harsh world.'

Harold was afraid and shocked, but he managed to stand up and then forced himself to turn round. He was alone.

He sighed, walked down the aisle, left the church, and stood in the cold autumnal night air looking out to sea. A hunter's moon was shining brightly. It threw a ghostly blue light over the water and onto the shore. Harold's imagination was racing. Could he see countless spectral ships full of armed men sailing towards him?

MATILDA'S PLAN TO PURGE NORMANDY

Duchess Matilda knew that Normandy needed to keep God on its side, otherwise even her best-laid plans would fail. The upcoming Mass of Christ would be critical to achieve this. In addition, all Normans needed to behave themselves, and that included her wayward husband and his half-brother Bishop Odo. She therefore decided upon a family meeting to be held at Caen Castle on October 30 1064. The invites stated that it would be a birthday party to celebrate her thirty-third birthday.

His whole family were present in the feasting room. William looked at them all, and smiled. He was so proud of his family. He would surely not die without a male heir, and his daughters would make fine wives. *And,* he thought, *there was still some years in me yet to add to my family.* In addition to his immediate family, others present included William's half-brothers Odo and Robert, William FitzOsbern, Robert de Beaumont, and Robert of Montgomery. The last three men were cousins and important advisors to William.

Once all had been seated, Duke William arose. 'Before we commence our feasting, I have something important to announce. I must—'

William was interrupted by a kick in the shins from Matilda. He lost his composure, pulled out his dagger and looked sternly at his wife. In return, she looked sternly at him and shook her head. When it came to stern stares, there could be only one winner. William sat down mumbling to himself.

Matilda stood up to her full short height. 'Duke William wants me to tell you what he wants to say as he has a sore throat.' She looked at William and smiled as she filled his wine goblet. 'There you are dear, sip this and rest your voice.'

William took a large loud gulp and sulked.

Matilda continued her speech. 'As you know, it's my birthday, and while I remember, thank you all for your kind good wishes and gifts, although I have to say that I do already have many bibles and crucifixes. Now I hope with God on my side, that I will enjoy plenty more birthdays, and it is on the topic of God that Duke William wishes to make an announcement that will affect all those present and the whole of Normandy and its army. God has spoken to me and to the living saint Priest Pierre, and He has confirmed that Duke William should be the next king of England. However, we must all ensure that we retain God's favour. Therefore, Duke William has laid out the following edicts:

'All Norman citizens must attend church at least once a week. All Norman babies must be baptised. Any pagan activities will be banned, and all witches and warlocks and heretics must be found, arrested, found guilty at a legal trial, and burnt at the stake. There will be a night-time curfew from the end of the Compline evening prayer service. No clergy will engage in any acts of debauchery, and this includes, you Bishop Odo. From now onwards the only laying on of your hands will be to do with religious matters. Do you understand?'

Odo nodded, and started sulking, thinking of all the good times he was now going to miss.

Matilda continued, saying, 'Well, you had better, since you will be followed day and night.'

'Finally, all my, eh, Duke William's children must be clean of mind and spirit, so they will be put under the strict supervision of vetted priests.'

'On a more uplifting note, we are all to be involved in the staging of the most lavish Mass of Christ ever to take place in the whole of France, let alone Normandy. I shall allocate your duties later.'

She then sat down while everyone considered the consequences of her announcement in complete silence.

Matilda stood up again. 'Oh, you can all start feasting now. Enjoy yourselves and the special treat that I have laid on. All the way from England and at great expense, the 'Pius Pipe Playing Pilgrims of Pevensey' will be entertaining us tonight.'

She sat down again.

Duke William gave a wry sneaky smile, thinking about the information that he had extracted that afternoon from those ever-so-boring pilgrims. He now knew much about the large harbour at Pevensey, including its tides and currents.

The guests ate in stunned silence. They would surely remember this miserable birthday party.

There was a great deal of both sighing and sulking throughout the castle that night, but only Duke William was allowed to mutter. This feeling of gloom would spread throughout Normandy over the next few months.

However, the Normans were great organisers and problem solvers, as well as determined, and by January 1065, several illicit establishments providing all night drinking and entertainment had been set up outside the main towns and cities. Most included confessional rooms run by opportunist priests who provided the means for the penitent to obtain absolution for the price of a large glass of wine. This they hoped would result in God having mercy on them, forgiving their sins, and leading them to eternal life. Matilda's spy network worked hard to discover and close these dens of iniquity, thus minimising the negative effect of these activities on Normandy's standing with God. To avoid the inevitable increase in unemployment amongst the female population, under-utilised females were put to work making sails for the new ships under construction. Other consequences were the establishment of recreational facilities by entrepreneurs living in lands bordering Normandy. This resulted in an increasing popularity amongst the Norman soldiers to be posted to the various border forts, especially those defending the border with Ponthieu. It seemed that Count Guy was willing to supply anything that a soldier would ever need as long as he had sufficient money.

HAROLD'S RETURN TO LONDON

Harold had now been at home with his family for three days. During those days, he dealt with many important matters but there was one major problem that needed his attention. Harold had to take the threat of invasion from Normandy seriously, so he decided to ready the English fleet and armed forces along the south coast of England. For now, he decided that he would advise King Edward that some of the English fleet should base itself in the area of the Solent and Isle of Wight while small contingents of the army would be positioned from the Solent to as far as Dover. The rest of the fleet would be based in the Thames along with the majority of the English professional army. He had concluded that he had to assume that William could invade after winter as soon as he had his forces in place whether King Edward was alive or dead.

His stay with Edyth and the children was all too short as far as he was concerned when he received an urgent message from King Edward. He had been summoned to immediately attend a meeting with Edward at Westminster Palace, and so had to ride there as fast as possible. It seemed that his master was impatient to hear the news of his mission to Normandy.

As he kissed Edyth for the last time, he said, 'Take our dear family to our manor house at Maidenhead and wait for me there. I shall be with you as soon as possible.'

'Dear husband, I'm sure that you have still not told me all about your time in Normandy. I have had visions.'

'Edyth, please don't ask again, and please don't tell me about your visions. Just know that I love you and my children more than anyone on earth!'

He gathered a contingent of heavily armed men and set off directly towards London. He continued to consider the whole problem regarding the Normans and in particular William and Matilda. He was mindful of his father's philosophy, he often said, 'Follow the power and do not concern yourself about the consequences to your soul.' Harold had to laugh, yes, his father was damned by his actions and had lost his poor soul. However, perhaps his father was correct. At the end of the day the crown best lay with the strongest candidate and not the rightful one. If his father had been alive today, he would have already sided with William, Edward would be dead, and William his successor. *No*, Harold thought, *I could not betray King Edward. So instead, perhaps I should take the path of becoming King Harold of England, with young but determined Adel as queen.* He thought on, his mind twisting this way and that just like the road. *Just another moment*, he thought, *of course, none of this is my fault. I am just in the wrong place at the wrong time. The ambitions of the Normans started way back when Ethelred the Unready was king and married Emma, the daughter of Richard I, Duke of Normandy, Duke William's ancestor. That family had Viking blood and an excessive thirst for power and many of its dukes were considered devils incarnate. Emma was of similar ilk and saved her skin and position on the death of her Saxon husband by later marrying that Dane, King Cnut. The whole family were the same, they wanted power at any cost, and wanted England. There could only be one conclusion, that ambitious family had had designs on the English throne for years, and on top of that, when in exile in Normandy, Edward promised the crown to a then young ambitious William who would have been indoctrinated in the philosophy and history of his family. Then there's the ambitions of Matilda! No wonder the now powerful and determined Duke William wants to be the next English king,* Harold concluded. *It all makes sense now. It is not my fault. It's the fault of others including King Edward.*

By dusk Harold and his men were just south of London and from Biggin Hill Harold could see the town below. It was a bustling town of some 26,000 inhabitants, most living in small wooden buildings. He could make out some imposing churches and other dwellings made of stone but by far the largest structures were on the Isle of Thanet that stood in the river Thames. Here the royal palace stood in all its splendour. He could also see the new part-built Abbey of Westminster next to the palace. Along the Thames, Harold could see all the lights, fires, and the silhouettes of boats at anchor or being loaded and unloaded at the quaysides. London Town was a busy place, night, or day. Harold could not understand why so much money and effort was being put into the abbey project when the money and resources would be better spent increasing the kingdom's armed forces and defences. *King Edward,* he thought*, cares little for England and more for his own soul. He's selfish in the extreme.*

The group continued their journey down the hill into London and on to the Isle of Thanet.

King Edward was advised of his arrival, and once fully awake and dressed, he asked for Harold's presence. Harold knocked on Edward's bedchamber door and was let in by Edward's servant. Harold approached Edward, bowed low, and kissed his ring. King Edward looked so much older than before. He was gaunt and wrinkled and he had a walking stick in his hand.

Edward arose with great difficulty, and hugged him as if he were his long-lost son. 'Harold, my son, I was thinking that I would never see you again. But here you are, all safe and well. I hear that you have returned with some success, as your nephew has landed on English soil. However, there are rumours that all did not go well, so please do provide me with a true and frank report.'

Harold cleared his throat. This was going to be a difficult speech although he had rehearsed it many times. 'Your Grace, my ships were blown off course and we ended up in the sticky hands of Count Guy. Fortunately I got word of our capture to Duke William who immediately sent men to rescue us. This rescue was successful and William brought us all to his palace. We were well looked after but held like prisoners by William and Matilda. They made it quite clear that William should be the next king of England. He said that you, Your Grace, promised it to him all those years ago.' Harold paused.

Edward nodded his head and sighed. 'Pray continue. I understand the tale so far.'

Edward coughed and spluttered and spat into his bucket. His servant came over, wiped his mouth, and gave him a spoonful of very dark liquid. Edward gulped it down, screwing his eyes as if in pain.

Harold continued. 'Unfortunately, he had me at a great disadvantage and basically would not let us return to England before I swore allegiance to him and his aspirations.' Harold paused again.

Edward became animated, throwing his spindly right arm about while gripping his walking stick in his left hand. He then pointed his hand at Harold, who was now bowing so low as to be nearly touching the king's foot. 'You fool, I told you that he and his wife would spin a web that you would find impossible to escape from without losing something precious, which it seems is the crown on my head.'

Harold continued. 'I swore that I would support him in his ambition to become king, but I also told him that under English law only you on your deathbed, and the Witan, could make the decision. However, I've thought long and hard about the crown. I believe that William would prefer to become king of England without a fight, but he's prepared to fight if he must. He is strong and has many allies in the north of France. England, I am afraid to say, is weak, and there's also a great threat of invasion from both Norway and Denmark. In my view, it may well be in the best interests of England to accept a Norman king. William will provide the strength that quite frankly, we are lacking at present. I also must remind you that England is still divided. Both the Mercians and those in Northumberland do not like being ruled by the royal family of Wessex. I cannot see any other way out of the current situation. If our enemies see an opportunity, they will exploit any weakness. I believe even as we speak, William has plans for an invasion, and only lacks the ships to do so. If he invades, we may be able to defeat him, but at great expense in men and materials, leaving England open to invasion from the Vikings.' Harold paused again, this time wondering whether he had gone too far or whether King Edward had grasped the problem.

Edward spoke at last, following another coughing fit. 'I have tried to be a good king, and as God knows, I've confessed my faults and weaknesses and asked forgiveness. I have also prayed for England. I can do no more.'

Harold interjected, trying to lighten the mood, 'Perhaps Your Grace, you will be known to future generations as Edward the Confessor.'

Edward chuckled and agreed, 'Yes, Harold, better that than Edward the Weak. I know I'm no soldier, as was demonstrated when I made my own attempt at grasping the crown off the Danes, fleeing at the first opportunity, and leaving my poor brother Alfred to take the consequences. I know this England remains divided. I've tried to keep its enemies at bay through diplomacy and promises, but I realise that this has only delayed the inevitable. I thought that you would have a chance of standing up to England's foes, but from what you've said, it seems that England is doomed to be ruled again by some foreign power. I think it best that we retire and speak more tomorrow.'

As Edward lay in his bed, he was deeply troubled. He could not sleep, drink, or eat, or obtain any comfort from his bible. He tossed and turned, sighed, and wept, and his mind became increasingly agitated. It was all too much for the body and mind of the frail king. His heart could not cope and he had a seizure. He collapsed and closed his eyes.

EDWARD THE CONFUSED

It was the middle of the night when Edward suddenly awoke confused and angry, shouting, 'Where's my jester and where's my present? Thomas, Thomas, come here!' A few moments passed, then Edward could hear a skipping footstep from the direction of the corridor, and Thomas, Edward's personal night-groom, burst in on one foot, while trying to put his hose on, but failing and ending up on his face. 'I'm here Your Grace!' he muffled with his mouth on the floor.

Edward exclaimed, 'I want my Turold and my gift from Harold immediately. See to it.'

Thomas got to his foot, bowed, and skipped out still trying to get his hose on. Eventually, fully hosed, he rushed down the corridor and banged on Harold's door. 'Sir, sir King Edward wishes an audience. He wants to know the whereabouts of his jester and his gift. He always gets a gift from a noble who's travelled abroad, even if it's just a piece of a saint, a vegetable, or a plant.'

Harold stirred from his slumber. He had been thinking of his one true love. He got out of bed, in his nightshirt, washed his face to cool his ardour, and shouted, 'I'll dress and come immediately!' He started putting on his hose, but that was not easy.

Thomas banged on the door. 'Come quick, please sir.'

So, Harold finished putting on his hose and scratched his head, thinking *what present can I give the king?* Then he remembered the vial that Turold had given him, and in his panic, without a moment's hesitation, took it out of his luggage, opened the door and followed the servant back to Edward's bedchamber.

Harold entered and walked up to Edward who had propped himself up in bed, 'Your Grace, you called?'

Edward looked confusedly at the stranger in front of him. 'Who are you?'

'I am Harold, Your Grace.'

'Harold who?'

'Harold Godwinson, Earl of Wessex, Your Grace.'

Old Edward laughed. 'No, you're not, he's just a boy. In any case, who's this Harold Your Grace?'

'I assure you, I am Harold Godwinson, son of Earl Godwin.'

Edward closed his eyes, thought awhile, and then replied, 'Liar. Well, if you are young Harold, please answer me this. Was your father that traitor who had my brother killed?'

Harold sighed, thought for a moment, then replied as simply as possible, 'Yes.'

'And what was my dear martyred brother called?'

Harold replied, 'Alfred, known also to you as Samson due to his fighting abilities.'

Edward clapped his hands. 'Correct! Now be on your guard next time, the questions may be more difficult. Good night and see you tomorrow.'

Harold sighed yet again. Edward was losing sight of reality.

He sat for some five minutes and then said, 'Your Grace, you called for me.'

Edward stopped snoring, woke up, coughed, and looked at Harold and Thomas in total confusion.

Thomas was on hand to help. 'Your Grace, you wanted to know where Turold was and you wanted your gift from Earl Harold.'

Edward had another think and a little snooze and then woke up, coughed, and replied, 'Yes, Yes, eh who's Turold?'

Harold was thinking perhaps Edward should be known as Edward the Confused not Confessor. 'Your Grace, your jester.'

Edward quickly replied, 'Yes, my jester, why didn't you say so to begin with? You are both just wasting my time. I would have you both fed to the wolves if I had any. Thomas, do I have any?'

Harold said slowly, 'Your Grace, your jester Turold decided to stay in Normandy. He is now the court jester of Duke William.'

Edward went red and screamed, 'What? Send an invasion force immediately and get the poor man back! He's my only friend.'

Harold considered his reply carefully. 'Of course. I will make the arrangements in the morning if you still wish to fight Duke William. It's very late and all your sailors and soldiers are in bed.'

Edward nodded. 'Yes, we will make the plans tomorrow. Now about the gift.'

Harold produced the vial. 'Your Grace, I managed with great difficulty to obtain a vial of holy water that has been blessed by both a living saint and God.' He handed the vial to Edward.

Edward looked at it with extreme distrust, since so many people had died from poison at the hands of the Godwin family. 'Will it do me any good?'

Harold replied, 'Well, it will not do you any harm I can assure you.'

Edward was not convinced. 'You take the first sip then.'

Harold removed the stopper and took a small drop of the holy liquid, then sat still and crossed his fingers and prayed to God. After five minutes of nothing, and being still in the world of the living, Harold stood and gave a smile of relief. 'See Your Grace, I still live!'

Edward was very suspicious, but thought, what did he really have to lose, he was dying anyway and if he remembered rightly, he had already decided that this man Harold who stood in front of him would be his successor. He took the vial and drank the contents.

King Edward's last words were, 'I confess—' then he collapsed and shut his eyes.

Thomas ran over to his master screaming, 'He's dead, he's dead, he's been murdered!' then pointing his finger at Harold, 'you killed King Edward. It's treason.' However, on inspection he found that Edward had a weak pulse.

Thomas turned to Harold and pointed at him accusingly. 'If you've given him poison, you'll pay!'

Thomas then left the room to report the events to any members of the Witan in the palace.

Harold looked down on Edward and said, 'If I have given him poison, I'll soon be King Harold of England, alive or dead.'

Harold was now wondering whether William and Matilda were behind this. He should never have trusted that so-called saintly priest. *What a fool I've been.* He left the king breathing deeply, and thought that tomorrow would be a very interesting day one way or another, but now it was time for a few glasses of wine.

Later, Edward's doctors, three members of the Witan Council and two priests entered Edward's bedchamber. The three wise earls were covering both possible outcomes. The doctors applied their normal medieval cures, such as a bit of bloodletting by leeches and the study of the pee and stool, and left, tasks complete, but with no idea what to do to help the poor old king. The two priests prayed to God, and gave the last rites just in case. One earl and two servants were left on guard and given the task of reporting anything that the king said, especially when it came to his successor. Four guards were stationed outside Earl Harold's bedchamber just in case he had to be arrested for treason. Edward remained in a deep coma all night.

The queen was entertaining company when Thomas knocked on her bedchamber door.

She did not like being interrupted, and shouted, 'Go away, I'm, eh, busy, eh carrying out my, eh, devotions,' and then she giggled, 'so go away.'

Thomas would not go and shouted through the closed door, 'My Queen, the king is gravely ill.'

'Is he dying?'

'The doctors do not know.'

'Does he have a priest?'

'Yes, two.'

'Then he has everything he needs. If he dies, let me know,' and she and her guest giggled again.

EDWARD THE REJUVENATED

Harold was rudely awoken mid-morning by a slap on the buttocks. 'Get up, son and heir, I've things to do and I want you with me. First, we will have a hearty breakfast and then I want to show and discuss the new abbey with you.'

Harold looked over the bedsheet and rubbed his eyes. In front of him was a pink blotchy skeleton wearing just slippers and a smile. This apparition turned and skipped out of his room cheerfully singing a hymn. Harold put his head in his hands and closed his eyes thinking that picture would stay with him until his dying day, which luckily, it seemed, would be sooner rather than later.

He sighed and got out of bed, saying to himself, 'Oh well, time for the condemned man to eat a hearty meal.'

He put on his best clothes and went to Edward's feasting room, where he found the pink skeleton now partly clothed, tucking into all sorts of meats and fruit while drinking a glass of the finest ale.

King Edward smiled at him, and patted the seat next to him. 'Sit here my boy. There is much to discuss, but first help yourself to some food and drink.'

Harold complied with Edward's command and soon he had a glass of ale in each hand, a glassful in his stomach, and some wild boar in his mouth. Harold looked at Edward. He was a changed man. He looked in Edward's bucket and could see that it contained a great deal of red and green sludge in which several worms seemed to be merrily diving in and out of. However, Edward was not coughing and it seemed as if he had had a complete internal purge, the result being a jovial lively pink skeleton.

The king spoke again. 'Now, I've been remiss with matters relating to the kingdom, but with your return and my new-born vitality, this can be put right. As you are now my heir, you must learn what's involved in being a king. I'm not so stupid as to not realise that I'll probably be dead by the end of 1065, but I intend to make the most of the spring and summer sun before the cold, frosty fingers of winter returns.'

Harold swallowed his boar with the help of another ale. 'But Your Grace, as I said yesterday, would it not be best for you to name Duke William as your successor?'

Edward turned to Harold, slapped him on the back and replied, 'You're by far the strongest Englishman in England, so I'll leave the kingdom to you to defend. I'm sure you'll do your best. That's my final decision.'

Harold sighed (again) and poured another ale, feeling death's hand on his shoulder.

Edward continued. 'As to the question of defence, I've thought long and hard, and have decided as follows. You will command all forces. You will divide my fleet between the Solent, the Isle of Wight and the Thames so as to see off any attack by William or others. You will also place men along the south coast. My main army should be placed close to London to protect me and England from both enemies to the south, the east, and the north, and place a smaller army close to York to rebuff any attack from Norway. We will need to get the Mercians to help with that.'

Harold swallowed his ale, rolled his eyes, and replied, 'Your Grace, that's a good plan. I wish I'd thought of it.'

The king chuckled. 'It's that tonic you gave me. My mind is as clear as a church bell.'

Harold poured another ale.

Edward continued. 'We must visit my abbey today. I need to go through the plans with you in case I'm not here to see it completed, and I also need to discuss my tomb. I wish to leave three legacies of my reign, you, my abbey, and my tomb.'

Harold mumbled under his breath, 'And I know which two of the three will last the longest. In any event I surely will not be here myself to see the abbey's completion.'

Edward chastised Harold, 'Don't mumble son, it's not becoming of a king-to-be. Now we must get going.'

Harold gulped down the remains of his two glasses of ale, squeezed some more boar meat into his mouth, stood up and immediately fell over. He thought, as he lay on the floor looking at the brightly coloured ceiling, *perhaps I have drunk too much ale.*

Edward came to his assistance and pulled him to his feet, giving him a hug. 'Let's go and have some fun.'

Hurrah, thought Harold.

Harold sat in the receiving hall while Edward dressed, head swimming. He thought of asking for some water but then no, knowing his luck he would get the plague. Eventually Edward came regally down the stairs in fine royal red robes. He dragged Harold across to the waiting horses. They mounted and rode the short distance to the building works with a contingent of the guard. All the workmen were amazed to see Edward looking so well. The two dismounted and Harold propped himself up against a part-completed wall while Edward showed him the plans and described what was to be built, based mainly on cathedrals Edward had seen during his exile in Normandy. However, this monstrosity would be one of, if not the largest, abbeys in Europe.

One thing Harold could remember later in the mist of his drunken memory was that it was Edward's wish to have that priest who provided the vial of holy water attend his court as soon as possible. Harold had agreed to do his best to make the arrangements but said that it would depend upon the agreements of both Duke William and Duchess Matilda.

After the abbey, Edward discussed his tomb and showed Harold its plan. Harold thought it seemed a little ostentatious but that, he decided, was just typical of Edward. He got the distinct impression that Edward wanted his tomb to become a glorious place of pilgrimage, so that Edward's people would remember him for all time, especially if a miracle or two occurred at his tomb.

These matters concluded, they returned to the palace where Harold could finally collapse on his bed and recover from the events of the last twenty-four hours.

Edward went to his desk and commenced his paperwork. That evening Harold had supper with Edward and tried again to change his mind but to no avail. Edward's mind was made up. Edward advised Harold that he would begin his apprenticeship tomorrow, and from then onwards Harold would remain at his side for all to see how things stood.

Harold did enquire whether anyone knew yet about his decision, and Edward replied, 'No, but they soon will.'

That night as Harold lay awake unable to sleep. Suddenly a sinister thought entered his head as if from Satan, '*Do away with the old man before it's too late. It would be kinder for him. Don't let him suffer. Then you can quickly contact Duke William and help secure a suitable landing place for his invasion. Poison would be the weapon of choice.*'

Harold mulled it over but he couldn't kill his adopted father and friend. *No, I love him, and in any case, he is my King. I will not be a traitor. I would prefer to die rather than jeopardise my soul. I'm beginning to believe that I am doomed whatever I do. I must do all I can to save my soul.*

Harold fell into a fitful sleep. At first light, Harold awoke with a start and sat up in bed. *There is perhaps still a third way out of this mess, if I could obtain the permission of King Edward to marry William's daughter Adel, then maybe I could somehow manipulate events so that I and Adel could rule England after Edward with the support of Normandy. Oh, I've not yet told him that I'm engaged to William's daughter! I'll tell Edward first thing today and hopefully receive his blessing.* He prayed to God for His help, and feeling a great deal more optimistic, fell asleep.

HAROLD IS TO BE BETROTHED AGAIN

It was not long before Edward was bouncing up and down on Harold's bed. 'Wake up, wake up sleepyhead! Listen carefully!'

Harold pretended to remain asleep

Edward dug him in the ribs, then pulled his bed sheets off. 'Come on son, you can't stay there all day!'

Harold couldn't see why not. He opened his right eye just as Edward hit him over the head with a pillow. 'Alright Your Grace, I surrender!' Harold sat up in bed and tried to look fully awake and attentive.

'Harold, I've decided that as heir to the crown, you must marry an appropriate woman, and I have in mind just the one for you. That previous Welsh king, Gruffydd, you know, the one you killed, has left a widow, Ealdgyth, who is the sister of those two powerful earls, Edwin, and Morcar of Mercia. It's an excellent political match. You can discreetly continue your relationship with that Edyth Swanneck woman, but you must marry someone suitable of being a queen, and then start a proper royal family. You must have legitimate sons to continue your line. Don't do what I did and end up heirless.'

Harold thought, *you'll make me hairless with all these so-called good ideas, then eyeless, and finally headless! I don't think Duke William, Duchess Matilda, and Adel are going to be too pleased about this! Oh well, it seems God is not on my side and things can get worse.*

Edward was waiting for a response. 'Well. Harold, what do you think? I knew you would think it a good idea!'

Harold felt he had to at least suggest an alternative, and replied, 'Your Majesty, I must advise you that I'm already engaged. Duke William has already given his consent for me to marry his daughter. In the circumstances, I think this would be a much better match.'

Edward patted Harold on the head and said, 'Best if you leave all the thinking to me dear boy.'

Harold sighed and said, 'Whatever you advise, Your Grace, and lord and master.'

Just a moment, Harold thought, *perhaps this ex-queen will not like me, especially as I was the cause of her husband's death. I'll not last more than a few days in her presence, probably coming down with some strange digestive disorder leading to my premature death. I'll just have to starve when visiting her.* Harold continued musing about the various methods she could use to end his ability to breathe. He was also worried about the reaction of his fiancée and her parents when they found out.

King Edward smiled broadly. 'Excellent, I'll arrange a hunting party in South Wales for next spring or summer. Now we must meet with the Witan and my advisors. We have so much to discuss.'

Harold trotted off behind Edward, thinking *I wonder if I could be the prey for the hunt and get it over with.* He also felt sorry for his bride-to-be who would only too soon become a widow again.

Edward added, 'Oh, I have sent a request to Duke William to allow that Priest Pierre you talked about to be sent to me so he may attend to my body and soul.'

EDGAR'S NEW FAMILY IN NORMANDY

Edgar was busy in the kitchen with Marie's mother, Joan, while his new half-sister Aedre sat in the corner working on a small tapestry. He had found great solace in the creation of cakes and bread. It reminded him of his youth when he spent many happy hours with his mother helping her bake bread and cakes that she sold in the market along with her needlework. He just loved the smell of both the ingredients and the finished product, and his mother always made sure she made a couple of underweight items for him to sample. He did not remember much about his father. His mother said that he was from North Africa, and had emigrated to England where he became a soldier in King Cnut's army. Edgar's father died when he was only five. He could only remember his father telling him, 'Live well not long.' He had only just recently realised how good this advice had been. He took Marie's father, Louis, his supper. Louis looked at Edgar and smiled. It was an odd arrangement but it worked. His wife was certainly happier now she had her adopted son and daughter, and so was he. He started to eat his moules in garlic and smacked his lips. *Delicious,* he thought.

Suddenly Marie entered the house and hugged her mother, hugged her father, and slapped her new brother Edgar on the back. 'I can't stay long. I have brought you some leftovers from the castle kitchens,' she placed a basket on the table, 'and a message from Turold for Edgar.' She turned to Edgar, 'Vous eh, meet 'im au church with Par Pierre sur Demarche mooning.'

Edgar and his new family were getting used to this strange combination of languages.

Edgar considered the message and clarified its meaning. 'I am to meet Turold at Priest Pierre's church on Sunday morning?'

Marie clapped her hands. 'Oui.'

That over, she had a chat with her parents, but spoke so quickly in French that Edgar was left far behind trying to understand the first few words while they had galloped across several hundred. He went back into the kitchen, scratching his head and thinking that he would never master this strange language. He was experimenting with a pancake mix, creating a special flat savoury that his new mother christened 'crepe', to which he added all sorts of savoury and sweet fillings. This, along with other baked products that they had already produced and tested on Louis, could well form the basis of the stock of a bakery shop that he was thinking of setting up. All he needed, he thought, was a small, kind, intelligent, French-speaking woman who did not find him too old and grotesque, and it would be like heaven on earth. *Finally*, he thought, *I'll be able to forget my past misdemeanours.*

THE THREE ENGLISHMEN ARE UNITED

Edgar attended church on Sunday morning with his surrogate parents, and on completion of the service led by Priest Pierre, he stayed behind. He looked around the church. There was no one else left except a small, cloaked figure in the far corner. At last, Priest Pierre came from the direction of a little room in the front right-hand corner, stopped a while at the statue of Mother Mary and Jesus, and beckoned the two over to him. Edgar and the small green robed woman approached him.

'Come with me, and we will talk together. Large walls have ears you know,' and as the priest took them into the vestry he continued, 'come, I have a surprise.'

The woman removed her cape. Edgar looked astonished, thinking, *she looks like a female version of Turold!* She smiled at Edgar. *How unusual, he thought, a woman actually smiling at me! I've not felt this strange tingly sensation since visiting Turold's wife! Is this the one?* She seemed perfect for him. The two strangers looked at each other.

The priest said in English, 'Miss Jeanne, this is Edgar, your cousin Turold's best friend from England. He is currently living with Marie's parents. You should get to know each other before the others arrive.'

Jeanne presented her hand and Edgar held it in his and kissed it. Jeanne continued to hold his hand as if assessing it. Edgar wondered whether she was looking for scars or checking his nails for cleanliness. Eventually she let go and nodded to the priest. She then went over to the holy statue back in the church and said a little prayer, before returning.

'I am honoured to meet you sir,' she said in a thick French accent.

Edgar was amazed. 'You speak English!'

'Un petite, I was taught by your mother.'

Jeanne now knew Edgar's fate as if his final hours on earth had already happened. She would of course never divulge what God had told her. She also knew that his heart was true and kind, indeed the type of man that any middle-aged Norman woman would be happy to marry, even if their shared lives would be oh so brief. A tear came to her eye as she thought about it.

Meanwhile, Edgar thought for a while and then scratched his head nervously. 'Voulez vous aller avec moi sur mon maison por patisseries? Amez vous patisseries?'

She replied immediately, 'Oui et Oui.' There followed a conversation in which arrangements were made.

The priest took Edgar to one side. 'Is your sister Aedre safe and well?'

Edgar nodded. 'Yes, she is so like my mother when she was young and had two eyes, and I must thank you once again for saving her from Duchess Matilda's agents when she was thrown out of the castle.'

The priest smiled. 'You must promise to protect her. She and her unborn son have destinies to fulfil.'

Edgar looked quizzically at the priest, then replied, 'I swear before God.'

After a few minutes, there were new voices in the main church. The priest went to investigate. Wadard and Vital stood with Turold and Rufus. 'Duchess Matilda has commanded us to bring these two fine fellows to see you. We will leave them in your tender care. Make sure no harm befalls them.'

Vital, having delivered his speech, nodded to Wadard and they both smartly turned and exited the main door, which they shut behind them. They then remained on guard at the large ancient carved wooden doors of the church, while a shadowy figure observed the events from across the street. To complete Matilda's surveillance, another agent kept watch from the graveyard.

Vital and Wadard recognised the agents and continued their debate about the best way of killing one of those heavily armoured and armed English professional soldiers, known as housecarls.

Priest Pierre welcomed the new guests saying, 'Good day to you both. Edgar and Jeanne are in the vestry, walk this way,' and he led them towards the small room where they could not be overheard.

Edgar was pleased to see Turold and at last speak to him. He still felt very guilty about his role in the many royal court secrets that ended up in the head of Duchess Matilda. Turold and his two friends brought each other up to date with recent events.

Eventually, Turold decided it was now time for the main business. He stood up, clapped his hands, and began his speech.

'As you may or may not know, until recently King Edward was my master. I have known him for a very long time. I also am aware of the politics and many of the royal secrets of England. I remain loyal to him and his wishes, although many other influential men in England do not deserve my loyalty. As you are all aware, Duke William and Duchess Matilda wish to rule England, and seem determined to achieve their ambition one way or another, whether England likes it or not. There is a good argument for allowing this to happen, especially if done peaceably. However, I know for a fact that my master, King Edward, wishes Earl Harold to be his successor. Truthfully, I do not understand this wish, although the earl is indeed the most powerful Englishman alive. Earl Harold has been forced to swear allegiance to Duke William. Whether Earl Harold stays true to his oath is another matter, especially if the crown is forced upon his head. I think it prudent for us three, with the guidance of Priest Pierre and Jeanne, to decide on our positions and courses of action. My position seems clear to me. I must remain loyal to King Edward. Perhaps you, Edgar, should speak next.'

Edgar thought for a few moments. Priest Pierre translated quietly to Jeanne during these discussions.

Edgar at last spoke, having gathered his thoughts. 'I was misled by Duke William and Duchess Matilda. They abducted my poor mother, and although she was treated well, and rose to a position of respect, I cannot forgive them for what they did or made me do. I do not believe that having England ruled by Duke William and his family is in the English peoples' best interests. Many will surely die.'

It was now the time for Rufus to speak frankly. 'I'm of the same mind as Edgar. I have been misled by the outward kindness of Duchess Matilda into helping her and her husband to construct ships capable of transporting an army and its equipment to England. I am happily married and love Normandy, and in the past have been cruelly dealt with while living in England, but I cannot completely abandon the country to these devils.'

Turold considered their replies. 'Well then brothers, we are all agreed that we cannot stand idly by, but the question is what can we do? It is perhaps time for some advice from these two people who seem to be able to look into the future with some accuracy.'

Jeanne and Priest Pierre discussed the matter at some length, in French. The other three continued to discuss other matters in English.

Eventually Jeanne and the priest seemed to reach a conclusion and the priest spoke. 'We of course cannot see all, but we have sufficient insight to be able to counsel as follows. Rufus, your objective must continue to be the preservation of Turold. Now you, Turold, can do no more than let God's hand guide you to your destiny. You, Edgar, must complete a task as penance for your betrayal. God has commanded that I must shortly return to my country of birth. You will be my guide and guardian.'

The three men considered his words. It all seemed very simple but Turold was still confused as to what he should do for the best. In the end he decided to leave his fate in the strong grip of God.

The group disbanded carefully. Turold and Rufus left by the main doors, where they were greeted by their Norman friends, who suggested some liquid refreshment even though it was Sunday. Edgar and Jeanne stayed a while, trying their best to communicate, while Priest Pierre went outside to see if there remained any of Duchess Matilda's agents. Luckily, they had both followed the other four, so Edgar and Jeanne were able to leave without being seen, and together they made their way to Marie's house. So began their friendship.

PRIEST PIERRE'S VISIT TO LONDON: PART 1 - THE CROSSING

It was late autumn 1064. Duke William and Duchess Matilda studied the request of King Edward. They were both bemused by its contents and had to read it several times to try and make sense of it. As usual, Matilda was the first to determine a course of action while all William could do was rub the short hair on his head.

She said softly to William, 'Well, dear, it seems that someone has been meddling behind our backs. Earl Harold must be behind it. Perhaps he is playing for time by trying to extend Edward's life. If so, then that is upsetting, but on the other hand, helps us gain more time in building up and training our forces. In addition, it does remove one thorn in our side. Priest Pierre is indeed a holy man honoured by the whole of Normandy, but as such does overshadow your debauched brother Odo, thus causing confusion amongst the men and women of Normandy. They seem to believe the priest to be the head of the Norman Church. I suggest dear, that removing this destabilising force from Normandy will help you elevate your brother's standing. Bishop Odo will be needed at any battle to add religious legitimacy to the invasion and help encourage the troops. One final thought dear, this Priest Pierre could perhaps be the subject of a cruel accident or incident that could not be traced back to you. Yes, he could become a Norman martyr killed by the English!'

William was still bemused but so liked the idea of a bit of murdering, especially, according to his wife, of such a troublesome priest that he immediately replied, 'I will reply to my dear friend Edward that arrangements will be made.'

Matilda arose from her seat. 'I will draft your reply for you to sign this hour. Later I will organise a warm welcome in England for our dear, but not long for this world, priest.'

William laughed. 'I love you so much when you are decisive and cruel, come here my beloved!'

The document was despatched to King Edward the next day.

A week later, Priest Pierre had a visitation from an official of William's court. He had brought a document for him to read. The priest read its contents and smiled. *The time has come*, he thought. He informed the official that he and his servant would make ready immediately, as the weather was unusually settled at present.

Two days later Edgar said his 'Au revoirs' to his adopted mother and father, Jeanne, and his sister Aedre, as he and the priest boarded the ship bound for London. There were a few other passengers on the brand-new vessel. Amongst the other passengers was a middle-aged monk who seemed to show a great deal of interest in Priest Pierre and Edgar. As the ship sailed towards the river Thames, Edgar used his time wisely by thinking through his plans of opening a bakery and pastry shop, whilst Priest Pierre offered religious guidance to the fellow travellers. The crossing was uneventful until they reached the mouth of the river Thames. Priest Pierre noticed that the ship was drifting dangerously close to the sandbanks that restricted the entrance. The sailors were preoccupied with sorting out teething problems with the new ship, including leaks and rigging issues. It was the sail rigging that was affecting the direction of travel.

Priest Pierre had been daydreaming as he looked at the English countryside. It would be the first time that he had been back in England since he had fled all those years ago. Suddenly God seemed to whisper to him, so he looked carefully ahead, and immediately saw the danger. He shouted loudly, 'Sandbanks ahead. Rowers on the left row stronger and faster.'

The sailors did immediately as commanded. There was a loud scraping noise as the hull of the ship's keel hit the sand but as the vessel did not ground on the bank itself, it was soon continuing its journey. All those on board congratulated the priest, and many thought it yet another miracle and thanked God for their deliverance, especially as most could not swim. He remained humble, saying, 'You were in God's hands. He decided to save us all. Once ashore, you must go to the nearest church and thank Him.' The whole event was made even more spiritual for all aboard when a rainbow appeared after a short autumn shower. They all agreed that there had been divine intervention.

PRIEST PIERRE'S VISIT TO LONDON: PART 2 - VISIT TO TUROLD'S HOUSE

Eventually the ship reached London. Priest Pierre and Edgar disembarked the ship first, with the rest of the travellers kneeling as they left. The priest would now be referred to as Peter, being his English name. Edgar knew where the palace at Westminster was, but first he decided that they would have an English breakfast, and then they would head for St. Mary's at Cheapside, visit the church, and then go to Turold's House. They would be followed all the way by one of Duchess Matilda's agents. Some of the others on board did indeed go to church, but most of the crew ended up at the nearest alehouse where they planned to get drunk and legless.

Once Peter and Edgar had fed both their bodies and their spirits, they walked down the track to Turold's house. By now, they were being followed at a discrete distance by Duchess Matilda's agent from Normandy and two local assassins hired by her London spy, Agent Cecil.

Edgar knocked on the door. He and it fell into Turold's house. He got up and brushed the straw off his clothes. The barmaid, Betty, rushed towards him, carrying one of the twins. 'Well, if it 'aint dear Edgar.' She gave him a big kiss, while the twin, after sniffing him, gave him a big lick.

Edgar was embarrassed, and was quick to introduce the pious priest, which vastly reduced her enthusiasm. She showed them into the main room, which was now transformed. There was no longer the smell of dog or twins, there was order rather than chaos, bright curtains in the windows, and two very nice chairs which replaced an upturned barrel and an old chair which had been held together with a great deal of luck. *Shame,* thought Edgar, *that the door remains unrepaired. I'll fix it whilst here. After Peter, the safety of Turold's family must be my priority!*

Megan sprang up from her chair and hugged Edgar. Edgar was embarrassed again, but this time, he enjoyed it.

He was first to speak. 'This is Priest Peter from Normandy. He has been summoned by no less than King Edward to come to England and do God's will.'

Both women were immediately in awe of this stranger and were unsure what to do with him. They curtsied and beckoned him to sit down near the fire. He thanked them in perfect English and sat. He was offered some of Megan's special pottage, which he accepted with grace, but not much eagerness, so as not to offend. He said a prayer and took a spoonful. It immediately hit the back of his throat with a tingling warm feeling that then permeated throughout his body, and although not very hungry, he ate some more.

Edgar was also enjoying his bowl of pottage. 'You must give me the list of ingredients as I could sell this in my bakery shop.'

Megan was more interested in news from Normandy.

'How is my Turold?' she asked.

Edgar replied, 'He's missing you and the twins, but where have they gone?'

'Oh, they are playing in the back yard.'

Edgar had to get up and see. The twins were quite a bit larger than when he last saw them, accentuated by the fact that they were no longer on all fours, but upright. They came over to Edgar and smelt him, and he patted them on their heads. *Well*, he thought, *they are not fully recovered but certainly improved.* The boys remembered his scent, and went back to their game of kick the dead rat. Edgar went back into the house, and started to repair the door.

The priest was chatting to the women and they were both giggling. It was probably something about him, Edgar thought.

Megan laughed and said, 'I hear you have a sweetheart who happens to be Turold's cousin.'

Edgar was embarrassed again, put down the hammer, and replied, 'We are just good friends.'

Priest Peter went on to explain to Megan. It is God's will that Turold stays in Normandy. It may be possible for you to visit him, but there is always a risk that you will end up in the same predicament as your Husband.'

Megan thought for a while, then replied, 'My place is with the twins, and although very painful to be without my husband, while the money lasts, I will stay in England.'

Priest Peter held her hand and said softly, 'Perhaps you may find solace in the house of God, or at least pray to Him for strength and guidance.'

Megan immediately felt God's presence in the priest's body and replied, 'I will.' She could now understand why King Edward wanted to meet this man.

Both men recovered from their journey while they had another bowl of Megan's special pottage.

It certainly helped Edgar's brain, and he soon fixed the front door, although there was much swearing when he hit his thumb with the hammer.

Priest Peter was not amused. 'That will require another visit to St. Mary's church!'

Edgar changed the subject. 'I have an idea. Perhaps Duchess Matilda could be persuaded to allow Turold to visit Megan, but who would she listen to?'

The priest wiped the pottage from his lips and suggested, 'Perhaps we could ask the old King Edward to write a request. I know that for some reason, she wishes to keep Turold under her control, but in certain circumstances she may be willing to let him out of Normandy although I am sure she would supply some bodyguards, and her agents would keep close watch on him.'

'Don't mention her agents in my presence. I am still of a mind to do them harm,' Edgar replied.

The priest shook his head. 'I can assure you that God will look badly on you if you do so. You must turn the other cheek. If they have done wrong in the eyes of our Lord and not repented for their actions, they will pay the price.'

Edgar relaxed but snorted, thinking he could easily do God's work for Him.

Luckily for Priest Peter and Edgar, Betty was looking out the window. She was seeing whether her friend, who she called Ethelred the Ever-ready, was still there, but all she could see were three men wearing black cloaks and looking furtive. 'I think those agents of hers are across the track, look, there they are, next to the decaying dung heap!'

Edgar looked and decided that evasive action was required.

PRIEST PIERRE'S VISIT TO LONDON: PART 3 - VISIT TO THE PALACE

When Edgar and Peter finally left Turold's house, they went out into the back yard, said their farewells to the twins, and climbed over the wooden fence into the yard of a blacksmiths. He was busy making a sword so did not see the two intruders as they went through his workshop and out onto the track beyond. From there they went past the slaughterhouse whilst holding their noses and looking the other way, and back to St. Mary's church. Once Edgar had confessed his sins and Peter had asked God for guidance, they continued towards the royal palace. Edgar looked over his shoulder, *yes,* he thought, *we've lost them for now, but there'll bound to be more at the palace gates.*

As they walked, the priest could not help notice that these Londoners were indeed a strange mixture of humanity, not only in terms of social standing but also nationalities. He had not seen so many people in one place since he had left England all those years ago, nor experienced such a pungent air made up of so many terrible smells, which a nose should not have to deal with all at once. He wished he had an incense burner in his tunic. As for the noise, it was deafening and so confusing. Edgar pressed on, and eventually they reached a bridge leading to the palace, guarded by several heavily armed English soldiers.

Edgar did the talking. 'We are here to see King Edward at his request. Here is our invitation.'

The sergeant looked at the document as if he could read, and scratched his forehead with his battle-axe, not looking at all impressed.

Eventually he said, 'Wait 'ere, I'll get someone official like.' He looked carefully at Edgar. 'Just a moment, is that you, Edgar the Assassin? Well, it's been a long time no see and no mistake. I thought you were dead, old friend. Don't you remember me? It's Grimbold the Brutal, your assistant!'

Edgar looked extremely uneasy, especially as he was in the presence of Priest Peter, but replied in a friendly tone, 'My friend Grimbold, life seems to have been much kinder to you than me! You look so well!'

Grimbold nodded and smiled. 'Three square meals a day, no battles to fight, and as many women as I can handle. This duty may be boring but it does have its advantages!'

Grimbold sent one of his men off and after quite a long time, during which Priest Peter had managed to convince at least half of the guard that they needed to attend church as soon as their shift was over, they could see a young man wearing official-looking robes walking towards them, following a gesticulating guard.

The clerk looked at the two strangers quizzically and commanded, 'State your business sirs.'

Priest Peter spoke. 'King Edward has asked that I attend court and have an audience with him. This is the request.'

He handed the clerk the letter. Luckily the clerk could read, and recognising the seal, the letter, and King Edward's signature as being genuine, immediately commanded the guards to let them through.

The clerk then announced to the priest, 'Sorry about those barbarians but they have their uses. Follow me please and I will take you to an antechamber, supply you with some refreshments, and see what can be arranged. King Edward is with his advisors now but will be shortly in need of a comfort break because of his age and frailty and lack of control of his bodily functions.'

The two were taken to a small but elaborately and colourfully decorated room. One guard remained inside the room, whilst another was placed outside the now closed and locked door. After some food and excellent beer, Priest Peter spent the time reading his bible and studying the selection of books on display. Edgar sat next to the fire and counted the logs while thinking of Jeanne and his past life as an officer in the King's Special Forces. *Grimbold had been a good assistant but perhaps a bit too enthusiastic when it came to killing people. There tended to be a great deal of collateral damage when he was around! Still, he did save my life on several occasions!*

One of the guards gave them a look and whispered, 'Bloody foreigners.'

Edgar could not resist saying, 'Don't be fooled by my haircut. In the old days I could have you hung, drawn, and quartered with a mere gesture to my assistant, Grimbold!'

The Guard tutted and continued to pick his nose with his dagger, while Priest Peter looked at Edgar disapprovingly. Priest Peter was becoming increasingly worried about

Edgar's standing with God. *I think poor Edgar has indeed a short future! Jeanne I'm afraid is correct.*

Eventually the clerk returned and unlocked the door. 'King Edward is busy at his toilet but will see you for supper. Please follow me.'

As they walked, the priest asked, 'Is Earl Harold here?'

The clerk replied, 'Yes, as the heir to the crown, he is at King Edward's side at all times.'

Edgar could not resist, 'What, even at toilet?'

The clerk was not amused and responded with a frown. 'Earl Harold will be present at supper.'

The priest was pleased about the presence of Harold as he had business with him too, but was taken aback by Harold's status as heir to the throne. Events had certainly gathered greater pace than he had expected. Their rooms could only be described as opulent. Neither had ever seen such furnishings before, and together with the exquisite wall coverings, including fine tapestries from Flanders, they made it the most wonderful lodgings imaginable. The clerk asked whether either wanted anything, and Edgar requested some ale, and some more food. He was determined to take advantage of anything on offer.

It was later that evening when the two visitors were escorted to the royal chambers where King Edward sat on his throne with Harold at his side. He graciously welcomed them. The priest kissed Edward's royal ring, and then held his hand, which was against all etiquette but necessary from the priest's point of view. Edward's royal steward and two guards rushed to Edward's aid but he held up his hand and commanded them to return to their places. The priest could feel Edward's spiritual essence, but also that he was full of remorse and regret. Priest Peter could also sense that the holy water had done its job of purging him of all the stagnant and malicious impurities that had infested his body, but he knew that this had been purely a temporary cure. He looked up to heaven and silently asked God for His helping hand in ensuring that Edward would just be able to take part in the Mass of Christ at the end of 1065.

Meanwhile Edward, on the other hand, could feel the flow of goodness throughout his body, and his soul seemed to expand until he was full of joy. He could not help but laugh and cry, 'Praise be to God!' He turned to the priest and declared, 'You surely are a messenger from God.'

Priest Peter replied, 'No Your Grace, but I try to do His work on earth.'

Edward led the small party to a table that had been laid out simply. They were then served a wholesome meal, much to the disappointment of Edgar. The priest and Edward talked at length about ecumenical matters, the state of the English Church, and Edward's grand project, Westminster Abbey. The priest advised Edward that he must resolve the problem of the corrupt Stigand, Archbishop of Canterbury as both the Roman Catholic Church and God considered the current situation intolerable. For some reason Edward seemed unwilling to consider removing the dastardly Stigand from his position, and Priest Peter got the distinct impression that somehow the archbishop had a hold over Edward which meant that he was powerless to do anything without some dirty secrets being made public that would badly tarnish Edward's reputation and perhaps undermine his ability to rule. Finally, Edward merely thanked him for his concerns but underlined the fact that he was King of England and knew what was best. The priest wondered whether he was getting confused between what was best for Edward and what was best for England and its people. *Unfortunately,* he thought, *no one's perfect and despite being so pious, Edward is imperfect in very many ways.* Priest Peter sighed.

The king continued his discussions about religion and his haughty self-aggrandizement building project, touched the priest's hands as much as he could, and asked him to say prayers and read from the good book. Edward was oblivious of the holy man's concerns as he was just thoroughly enjoying himself. At one stage he even offered to make Priest Peter an English bishop. The priest gently declined, but eventually promised to be at Edward's bedside during his final hours on earth. This gave Edward great comfort, as he believed that this great man of God would be a much better guide to the afterlife and would be a much safer pair of hands for his immortal soul than that evil Archbishop Stigand.

Meanwhile, Harold and Edgar had been talking about various matters, including the weather (always a safe topic, Edgar found), bread and pastry making (Edgar found that Harold strangely had no knowledge of this art form), and matters of war and defence that Harold could talk the hind leg off a donkey about. From these topics, it was agreed that the weather was unseasonably sunny but cold, that Harold should find someone to advise him about setting up a bakery business for his common law wife, and that one must keep one's weapons and armour in tip top condition and close at hand at all times.

Something significant did arise from their discussions regarding the Norman question. Edgar was able to provide the earl with various useful pieces of information, that

Duke William was indeed building a fleet of ships capable of invading England and although not yet in sufficient numbers, this would be rectified given time and resources. Also, Edgar was able to advise Harold that it was rumoured that William was in discussions with his neighbours about the possibility of their involvement in any such enterprise. There were also rumours of secret army training camps being set up in remote areas in the dukedom. As regards Duchess Matilda, Edgar informed Harold that she had agents throughout England gathering secrets and information. The earl found all this of great interest and requested that Edgar keep him informed of any developments during his stay in Normandy. Edgar was pleased to be of assistance and saw this as a way of redeeming himself. The earl handed him a bag of gold coins and advised him to be careful. Edgar thanked him for his concern and looked in the bag. He now had the capital required for his bakery business.

Edward eventually declared that he was tired and as any old man, needed to undertake certain bodily functions prior to retiring to bed. The priest gave him a final blessing and said a prayer for God to watch over him, and with that, Edward left with his steward and guards.

Priest Peter was now able to turn his attention to Earl Harold. 'I understand that King Edward has announced to the court and the Witan that you should be his heir. I expect this has unsettled you somewhat.'

Harold nodded. 'Certainly, I tried to argue that perhaps Duke William would be a better heir, but I was unable to change his mind. As you yourself have found out, he is very stubborn on certain matters. He seems unwilling to treat seriously the threats of other contenders to the throne and I regret that this will inevitably lead to disaster. In addition, he is now trying to arrange a marriage between myself and the widowed ex-queen of Wales.'

Priest Peter softly patted Harold on the shoulder and consoled him as best he could. 'You can do no more and God knows that.'

Harold shrugged. 'He may, but I believe my soul is lost unless there is any redemption for me. Is there anything I can do dear sir? I will do absolutely anything!'

The priest walked away, knelt, prayed, and contemplated for a while, then said a prayer to God and waited for any response from Him or the Lord.

He then arose and returned to Harold. 'Christ has answered my plea and prayer. Next year Edward will be taking you on a journey through the west of England. On your way you must do penance at all the holy shrines and churches, including those at Winchester, Salisbury, Glastonbury, and Bath. You must walk on your knees from the doors of the churches to their altars, be humble and pray for forgiveness. You must give gold to the abbots or priests on the strict understanding that it be used for looking after the poor and needy of the parish, and for the education of their children. In addition, you will give one twentieth of your wealth to Turold for him to use in providing for the poor and needy when he returns to England. This will be done by you depositing the money with a good friend of mine, Abbot Matthew, at the abbey of Shaftesbury. You will deliver the money and the letter that I will write tonight when you journey through Wessex. This is the will of Christ and you must obey him in order that your soul is saved for all eternity. Unfortunately, I must leave the safety of your body to you and those who guard you!'

Harold considered this penance carefully. It seemed all very clear and reasonable in the circumstances, and he was happy to agree. 'I agree to carry out Christ's punishment for my many sins. In addition to these actions, I will also provide sufficient money for completion and maintenance of the abbey at Waltham, where in childhood I was miraculously cured of paralysis by its great golden holy cross. Now, dear priest, what can I do for you?'

'You can come with me and pray in the palace chapel, and then ensure my safe return to Normandy. I fear that there are strong foreign forces in England who mean me harm, and God's work is not yet complete. By ensuring my continuing heartbeat, you will indeed improve your standing with God. In addition, any harm to me on English soil will surely be used by Duke William and Duchess Matilda in furthering their ambitions.'

Later, Earl Harold would make the arrangements for Priest Peter's and Edgar's journey back to Normandy.

PRIEST PIERRE'S VISIT TO LONDON: PART 4 - VISIT TO WESTMINSTER ABBEY

Early next morning King Edward, Earl Harold, Priest Peter, and Edgar inspected the building works at Westminster Abbey. The priest was able to offer some suggestions as to ways of improving the house of God from a religious point of view, and Edgar seemed to have knowledge of stonework, and offered his advice which Edward was only too pleased to accept, as much of what Edgar said would make the edifice even more imposing. It seemed that Edgar had a lot of knowledge about many subjects.

Suddenly an inspirational thought hit Edward's brain, and looking closely at Edgar he was able to confirm the fact that he had met Edgar on several occasions before.

Edward had to ask Edgar, 'Are you not Edgar my trusted agent regarding any, well let's say, sensitive matters?'

Edgar nodded and replied, 'I am, Your Grace, but I prefer to forget those years in your service!'

Edward smiled. 'I wish I could forget those times, but I do find that continual confessions are good for my soul! Yes, I remember now, they called you Edgar the Ass—'

Edgar quickly interrupted and tried to divert Edward's attention. 'I think Your Grace you should look at the wall behind the altar; in my view the opening for the grand stained-glass window should be larger. Just follow me, Your Grace ....'

And the two of them left the priest with Earl Harold.

Priest Peter looked into Harold's eyes. There was still no sign of his devil father inside that head. 'You should make good use of your time here by praying with me.'

Eventually all four men returned to the centre of the church.

The priest asked for one favour from Edward. 'King Edward, your poor jester, Turold, has been away from his family for many months now, and I know that both his family and you miss him. Would it not be advantageous to all if you write to Duke William and ask whether Turold can visit England? For some reason he is determined to keep Turold under his protection but he may be persuaded to let him stay in England during the summer.'

Edward considered the proposal. It seemed a reasonable one on the face of it, and surely would not antagonise Duke William or Duchess Matilda, and he did miss his diminutive friend and would like to see him one last time. 'I will consider you request, and Harold and I will make a decision early next year.'

The priest bowed and said, 'Thank you Your Grace, but one other matter has come to my attention and God's. It is time for Earl Harold to complete a pilgrimage during your next royal progress in readiness of his forthcoming responsibilities. I humbly suggest that you allow him to stop at the various holy places on the way, and for you to enlighten him as to their significance.'

Edward was delighted with this idea. Not only would this journey be a religious quest, but also both a hunting and a political expedition. This would indeed be a fitting end to his life.

'I agree wholeheartedly. Harold has not really shown too much interest in religion. I will educate him, and at the same time I myself will complete a final pilgrimage to those holy sites.'

Finally, Harold shook Edgar's hand, saying, 'Remember to keep me informed of Duke William's preparations.'

All four men were happy and content in their own way and for various reasons. At the palace entrance, Edward and the earl hugged the priest, and shook Edgar's hand. A special guard, commanded by Grimbold, surrounded the two men and marched them back to a waiting ship. They were to make sure that they were returned to Normandy still breathing and with no pieces missing. Edward and Harold turned towards each other and smiled broadly, each feeling a great deal more optimistic about the future. Meanwhile, Cecil and his assassination squad could do nothing but watch as Edgar and Priest Peter made their way to the ship. Cecil knew that Duchess Matilda would be very disappointed, and that meant that his life would be at risk. One more failure would surely mean premature death.

PRIEST PIERRE'S VISIT TO LONDON: PART 5 - THE RETURN

With such an armed guard, the assassination squad sent by Duchess Matilda could not get close enough to cause mischief. She later regretted not sending one or other of the Richards to do her bidding. The heavily armed procession walked briskly down to the docks. Many people stopped and watched, thinking it must be King Edward himself on some important royal mission. They were surprised and disappointed to see that the dignitaries consisted of merely a cleric and a servant, both of whom seemed to be of Norman blood. Edgar thought it quite humorous to wave his hand royally as he walked, until Grimbold advised otherwise, saying, 'Not everyone in London supports the Saxon King Edward. There are still a few Danes about who would cheerfully kill anyone associated with King Edward, especially if they knew who you were and what you had done to two of their kings!'

At London docks, Priest Peter, Edgar, and their guard boarded a ship provided by Harold, bound for Caen. Unlike Harold's crossing, the trip across to Normandy was a good one, as the winds were from the north west and the seas slight. They made good time and reached landfall by late afternoon. The guards handed their charges over to a port official, then quickly embarked on their ship for the return trip to England before they could be detained, arrested, and held hostage. Grimbold shouted to Edgar, 'Farewell, dear friend, may the gods be with you. May Odin be at your side always, and if you ever wish to resume your previous occupation, come, and see me! There's always a need for someone with such talents in the English army!'

As the English ship left, Grimbold could see a great deal of new ships laid up along the sheltered shoreline. That information would soon be given to Harold. One Norman ship full of burly soldiers did try and intercept the ship as it left the harbour walls, but the English ship was already under sail and with the wind now from the west, it was soon a faint dot on the horizon.

Edgar accompanied the priest back to his little church.

Inside, the priest turned to Edgar, gave him a hug, and blessed him. Then he said, 'Thank you dear Edgar. God is surely pleased with you. Now go and see your friends and family. Oh, and remember I'm now to be called Priest Pierre! God be with you always, Edgar!'

Edgar smiled, saying, 'It was a pleasure not only to help a living saint but also a fellow Englishman!' He then left swiftly since he couldn't wait to show Jeanne the bag of money. Perhaps she would agree to a marriage proposal.

Priest Pierre knelt in front of the altar and prayed. He was very unhappy. *If that Grimbold is a true reflection of the attitude of the English fighting men towards religion, then they're surely going to be punished by God!* He sighed, and asked God to forgive the English sinners, but he was sure that God was unlikely to listen to his plea.

Edgar received a warm welcome on his return to the house of Marie's parents. Her mother gave him a great big hug that lifted him off the ground and she was soon providing him with some lovely baked delicacies. The English, he thought, did not know what they were missing.

NOVEMBER AND DECEMBER 1064

Matilda looked out of her window upon another stormy and rainswept day, sighed, and then returned to reading her bible. The book of Genesis verses 6 and 7 had been an obvious choice, given the weather since the return of the priest. For the whole of November, one storm after another had swept up the Channel between Normandy and England. All the tracks and roads were just muddy streams and the ship builders had run out of materials. Everyone was depressed and the whole of Normandy was flooded. Even though Matilda had instructed Bishop Odo to have continuous prayers said, and to have daily services where the bones of saints were blessed, and prayers said to the saints so that they may intercede and bring an end to the flooding, the devastating weather would not cease. Matilda put down her bible. *At least*, she thought, *we have the ships in case we must take to the water*! She laughed. Perhaps, she thought, she was to be the new Noah, and she and her family would become the sole survivors of humanity. She sighed again and then meditated, and prayed to God. Suddenly a thought hit her mind like a thunderbolt. She had been given the answer. She thought, *how stupid have I been! I had the answer all the time!*

Matilda made the arrangements. The so-called miracle would occur on 30 November. This was the day of the feast of Saint Andrew the Apostle. The feast marked the end of the Church year and the beginning of Advent, so it would be an opportune time for the weather to suddenly improve. She decided that the venue would be Rouen Cathedral, and that Archbishop Maurille, assisted by Bishop Odo and Priest Pierre, would conduct the service before the feast. In common with most important religious Christian sites, bones of the various apostles were already available, so those supposed to have belonged to Saint Andrew were to be especially cleaned, and displayed in a small gold-framed glass reliquary.

On 30 November 1064, the congregation struggled through the floodwaters, with the rain beating down on them and the wind doing its best to blow them all off their soggy feet. Bishop Odo and Priest Pierre welcomed each pilgrim as they entered the cathedral, a magnificent structure built in the Romanesque style. Many parts of the remodelled cathedral were only just over a year old, so as the congregation sat and dried off, they were able to admire the Norman workmanship. William and Matilda were seated at the front with their family, with the other dignitaries seated behind them. All was ready. Archbishop Maurille came through from the sacristy and the service commenced. Maurille was one of the most venerated men in Normandy and his presence, along with Priest Pierre, made the whole service an inspiring spiritual experience for all those present. Then, when the reliquary was displayed, and the congregation was asked to come forward and take the sacrament of the Eucharist and touch the casket, many were overcome with spiritual joy. Matilda was extremely pleased as the service reached its conclusion. It was nearly time for the final prayers. Unfortunately, most in the congregation were turning their attention to the sounds of the storm raging outside, and thinking that surely God had abandoned them. It was time for Matilda's miracle. She nodded her head to the choir leader who had been commanded to wait for her signal, and then the choir started to sing Psalm 23. The uplifting words filled the cathedral. This was the cue for Master Perciville to undertake his task as he and the two Richards stood on top of one of the two towers. The twins were soaked and cold and miserable, and this did not help at all as regards the weather.

Master Perciville said commandingly, 'Men, it is time. For your sakes and the whole of Normandy, do what you must to change the weather!'

Richard the Last looked at his brother for inspiration, as he had no idea what to do. Richard the First opened his bible and read out loud Psalm 40, including the words, *I waited patiently for the Lord; and He inclined to me, and heard my cry; He also brought me up out of a horrible pit, out of the miry clay, and set my feet upon a rock, and established my steps.*

He then held hands with his brother and they both looked up into the rain and grey clouds and said the Lord's Prayer. Once their task was complete, they both collapsed on the stone floor.

Master Perciville waited. Nothing happened. He waited some more, frowned, and sighed, and turned to the Richards. 'You have failed! We are dead men walking! You are complete and utter—'

His words were cut short as a gust of wind blew him off his feet. He flew through the air, knocking his head against the low stone wall. He was very lucky not to plummet off the tower.

Then the miracle happened. Initially the wind dropped to a gentle breeze and the rain to just a light drizzle. Next, the wind altered its direction so it now blew cold clear blue skies from Scandinavia.

When the three men awoke and looked up, all they could see was an orange sun in a blue sky. Master Perciville was still concussed but was able to vocalise, 'Praise be to God, I am saved!'

Down below, the congregation were hearing Bishop Odo say a special prayer that Matilda had composed, which finished with the phrase, '…. and God and Jesus will listen to our prayers because we Normans are devout and Duke William and Duchess Matilda are here on earth to do Their bidding. Praise be to God! Amen.'

Just as he finished, the congregation got ready to go. They were amazed to see William, Matilda and their family lead the way in their finest clothes with no protection from the wind and rain outside. One by one they realised that the noise of the weather had ceased, and the sun was shining through the stained-glass windows. One shaft in particular lit up the faces of the statue of the Virgin Mary holding baby Jesus. They all fell to their knees and gave thanks. There had indeed been a miracle.

The good weather would last until after the Mass of Christ, as commanded and orchestrated by Matilda, using her twin instruments of God as required.

THE MASS OF CHRIST 1064

During December 1064, Duchess Matilda, her family, and
Turold had been very busy with the rehearsals for the Mass
of Christ feast. Her elder children Robert, Richard and
Adeliza had been most enthusiastic once incentivised. In
addition, Young William, even though only eight years old,
was in his zone, what with designing the costumes with
Adeliza and deciding upon the musical content with the
help of his elder brothers. Turold was given the job of
director and choreographer, given his wealth of experience
in putting on an impressive show. When Matilda saw the
last rehearsal, she broke down and cried. She was so happy.
She congratulated all the participants, and then followed
the presentation of valuable gifts to all with a promise for
more to follow if things went well.

Duke William was not interested at all. His only
stipulation was that 'The Pius Pipe Playing Pilgrims of
Pevensey' were not to be invited to perform.

The formal Christmas midnight mass took place at Rouen
Cathedral. Now was the time for Matilda's nativity play.
All the participants were dressed and ready. As well as
Normans, the audience consisted of representatives from
the neighbouring lands, together with ambassadors from
England, Rome, and France. Part one consisted of
Matilda's interpretation of the Nativity, starring Adeliza as
Mary, and young William as the Archangel Gabriel. All
gave stunning performances, especially William, who sang

a beautiful song while being suspended from the ceiling. It bought a tear to the eye of even the most bloodthirsty men present, except for Duke William who considered such a high voice inappropriate for one of his sons. He wondered if he could disown him as not being his, but then he could not believe that his wife could ever be unfaithful. Matilda, God, and Bishop Stigand knew otherwise.

Part two consisted of a pageant of past English kings, from Alfred the Great through to the present King Edward. Alfred the Great was played by the eldest son, Robert and accompanied by Matilda who made a short speech underlying that she was a direct descendent of the great king himself. Richard was King Ethelred and was accompanied by Adel who played Queen Emma and who gave a short speech outlining the fact that her father, Duke William, was related to Queen Emma and therefore to her son, King Edward. Cnut was played by young William while again, Adel, played Emma, now King Cnut's wife. Surrounding them were pigs wearing Viking helmets and representing Cnut's devilish Viking Danish offspring. The sight and tricks of the pigs created a great deal of amusement amongst the audience and participants. The pigs were controlled by no less than Turold, who had found during rehearsals that these animals were particularly friendly towards him. Unfortunately for the pigs, this would be their last performance as they were destined to be part of the forthcoming feast's menu. Finally, William FitzOsbern played a decrepit and senile King Edward. He was very convincing in his regal clothes and heavy makeup. He finished his performance by reading from a document written by Duchess Matilda. 'I, King Edward, swear that if I die without male issue then Duke William should be the next king of England. May anyone who defies me and the will of God be excommunicated by the Church of Rome, struck down, and their soul lost for all eternity.'

Matilda closed the show with a speech. 'Duke William and I are related to King Edward, and in the fullness of time we have all these talented and educated sons ready to succeed their father. Duke William and his family will make England strong and pure. He will end any lingering paganism. He will have magnificent cathedrals, churches, and castles built throughout the land. England is to become a glorious Christian land never to be invaded again. This is the will of God, and no man should defy God. Duke William will wage a holy crusade on any who disobeys God and seizes the English crown. They will be damned.'

This whole show was intended to sow seeds in the minds of the nobility and the ambassadors present. Soon, the whole of Europe would know that Duke William intended to take the English throne one way or another.

There followed a performance of jester skills by Turold and, unfortunately for Duke William, a performance by the 'Drum playing Jumping Priests and Nuns of Duiblinn'.

Bishop Odo closed proceedings by saying a few prayers, with one asking for God's continued protection of King Edward, Duke William, his wife, and their family, and Normandy.

Later, the feast and festivities took place, much to the relief of all present. It had been a long day, and now it was time to enjoy themselves. There would be much food, wine, music, and dancing, under, of course, the watchful eye of Duchess Matilda. In particular, she kept Duke William within chastising distance, much to his annoyance. He had seen a young maiden ready for him to conquer.

THE MISSION FOR ONE OF THE RICHARDS

Months had passed. It was the middle of March 1065 and
Duchess Matilda had summoned the Grand Spy Master.
He gave the secret knock and entered through a concealed
door into a small room at the back of the palace. 'Good
evening Your Grace, and what are your orders?'

Matilda was seated at a small writing desk with two
candles lighting it, and had been busy with some papers.
She turned the papers upside down, took a key that she kept
around her neck opened the top right-hand drawer and took
out a sealed parchment.

She looked at her visitor, standing there in his fine white
robe with its embroidered red dragon, and handed the
document to him, saying, 'These are the sealed orders for
one of our Richards to perform. They must not get into the
wrong hands. You, Master Perciville and whichever
Richard you select must read and memorise the contents
and then the paper must be destroyed, do you understand?'

'Yes, I will carry out your request immediately. Is there
any other matter for discussion?'

Matilda stood up and walked over to him, and said
quietly, 'Yes, have our agents continue to discreetly watch
that troublesome priest, and put our agents in England and
Wales on full alert. I want Earl Harold followed, and our
agents in Winchester and London to closely monitor the
condition and bowel movements of King Edward.'

'All will be done as requested,' he replied, and
disappeared through the concealed door, turning it back
into a bookcase.

Matilda went back to her desk, sat down, and turned her papers back over. Even the Grand Master was not privy to all that she conspired to do.

Master Perciville read the orders. In front of him stood the Richard twins. There was a big sheet of lead metal between the two. This helped reduce their combined powers. Previous attempts in using other materials had all failed miserably. The agency building no longer had an east wing, in fact, it no longer had an east wall.

He needed to be quick and try not to upset or disturb the two destructive forces standing in front of him at attention. 'At ease, agents.'

The two Richards obeyed, vigorously saluting as one.

This action seemed to cause the formation of a thunderbolt that destroyed a potted plant and its stand directly behind the master. Luckily his reflexes were quick, and as he dived for cover behind the bath sitting in the middle of his bedroom, he thanked God for the armour he was wearing and his speedy reactions. The Richards leapt to his aid, both falling into the bath which then commenced to vibrate, and with the master holding his shield against the bath, caused that to vibrate as well while seeming to whistle a little tune, making his body shiver and shake uncontrollably, until he thought his heart was going to end up in his head. He was able to concentrate all his strength and managed to roll over and throw his shield away. It whistled and twisted and span through the air and decapitated his ceremonial armour that was standing upright in the far corner of the room.

After sanity was restored, Master Perciville continued, 'Just stand there and do not move or speak.'

There was silence as the twins were still admiring their master's skill.

'Now please concentrate. One of you has a mission. Who's the best sailor?

There was no reply. Perciville sighed and said, 'You can now raise your hands but slowly and under control. Who's the best sailor?' They both raised their hands slowly.

His next question was in English. 'I believe you are both trilingual, so who—'

He did not finish his question. The two were looking at each other and getting angry, the floor was starting to shake, and Richard the Last announced, 'That's a lie, we are just shy when amongst women.'

Perciville had to be quick to disarm them. 'What I am asking is who speaks English the best?'

They realised that they had got the wrong end of the sword, calmed down, and both raised their hands.

Perciville thought for a moment, *this is not getting us anywhere and my person and this house are both in serious peril.* 'Richard the First step forward one pace.'

He complied while his twin looked totally dejected.

'Richard the Last, you are dismissed. You will continue your training for your forthcoming mission which is more complicated and important than your brother's.'

Richard the Last poked his tongue out at his brother.

Richard the First now looked forlorn and slammed the door loudly behind his brother, splintering the wood around the hinges and causing it to topple over with a clang and clatter. It then continued to slide down the stairs closely following his twin, who was now leaping down them two treads at a time, rolling to one side as he reached the bottom. The door continued its escape, through the front door which a servant had opened for the agent, and out into the street where it came to a halt beside a pair of young boys with time on their hands and mischief on their minds.

They both looked at it in amazement and one said to the other in French, 'Well if it 'aint our lucky day, thank the Lord.' They each took one end of it and trotted off home with their prize.

Once he was left with just one Richard, Master Perciville continued, 'I only said that so as not to upset your brother. Now, your assignment is outlined in this document. You and I will memorise it and then it will be destroyed. You will be fully trained and briefed, but in the meantime, you are strictly prohibited from removing any hair from your head. You must look and act an Englishman.'

Richard the First rolled his eyes, spat into the corner, and declared, 'I hate the English. They are so uncouth.'

Master Perciville sighed again and sank into his chair, which then collapsed from a strange form of wood fatigue. He thought, while lying on the floor, *bringing them to my house was not such a good idea after all. I had better get some men in tomorrow to check the stability of my home, but tonight just in case, I will stay with a fellow spy master.*

Next day the sun rose brightly and beautifully over a pile of wood, tiles, stone, and brick that was once Master Perciville's house. All that was left intact was his bath, in which sat his ceremonial armour as if waiting for its back to be scrubbed. The door had definitely had a lucky escape, as it was now the front door of the urchins' hovel.

EDWARD'S STRANGE REQUEST

It was the end of March 1065. Duchess Matilda could not concentrate on her embroidery. She had devoted a great deal of time to the subject being sewn. It was supposed to be the life of Saint Pierre, from his humble beginnings to his martyrdom in England at the hands of the dastardly English. Unfortunately, her plan had failed, but there was still time. She believed that his death at the supposed hands of the pagan English would not only be convenient to her, William, and Odo, but also help elevate Normandy as being a true Christian region, and secure the support of Pope Alexander himself. She had already instigated the building of magnificent religious buildings to the glory of God and the Roman Catholic Church (and Pope Alexander), and creating Norman Martyrs would surely improve William's standing further. She had to try to convince Pope Alexander and other powers that William was not just a ruthless butcher of dubious birth. He was instead a strong upholder of the true faith who occasionally had to make examples of those who strayed from the narrow path of the Church of Rome and God. She also had to try to make the world forget about the past members of William's male lineage who, to a man, were quite frankly devils incarnate.

She put down her sewing and studied the letter she had intercepted on its way to her husband. *Yet another strange request from that old senile King Edward*, she thought. *He now wants Turold to visit him. Whatever next?* She shut her eyes and considered for quite a while before deciding as to what William's response should be. *Now*, she thought, *where is my husband?*

Matilda arose from her comfortable chair and asked Adelaide, her lady in waiting. 'Do you know where my wayward husband is, dear?'

Adelaide, dressed in a lovely clean white dress with a red apron and red shoes, stood up from her wooden chair and came over to her, helping to rearrange Matilda's dress and hair so she looked 'just right'. Her mistress was normally mild and gentle but she hated mess and dirt and untidiness, and if she found any, there could be consequences.

'No mistress; I shall make enquiries immediately. I believe he's in the palace somewhere.'

Matilda frowned and replied, 'I'll come with you and see what he's up to.'

The two walked gracefully out of Matilda's day chamber, immediately followed by another two ladies in waiting, again dressed immaculately in the same outfit as Adelaide's. The resulting party was followed by four armed guards, and at a distance two members of the spy agency. It looked like a royal procession as they started their hunt for Duke William. Matilda knew that to find William meant doing a lot of listening since he never did anything quietly, including sleeping. Now and again, she told her party to stand still so that she could try and pick up his noise. Eventually she heard his voice and a certain amount of clanking coming from the large feasting room. She told the party to remain outside, and she made a quick entrance. She found William engaged in what could only be described as the manly chasing of male and female servants, while some of his senior knights looked on.

Matilda had to shout above the screams and roars and obscenities, 'Sir, what are you doing?'

William dropped a scullery maid, picked her off the floor, and dusted her down. 'Madam, I'm instructing my men in the art of rampaging. It is an important part of war, as it not only helps secure the loyalty of the local peasants and low life but also gives the men some recreation and diversion from the cruel aspects of battle.'

Matilda walked up to William and looked him sternly and squarely in the chest. 'Well, I suppose it'll make the dead peasants less rebellious!'

The onlooking knights chuckled. They so loved rampaging after battle. It was their most favourite pastime and diversion, after hunting of course.

William shook his head. 'No madam, you don't understand the subtleties of warfare. It makes the survivors and those who hear of the devastation caused by my conquering army more amenable to being persuaded to accept the inevitability of the conquest. In the long run, it reduces casualties on both sides, so it's really very humane and worthy of God's acceptance.'

Matilda sighed, but there was some underlying truth in what he'd said. She decided she would pray to God on the matter and ask for guidance. 'Sir, we need to talk about an important matter needing your immediate attention. We have another letter from that decrepit King Edward.'

William put down his sword and left with Matilda, turning to his knights, and shouting, 'Carry on men!'

The knights cheered and set to. The servants were less pleased, especially the women.

William was not happy with Matilda and decided, unwisely, to argue with her. 'You just don't understand what I must do to control my knights and men, let alone subdue my enemies. If I showed any weakness then my foes would be down on me in the slash of a sword. I keep a list of names in my head of those who wish us harm. When I was just a boy I was tutored by my great uncle, the Archbishop Robert of Rouen, right up to his untimely death that, some say, was due to poison although he was very old and ill. Coincidentally, between you and me, there was talk that my great uncle had my father killed by poisoning and then he himself succumbed to the same fate. I, of course, had nothing to do with my uncle's death.' William smiled as sweetly as his lips could allow while trying to look as innocent as an angel. It didn't work.

Matilda shook her head and replied, 'In some ways my dear, you think me very naive.'

'What do you mean?' William responded defensively, raising his voice.

'Never mind my dear, carry on if you must.'

'Well, where was I … I have now forgotten what my point was.'

He thought for a while as they walked back to her chambers. 'Ah, yes, I was saying that he taught me how to rule and be a leader, what to do, who to trust, who not to trust, and the art of warfare. I have of course modified certain aspects of my training, but I must follow the basic underlying rules, it is expected of me.'

They entered Matilda's chambers. She sighed and had to agree. 'I understand. Sometimes one must do things that are necessary but unsavoury.'

'Like eating English food?' William was now in a good mood, having won an argument with his wife at long last.

Matilda laughed. 'Now dear, read this letter from the old fool in England. Don't get angry or upset, just read it.'

She gave him the parchment with the English crown seal on it. He sat down, read its contents, and then thought for a long while. Matilda continued her sewing, humming a traditional Norman song about burning pagans.

Eventually William spoke. 'As far as I'm concerned, let Turold go to England to see his family, as long as he's back by the autumn. However, he must go with an escort, and I suggest his English sailor friend who's been so useful to our plans, and my knights Vital and Wadard together with some retainers.'

His wife put down her work. She was very surprised with his response. There was something behind this. *He's planning something behind my back*, she thought. 'Well, I'm more concerned than you obviously. Firstly, Turold is one of the keys to our, eh your, success and therefore should be kept safe and close at hand, and secondly, I'm worried that he may share certain observations and any known facts about our, eh your, plans and preparations with either the decrepit Edward or his puppet Harold.'

William laughed and responded, 'I don't fully share your convictions regarding that jester, and I don't mind if the powers in England do know what I'm up to, in fact I will take the opportunity to show Turold my preparations before he leaves for England. In my opinion if King Edward and Harold are made aware how seriously I take my wish to rule England, then we may be able to avert unnecessary bloodshed.' William knew this last argument would sit well with his meek and mild wife.

Matilda looked him in the eyes. 'What are you up to?'

'Eh, nothing dear, my mind is made up. I'll send word that the jester will be sent to England in the spring with some companions to ensure his safety during his journey. Now come here my love, that rampaging has got my blood up.'

Matilda put away her embroidery and sighed.

There was sometimes much sighing in William's castle, especially after rampaging lessons, but mumblings behind William's and Matilda's backs were never tolerated.

Later that day, William wrote his response to King Edward's request.

WILLIAM'S PLANS

Two months later, following further communications between Duke William and King Edward, detailed arrangements had been made for Turold's visit to England.

William was in a good mood. He was having a very good day and nothing was going to spoil it.

He looked down from his throne at the two knights summoned before him. 'You are instructed to make ready for a journey to England. You'll be taking that jester, Turold, and his sailor friend, Rufus, to London, where he will visit his wife and family and his old master King Edward the Dying. You'll hand pick two others skilled in the art of surveillance and armed and unarmed combat to accompany you. You'll be away for many months. You must return by the middle of September before the bad seas return. You must ensure the safety of both Englishmen on pain of death. Do you understand?'

The two knights nodded, and Vital enquired hopefully, 'Your Grace, do you really need two senior knights to babysit those two?'

William started to twitch, and stroke his sword. The two men knew the signs and started to back off a pace or three.

'Don't query my decisions, but I agree that if this was all that I required you to do, then I may well have considered others, however it's not all. At the same time, I'll be sending you on a secret mission. We'll discuss my requirements at length. Now go select two men.'

The two bowed and left. Vital looked at Wadard and said, 'What is the Red Fox up to?'

Wadard shrugged his broad shoulders. He had brawn but little brain so he found it easier and safer to just follow orders. He liked following understandable orders. It made him feel safe and secure, and had kept him alive since becoming a knight. Although very good friends, he always thought that Vital was too inquisitive and that this weakness would eventually lead to his best friend's downfall. Wadard hoped that he would not be around when that happened, but they seemed fated to be joined at the hip. He often wondered whether he could ask for a transfer.

Vital was worried. He was sure that this mission would lead to his death. *I'll go to church later and pray to God. I'll ask God to protect us from the dastardly English thugs. I don't know what I'd do if I lost dearest Wadard! Perhaps I should tell him, but, probably best not to. He may not understand!*

WILLIAM'S SHOW OF STRENGTH

One week later, Turold and Rufus were taken by Vital and
Wadard to see Duke William. Turold and Rufus
were worried that William had found out that they were
conspiring against him and wondered whether they would
ever see another night. They entered the throne room. As
usual William sat regally on his throne, but, not as usual, he
was beaming from ear to ear. It scared the two and shook
Vital and Wadard to their cores. None of the four had ever
seen this expression on William's face before. Turold
thought, *he's up to something, and he's probably looking
forward to seeing our insides on our outsides.*

'How lovely to see you both,' William exclaimed, still
grinning. 'I want you to come with me today. I am going to
inspect my military preparations. As you must be aware I
have many enemies, borders and interests that must be
strongly protected. I also have some good news for
you.'

He stood up and marched through the door accompanied
by his bodyguards, and the four followed. In the palace
courtyard, several horses awaited them, including a pony
for Turold. Turold looked at his ride, and the horse glared
back at him.

Turold knew the signs and enquired, 'Can I walk please
Your Grace?'

William laughed. 'Of course not, we've a long way to
go and your little legs will take hours to get there.'

Turold tried a last gambit. 'Your Grace, I can run fast
and long!'

'No, no, I insist, now mount your horse.'

All the horses had now surrounded Turold, and he felt like a maypole. His three friends saw the danger and Rufus quickly rescued him before things turned bloody. Rufus picked Turold up in his arms and rushed to the far side of the courtyard, then Vital secured the pony by its reins and brought it over. The pony strained and pulled as it tried to gallop headlong towards Turold, but with Wadard's help, Vital was able to keep control of the red-eyed sweating animal that now seemed to have eight legs and two heads. Turold hid behind Rufus but the pony was not fooled. Turold's scent was just too strong.

'Don't look scared! It's upsetting the beast,' Vital shouted.

'I'm as scared as I look, and there is nothing I can do about it! That animal has only one thing on its mind and that's me on the ground being trampled to death,' Turold replied.

'Come out from behind that sailor and stroke it,' Wadard suggested.

Turold knew he had to face the Beast of Normandy at some time or other, even with ten legs and three heads. He took one step to the right. Bluebell the pony neighed loudly and attacked with all its strength, its hormones being fully charged. It managed to break loose from the grasps of the two unfortunate knights who were both given a passing kick as a gift. Rufus was lightning quick in his reflexes and picked up Turold like a matador would use his cape, and the pony flashed past the two. It was Bluebell's speed that was her undoing. She could not stop on the gravel, and this affected her aim. She merely managed to get her teeth into one of Turold's shoes before disappearing into a cloud of dust. William and the onlookers were really enjoying the entertainment. The pony turned for another charge, still with the shoe in its mouth, which was now covered with white foam. Bluebell's nostrils were snorting like a raging bull, and her next charge was even less controlled. Rufus, in the meantime, had rushed over to the ornamental pond and fountain and now stood in front of it. At the last moment he and his load dived to the right and ended up in the pond while Bluebell headbutted the fountain and ended up in a stunned heap. The whole party clapped and cheered and laughed.

William thought that this was already turning into another great day and exclaimed, 'Well done you two, great performance and diversion but we must get going.'

Rufus and Turold emerged from the pond, and Rufus removed the excess pondweed and a frog that had lodged itself down his hose. The two drips were shaken but alive and basically unharmed, save a few bruises and a missing shoe. Rufus decided that he and Turold would ride the same horse and picked the most placid one available, Buttercup. Rufus calmed Buttercup down as much as he could, placed Turold on her back and then jumped up quickly himself. Buttercup knew something was not right, but because the pond water and mud masked Turold's scent, remained manageable.

The whole party set off. William had taken his hunting dogs and eagle. *Well, you never know*, he had thought, *you might as well try and kill two birds with one stone*. In fact, his tally for the ensuing hunt through the nearby forest was six blackbirds, three pigeons, two hedgehogs, three wild boars, a basket of truffles and one peasant who managed to get between the dogs and a fox.

Eventually they arrived at a clearing where a camp had been set up and many men were busy felling trees and working the wood into ships' timbers. It was very well organised and impressive. The finished planks were being loaded onto carts pulled by oxen. Rufus kept his distance downwind of these magnificent but muscular and potentially aggressive beasts. He thought, *if a small pony could cause so much havoc, what about a herd of charging oxen?* Turold made a mental note of the proceedings. They followed the carts down to the nearby shoreline, and on to the shipbuilding yards and facilities. Rufus immediately saw the part-built and fully finished ships as being of his designs, although with some notable modifications. Some of the ships were extremely large, and could have only been designed for the transportation of horses, equipment and even fortified structures. Rufus was given a guided tour, and was soon shown a large warehouse. Its large doors had been left partly open so he could see what looked like large sections of a wooden fort. Rufus was both amazed and sick to the bottom of his stomach.

Turold enquired of the senior carpenter giving the guided tour (the route of which had been strictly outlined by William himself), 'How many ships are to be built?'

The carpenter was sweating now, trying to be careful of his responses to questions, especially in front of William's men. It had been made painfully clear what would happen if he developed a loose tongue and he had the bruises to prove it. 'I am not privy to that information, but let's now go down to the shore where you can see the finished ships.'

Down on the shoreline Turold and Rufus counted forty ships already finished, and with the facilities set up, neither could see any reason why a great many others could not follow within the next year or so. William was pleased with the two Englishmen's expressions when they had finished their guided tour, and gave the carpenter a gold coin and pat on the back. The carpenter bowed as low as he could with such trembling knees, and walking backwards removed himself from William's gaze. He wiped his brow, walked over to his shed, and collapsed in a quivering heap. He could not believe that he had actually survived. His first thought was to give himself the afternoon off and visit a well-used entertainment and refreshment establishment. He thanked God for his continued breathing, and humbly requested that God made sure that lovely Emily was available. He promised to visit church afterwards and give a full confession.

Next on the agenda was a visit to a military training camp, where the party were given a performance by 500 heavily armed knights and soldiers. This show had been specially choreographed by William to impress, but mislead, the two guests. The men were formed up as foot soldiers in the style of an English shield wall formation that was now, quite frankly, obsolete given the continental way of warfare involving the use of castles, knights on horses, and archers. The shield wall was the traditional way that the English fought, and William wanted Edward and Harold to think it was also the way he would fight a large-scale battle. In some ways, the spectacle would have been familiar to the ancient Romans. This block of men proceeded to walk slowly from one end of the field to the other as if advancing on a corresponding defensive army while shouting, swearing, beating their shields with their swords, axes and spears and then at the end, changing the pace and rushing the pretend enemy positions, prodding and slashing with their weapons. The army then reformed and did the same in the other direction. It all looked very impressive. The theatrical performance over, the party left for the palace and a well-earned rest and feast.

Turold and Rufus both looked extremely worried, and talked little as they rode back. William thought, *job well done*. On the way back the pack of dogs and William's massive eagle increased their tally of unfortunate wildlife and peasants.

Meanwhile back at the training camp, any discipline was lost as all the men laughed and joked about their manoeuvres. The horsemen and archers were brought out of hiding and the afternoon training exercise consisted of the cavalry attacking an English block of 250 men, feigning retreat, and waiting for the English to follow. Then they turned, and together with Norman infantry, attacked and encircled the exposed undisciplined men, and finally the cavalry attacked the exposed flanks of the English shield wall. The tacticians knew that this would be the easiest way of defeating a shield wall. They knew that the English shield wall, composed mainly of a very large force of inexperienced and ill-disciplined men, would not stand up to the skilful use of archers and heavily armed mounted knights.

At the palace, Rufus and Turold dismounted. Buttercup turned and looked Turold in the eyes. She knew that there was something about the small man that she did not like, but couldn't quite put her hoof on it. Even so she decided to give him a parting present by turning away from him and relieving herself on his head. Turold was too slow to react and so soon resembled a brown two-eyed pyramid. He immediately ran to the pond and jumped in before he could be dragged there by the others.

William walked over. 'That's it, clean yourself up sir. You resemble a mobile compost heap.'

William thought, *great deception today on the battlefield, hopefully it will mislead Earl Harold, and all our ships should make his English chicken legs tremble!*

Before leaving, William announced to Turold and Rufus, 'I forgot to tell you, you're both going to England for a few months next week. Enjoy your time there and be sure to give my kind regards to King Edward and Earl Harold,' then he walked off holding his nose.

Turold sat in the water thinking. *Did I hear correctly, was I really going? I'll have to confirm the news with Vital. He usually knows what's going on.*

THE BOAT TRIP TO LONDON

It was now mid-June and all arrangements had been made for a boat to take Turold and Rufus and their escort to London. King Edward had guaranteed safe passage for them and his fellow travellers once they arrived in London, and provided papers as proof. They would be met at London docks once the palace had received word of their arrival. The ship was made ready and once a settled day arrived, set sail for the trip across the Channel then up the Kent coast to the mouth of the river Thames before heading upriver towards London. There was one unknown passenger amongst the group but he kept apart from the party. Vital tried to discover his identity and the purpose of his visit to England from both the stranger and the captain, but could only find out that his name was Richard.

Vital said to Wadard, 'That fellow looks very familiar. I'm sure we have met him before, but he will not talk to me and when I pressed him further, he looked at me curiously and said, 'Leave me alone, do not make me angry, you would not like it if I got angry,' and now he just sits at the back of the boat meditating, eyes firmly shut.'

Wadard looked at the man all in black with a large floppy hat on his head and a funny-looking English moustache and beard, and agreed. 'I know those eyes, but cannot place them. Perhaps he works for Duchess Matilda. If he does, then he must be considered dangerous, so best left to his own thoughts. We don't want any mishap to befall Turold. As a precaution, we will move Turold to the other end of the ship and keep us between the two of them.'

Luckily no unusual events happened during the journey, although before docking in London, the stranger vanished while the others were deep in conversation.

At the docks word was sent to the palace, and an escort soon arrived and took them to see King Edward. Edward was very pleased to see Turold and held him in his arms for what seemed an eternity. All six men then had a very pleasant evening. This involved a magnificent feast, and entertainment provided by the Viking Saga Theatrical Society whose performance of old Viking sagas, involving gods, heroes, bears, trolls, wolves, and much blood, thrilled the whole audience including Edward, who seemed to thoroughly enjoy the brutality of their art.

The whole party remained at the palace for the next few days while Edward and Turold renewed their deep friendship and Turold advised the old man on matters of state and updated Edward about William's preparations for invasion and war. In addition, Edward made Turold attend prayers and have Bible study periods.

However, after five days Turold had to make a request to Edward to let him and his party leave to see Megan and family. Edward knew he was being selfish, so agreed, much to the annoyance of Rufus, Vital, and Wadard, who enjoyed being indulged in such luxurious surroundings.

RICHARD'S MISSION AND NEW FRIEND

Richard lowered himself stealthily over the side of the ship while his travel companions were deep in conversation. He quickly swam to shore and vanished into the crowded streets. He had a meeting to keep with an agent at a small alehouse near Barking Abbey, to the east of London, near the Thames. He found a one armed, one-legged, peg-legged drunken sailor willing to take him there by row boat, and eventually after a great deal of him rowing around in circles until Richard volunteered to help row, arrived at Richard's destination via two alehouses.

As Richard entered The Merry Sailor alehouse, he was greeted by what he could only describe as an old woman covered with warts, no, worse than that, she had warts on her warts, and together with her hooked nose, would surely have been burnt at the stake in Normandy as a witch. He knew from his research that these alehouse women tended to be the widows of dead soldiers or sailors trying to make a living from making ale since their looks would never attract any man alive. He sat down in a dark corner and was served a flagon of ale that tasted fine, but smelt like the foul-smelling street outside. He was offered a bowl of festering meat stew, which he accepted, but after tasting a spoonful realised that he had made the wrong decision. His stomach was beginning to bubble and complain. He took another mouthful of ale. That was a mistake, as his stomach now grumbled like Master Perciville on a bad day. He had to get out of the alehouse before he destroyed it.

He sprang from his seat and rushed over to the old widow who was busy picking a wart. 'Quick, do you have a back yard?'

'Yes sir, through there, but don't....'

Richard could not wait so ran for the door, quickly opened it, and stepped out into the glaring sun.

'.... go out there, it's full of the live meat for my meat stew,' she finished replying.

Richard was greeted by a pack of dogs with vengeance and escape on its communal mind. He quickly focused his eyes on the dogs and used the strength of his mind to gain control of them. He then opened the back gate and gave them their freedom. All but one of the dogs stampeded for their lives. The remaining one, the leader of the pack, came over to him, licked his hand and sat down next to him wagging his tail. It seemed that Richard had a new friend. Richard staggered into a corner of the yard and emptied the contents of his stomach into a bucket. He sat down next to the dog and shut his eyes. The dog put his head on Richard's lap. After some while, Richard recovered his composure. He was so relieved. He could just see the report now. 'Agent Richard lost control of his senses. The Merry Sailor alehouse collapsed in a heap and caught fire. The fire spread throughout London, including the royal palace. King Edward and Earl Harold died of smoke inhalation and the English Witan has offered the crown to their conqueror, Richard, now to be known as Richard the First. His coronation is next week.'

His daydreaming was suddenly shattered by a croaking, crackling voice saying, 'Your friend has arrived and you owe me for the disappearance of the prime ingredients of my stew.'

Richard stood up and entered the alehouse, with the dog close by his side. 'I don't think your customers would be too pleased if they found out what your main ingredient was, but here's a gold coin for your loss.'

The woman took the coin and started to prepare the vegetarian version of her meat pies, consisting of day-old pottage and nettles. Richard saw the agent and went over to the table where the spy sat. It was the same agent, Cecil, that had dealt with Edgar so cruelly.

The agent said in French, 'Ah, Sir Richard, take a seat. We need to talk about the arrangements.'

Richard sat down slowly, sword ready just in case. The dog joined the two and lay at the knight's side, staring alertly at the stranger.

'Does your companion bite?'

Richard replied, 'I'm sure he does and you will find out soon enough if you upset him or me.'

The agent was uneasy. He hated dogs and this one definitely had an attitude problem. It unnerved him but he had his mission to complete, with dire consequences if anything went wrong. He had been warned.

'I've made arrangements for you to sail up the east coast of England from London where you'll be landed at Lindisfarne Island and met by a monk who will call himself Aidan after the saint who founded the monastery. You will be known as Richard Longshanks. He will escort you to the main band of rebels in Northumberland. You, I understand, have your orders as to what to do once you have made contact.'

'I do. I assume that there'll be no problem with me taking this dog with me?'

The agent thought for a moment. He certainly didn't want it left with him, although the old widow could surely put it to good use. However, this knight's reputation was well known in the agency and he didn't want to suffer the consequences of him finding out that his ex-companion had become an ex-dog.

'Just don't let him bite any of the resistance fighters. Now let's have some food and drink and I'll take you to your ship, it leaves at high tide.'

They ordered bread and cheese rather than have the remaining five-day old meat stew the old widow offered. As soon as the dog smelt the stew, it attacked the woman. She limped back to her kitchen with the offending bowls, pulling her bleeding leg with the dog still attached to it. Richard had to help her separate the dog from her leg by distracting the dog with some of the bread and cheese and a bowl of ale. The dog seemed to appreciate the ale more than the food, and so did Richard and Cecil.

RICHARD'S JOURNEY NORTH

The agent took the two travellers to the awaiting cargo ship. Its crew were made up of some of the worst-looking sailors that could ever be encountered. None of them had a complete body. Well actually one did, the ship's cat, but he fled the scene when the dog boarded. The ship's rats soon followed the cat. It seemed that the dog had a certain reputation too. The rats were soon infesting the immediate vicinity and in the forthcoming months their fast-breeding program led to an overabundance of the beasts, leading to a plague that swept across London killing several thousand people. It was indeed unfortunate that these diseased rats had come all the way from Constantinople.

God looked down and was extremely happy with the bond between his chosen ones. Hopefully they would help in His quest to purge England of its unchristian activities.

The crew looked at the passengers and started whispering to each other and pointing while they worked (well those that had a spare arm did). They were uneasy, having seen the way the animals had abandoned the ship, and being superstitious, immediately blamed these two complete strangers. The captain saw this and thought it best to remove the passengers from his crew's view, so installed them in a small cabin at the back of the ship. The ship edged away from the quayside with the agent, Sir Cecil, looking on. He was worried whether the knight would ever reach his destination, and feared the wrath of Duchess Matilda if anything went wrong. Luckily for him he'd never have to face that problem, as he would soon die of the plague.

The dog and Richard were extremely tired and settled down together for a well-earned rest.

When Richard awoke, all was eerily quiet, and so he went to have a look on deck. It was just before dawn. There seemed to be no one else on board. Here and there were splatters of blood and the odd body part, and he could hear a low moan from the prow.

Something was attached to the figurehead. It was the captain. 'Oh, thank God. It's you. The crew got restless during the night and fuelled by drink, some decided to throw you and your devil hound overboard. But before they got within three footsteps of the cabin, that beast launched an all-out attack on them. It was terrible and was over in minutes. They had no time to even scream. The rest of the crew abandoned ship thinking it best to take their chances in the sea, and I crawled up here out of the range of his teeth and claws. Luckily, he seemed satisfied with his efforts and left me unmolested, but I'm now stuck.'

Richard managed to help the poor man back onto the deck where he collapsed and sobbed. Richard found him some drink to comfort him. He then threw the remains of the crew over the side and went back to his dog. His dog looked at him innocently. Richard did not know what to say or do. It had saved his life but at a terrible cost. Perhaps it was best not to dwell on it, so patted his head.

He returned to the captain who had recovered somewhat, but was now drunk. 'Best if we make for shore, Captain.'

'Yes lad, best if we do. Where's the land?'

Richard pointed towards the west. 'It's the dark green outline off to our left in the distance.'

'Oh yes, I'll give the order. Change course towards those lights Mr Rye and get the men ready to row.'

'I don't think they'll be following your orders, Captain.'

'What, is it mutiny then?'

'No, it's death that keeps them from their duties.'

The captain broke down again and sobbed. Richard had no alternative but to make the course correction hoping that there were no unseen dangers under the waves between the ship and land. They were either lucky or watched over by God, and managed to round Landguard Point and enter Harwich Harbour by midday. Onlookers gazed in disbelief upon the ship, as it contained just two men and a dog. The captain was incoherent with shock and drink and in the confusion, Richard and the dog made their escape.

We leave the two on their adventurous journey up to Holy Island and Lindisfarne Priory, during which many English casualties were sustained one way or another. Their encounters with the inhabitants led to a rumour that the Vikings had landed and were making havoc in the lands of Essex and Mercia. By mid-July Richard and his devil dog had reached the river Humber. On they walked towards the city of York. An army was raised at York to defend the city from the rumoured approaching Viking army, and the soldiers were totally confused when confronted by merely a strange man with a funny English accent and a vicious English wolf masquerading as a dog. They were both barred from entering York so they continued their journey northwards.

TUROLD AND FRIENDS IN LONDON

Vital, Wadard and their two assistants were found accommodation on the upper floor of Turold's old drinking den. There they made contact with agent Cecil. They spent their days researching. Much of this was done in various alehouses where after a few ales, they found that King Edward's soldiers tended to relax and were quite prepared to discuss the army's strength, weapons, and tactics. Meanwhile, Turold was enjoying his time with Megan and his boys who he now named Peter and Paul after the priest and the saint.

One day, Cecil received a message from Duchess Matilda. It was a warning. She had been told by God whilst at prayer, that a plague was about to spread throughout London. Vital and Wadard must move Turold and his family away from danger.

Vital and Wadard immediately went to see Turold. Vital knocked on the door of Turold's hovel, and along with the door, fell into its interior. It seems Edgar's repairs had only been temporary. Vital was immediately set-upon by the twins who thought it great fun to jump up and down on his stomach, followed by much licking. Turold diverted the twin's attention by waving a massive dead rat in front of them. He threw it out into the back yard, quickly followed by Peter and Paul.

Turold helped Vital to his feet, and brushed the straw off his clothes. 'Sorry about that, but boys will be boys, or in their case, I'm afraid, dogs.'

Vital smiled, sat down, and he and Wadard were soon eating a bowl of Megan's special pottage. 'I suggest either you get that door fixed or move! In fact, I've some bad news. A plague is about to spread throughout London. You must indeed all leave or perish! Luckily, I have a solution, I suggest we all move to the south coast of England. I'm sure King Edward and Earl Harold will help.'

It was agreed, and Turold, Rufus, Vital and Wadard were soon on their way to the palace. At the main gate, a heated argument soon began between the Norman knights and the English guards, which although in two completely different languages, left neither party in any doubt as to the other's meaning. It seemed gestures and profanities were understood in any language. Luckily Edward's groom, Thomas, had just finished his shift and was leaving the palace to meet his sweetheart, Saucy Sal.

'What's going on here? Ah, Turold, it's you! Let them through you brainless oafs!

The groom had Vital and Wadard escorted to an antechamber where preparations would be made to keep their minds and hands and mouths occupied while Thomas took Turold and Rufus to King Edward's chambers.

King Edward and Earl Harold were finalising arrangements for their pilgrimage. Edward was still looking better than he should as he sat on his throne with Harold beside him. Edward was very pleased to see Turold again. He leapt to his feet and enveloped the dwarf in his embrace.

Harold was not so pleased. He merely nodded in Turold's direction, after which he enquired, 'Does this scruffy sailor have to be present?'

Turold replied, 'This scruffy sailor, sir, has saved my life on many occasions and deserves to be present! I am here to request that my family, my friends, and myself should be allowed to leave London Town and visit somewhere more conducive on the south coast of England.'

Edward looked at Rufus, smiled, slapped him on the back, and said, 'You, sir, have done me a good service in preserving this little friend of mine so you will be well rewarded, firstly with a bath and new, sweet-smelling clothes and then with a purse of money. I will even bestow on you some land near the south coast for you and your family. What do you say Harold?'

Harold had to think quickly, or he could see his beloved Bosham Manor being given to this troublesome jester and sailor. 'Eh, yes, Your Grace, if that's your wish, I'll have a think about the whereabouts of the land to be given to this eh, hero, yes, perhaps some remote place far from any danger. Pevensey or Hastings I think would be ideal.'

Rufus was very excited since he was to become a landowner. However, the idea of washing was not to his liking at all. Edward called Thomas over, whispered to him, and then the groom approached Rufus and guided him out of the room at arm's length, while holding his nose.

Turold wanted to find out what Edward had decided to do about Duke William, so asked, 'Your Grace have you commenced preparations to repel any Norman invasion?'

Edward shook his head. 'No, other than what I have already agreed with Earl Harold. I mustn't be seen to be preparing for war. I will pray for guidance from God.'

Harold sighed. 'In light of the detailed information we have learnt from Turold, I strongly suggest—'

'No, no, I refuse! My final decision is deferred until I've spoken to God or received one of my divine dreams. I will not be responsible for starting a war.'

Wonderful, Harold thought, *you'll die contentedly, ruling a peaceable realm to the end, leaving me to fight all those wishing to succeed you!*

There followed a period of reflection and silence, broken by the entrance of a good-looking clean Englishman in fine clothes. Rufus joined Turold. He was clean, but bruised since that washerwoman had muscles on her muscles and hands the size of a shield.

Turold looked stunned and laughed, joined by Edward, who announced, 'Now we're all gentlemen, let's eat and drink and be merry.'

Ho ho, thought Harold.

While at their repast, Turold advised Edward that Duchess Matilda had been told by God of a forthcoming plague in London. Edward thought for a while. I know she is close to God, so her warning must be taken seriously. 'I think, Harold, that the time has come for our pilgrimage!'

The next day, Turold spoke at length to Rufus who was still sulking but very clean, and they concluded that if indeed Rufus was to be given land on the south coast, then a little sun and fresh air would be beneficial for all. At their next meeting with King Edward and Earl Harold, arrangements were finalised.

Harold had found a suitable place. 'There is an old Roman fort in the port of Pevensey. Within it is a large house owned by me. It should be fine for your needs. I will arrange the transport and the guard to take you all there.'

King Edward was so pleased. 'Excellent, we will all go to church and ask for God's protection. Tonight, we will have a farewell feast at which Turold can provide the entertainment!'

Turold gave a great performance of the new material he had learnt while in exile, and King Edward laughed so much that he ended up rolling about the floor with his long, lanky, bony legs flailing about uncontrollably. It seemed he had the same sense of humour as Matilda. Harold could not really understand why it seemed so funny and requested leave to organise the transport and habitation. He was glad to get out of that mad room, much preferring to be doing something useful and quiet. He called his various clerks and servants, gave the appropriate orders, and then went to his chambers to lie down on his bed with a wet towel over his face. He had to consider all the news received and its consequences. *Yet again it certainly looks bad for me, especially as Edward will do nothing to help me defend England. I know, I'll speak to my brothers. We'll have a family reunion and conference.*

At the end of all the merriment, it was decided that the party would stay at the palace two more nights and this news was sent to Megan and the two Norman servants who had been billeted at the nearby alehouse. Megan was also informed that she should pack all her belongings for a move to the seaside. The news of their stay was given to Vital and Wadard who were both enjoying the various diversions on offer, mainly two young English ladies called Mary and Elizabeth, and so were delighted to have to put up with the inconvenience.

That night, Edward retired early. It had been a tiring day, and all that laughter had brought on a coughing fit. He also wanted to see if God would deliver another dream.

EDWARD'S DREAM

Next day the king rushed into Harold's bedchamber shouting, 'I have had a dream from God.'

He jumped on Harold and his bed and, smiling and giggling, lay down beside the trampled earl.

'Your Grace, it's still dark.'

'No, it's not, open your eyes.'

Harold complied, but could still see no further than Edward's bony face and knee. He'd last seen a knee like that when he was shown the bones of Saint David in Wales.

'My vision started with me inspecting my abbey when suddenly an angel descended and pointed to the sky where I could make out many ships full of the enemies of England being tossed about in a sea so turbulent that at times the oars made no contact with the water. Many of the men and horses were tumbling into the white foaming waves and were devoured. The hand of God pointed down on this scene that started to fade as several ships sank below the waves. Now this vision was replaced by one of Canterbury Cathedral, where Bishop Stigand was, well let me just say, entertaining a maiden on the altar. The angel pointed to the scene and a thunderbolt left his ring finger and hit the debauched cleric in the back. I then awoke. England is safe, Harold. God will protect my realm from the Normans if I deal with that bishop. Harold, England is blessed and is saved!'

With that, Edward leapt off the bed and left Harold on his own, pondering. *Another so-called divine vision! I'll see if once and for all he does what he should have done years ago. Otherwise perhaps he should give the order for some of his men to do the deed. But then this could worsen his relationship with God!* He sighed, got a damp towel, put it on his head and shut his eyes. *I'm getting a lot of headaches these days, perhaps I and my family should escape somewhere before it was too late. Denmark looks like the safest location given the circumstances. Yes, I could abandon England and live a quiet and long life in a remote castle somewhere in Denmark. I'll be safe there if Duchess Matilda does not find out where I am.*

Harold meditated for a while, then removed the damp cloth, and shouted, 'No, I cannot turn my back on Saxon England! I am not a traitor or a quitter!'

There was a knock on his chamber's door. 'Sir, are you unwell?'

Harold sighed and replied, 'Just a nightmare!' Then he mumbled to himself, 'A complete and utter nightmare!'

He reapplied his damp cloth and closed his eyes. *I know, I'll visit Edyth and the family in Maidenhead. But I'll insist she does not tell me about any imaginary visions from God! She's just as bad as Edward! I truly believe in God, but there just seems to me to be too many people receiving messages from God! That Priest Pierre, yes, but surely God has better things to do than provide all these people with predictions!*

MEET BISHOP STIGAND

A shifty-looking bishop stood in front of King Edward, who sat on his throne trying to look superior.

Bishop Stigand sauntered disrespectfully over to a chair and placed it next to Edward. 'What do you want? This is very inconvenient you know.'

Edward was livid and commanded, 'Don't you be so impudent. Get off the platform and don't speak until spoken to.'

Bishop Stigand had a body in the shape of a big ball with two lumpy legs and arms sticking out, and a round chinless head on top. He was certainly suffering from the various overindulgences of his extravagant life style, having contracted several diseases and ailments due to his excesses, including diabetes and gout. He waved his hand mockingly in acknowledgement of Edward's command, took his chair and placed it in front of him.

He then bowed low, grinned, sat, and said, 'Get on with it. I've got places to be and sinners to absolve.'

Edward continued. 'I have had a vision from God. You must change your ways and be humble and seek forgiveness from God. You must confess your sins.'

The bishop laughed. 'You don't actually believe in such things, do you? It is just a way of subduing the otherwise rebellious population so the likes of us can have a good and privileged life!'

Edward was astounded. He knew that Bishop Stigand was corrupt in many ways but for him to not believe in God was unthinkable. 'You must resign as archbishop immediately.'

Stigand laughed again. 'I don't think so, Your Grace,' he sniggered, 'I know of certain secrets regarding yourself that would surely create havoc if told. I've the evidence in a safe place with instructions for it to be made public if anything untoward happens to me. I'm sure both the Witan and Rome would be very interested to know how you cleared the way so you could become king! Now, I must go and attend to my flock!' With those words said, Stigand turned and laughed as he left the room, saying, 'What a fool, believing in God!'

Edward was left collapsed in his chair. He could do nothing about this problem, since the archbishop knew his secrets. All he could do was to pray to God for guidance and hope for God's mercy and patience. Alternatively, perhaps God Himself could remove the problem. Unfortunately, God expected Edward to take responsibility. God required Edward to remove Stigand as archbishop, and purify the English Church and its people, or England would suffer his inaction.

THE JOURNEY TO THE SOUTH COAST OF ENGLAND

Two days later, Edward and Harold held a meeting with Turold and Rufus.

Harold announced, 'The house inside the walls of the old Pevensey Castle is ready and will from this day onwards, belong to Rufus. I visited this area while reviewing the defences of the south of England. The fort was originally built by the Romans, extended, and improved thereafter, but became derelict as a military base for various reasons. You will all be safe and comfortable there. The transportation has been arranged and two of my men will accompany you on your journey and ensure you receive a warm welcome.'

Edward was pleased with the arrangements, said his farewells to his friends and left them in Harold's capable hands. The earl and the two men left the throne room and went to find the two Norman guests. Vital and Wadard were sleeping soundly in their chambers and were not too willing to wake up. The earl and two of his men had to drag them out of their beds, help dress them, and take them to Turold and Rufus for food and ale before their departure.

While sitting, blurry eyed and dazed, the Normans were advised of their forthcoming expedition. At that moment they would have agreed to anything to stop the grating voices, so accepted the arrangements with no hesitation.

Later that day, a horse and cart stood outside Turold's house while his family's possessions were loaded. Some of their neighbours were already hearing rumours of a disease sweeping across the docks, and looked enviously at the activities. Megan was tearful. She would miss her hovel, but it was for the best. There were so many memories being left to fade away, but she must look forward. She sighed as she was lifted onto the cart along with her twins. As the cart started moving, she looked back on her beloved house and waved. Her neighbours waved back, then just as the cart turned the corner, rushed into the house hoping to steal anything left of value.

Turold sat in the back of the cart as far away from the horse as possible, and was soon showing his boys some of his magic tricks to keep them entertained. One of Harold's men drove the cart while the other rode horseback along with the four Normans and Rufus, who still looked quite smart in his new clothes although some food and drink stains had already appeared here and there, as if to remind him of his various sumptuous meals at the palace. Vital was uneasy about the presence of the two English soldiers but tried not to show it. Nothing must get in the way of their mission. The party crossed the river Thames and left diseased London Town behind, travelling south towards the forested Weald and Sussex.

Unfortunately, both the security guards supplied by Harold had personality issues, mainly because they were single-minded housecarls, full-time paid royal soldiers who were more at home wielding their large battle-axes than being nurse wenches to foreigners, a family and one Englishman. To make matters worse, the foreigners were Normans who were considered potential enemies of England. If it were up to them, they grumbled, they would dispose of the lot and get back to the palace, reporting that outlaws had attacked and killed them all. However, they had their orders. The two men were large and stocky, and their clothing and appearance resembled those of the old Viking traditions rather than those of the Saxons. They were brave, over confident, foolhardy, and feared nothing except washing and a haircut.

As the group entered the land of Sussex, the escorts decided on a short cut. Rather than follow the safer, longer route through Kent, they decided to go straight through the wild, heavily wooded, and lawless Weald, and directed the party down a cattle track. The rest of the party were unaware of the potential consequences of this decision. The two housecarls, Asger and Bjorn, headed for a hunting lodge they knew where they could stay overnight. To begin with, the journey was very pleasant and picturesque but after a while, the trees became more oppressive and soon seemed to envelope the track so it resembled a green tunnel. Suddenly heavily armed men appeared as if they had set forth from the very trunks of the trees. They stood in the party's way and, from their threats and weapons, meant business. They were outlaws looking for easy pickings but they had picked the wrong travellers. Unfortunately for the four bandits, they were not quick enough to guard against the swift attack from Asger and Bjorn, who dispatched one and wounded the other three within the blink of an eye. Their axes were no match for skin and sinew. The three remaining outlaws limped screaming into the green of the forest pursued by Asger, whose name meant Spear of God, and the screaming soon stopped. Asger emerged from the forest looking very satisfied, and was given a congratulatory slap on the back by Bjorn, whose name meant Bear. Strangely as fate or God would have it, one big brown bear suddenly appeared from the undergrowth, attracted by the commotion and the smell of blood.

Asger looked at his friend and shouted, 'Over to you, Bjorn, as it's one of your relatives!'

Bjorn rushed at the bear which was now standing on its hind legs and growling, but at the last minute, as the bear's slashing claws moved at lightning speed towards Bjorn's body, he slid to the ground under the bear's paws, giving it a quick slash with his axe as he did so. Then emerging at the back of the wounded animal, he jumped to his feet and with four powerful hacks from his axe, put the bear out of its misery. Asger was extremely impressed. Megan got down from the cart and fainted as the blood and gore and screams had been just too much. The twins on the other hand clapped in admiration. Vital and Wadard were both amazed and impressed by this show of strength and prowess, and made mental notes for their report, including the seeming disregard for their own safety when the housecarls' blood was up. This could well be used against such men in battle by enticing them out of their formations. The party eventually recovered their composure and continued.

By early evening they reached the hunting lodge. Asger and Bjorn entered the lodge and made sure that it was safe, making a family of badgers homeless in the process. Then they opened the large courtyard doors so that the horses and the cart could enter. Megan took the twins inside and started to get a fire going while the men unloaded the cart. Turold decided not to get involved with this, due to the proximity to the horses. He and Rufus volunteered to fetch firewood and some feed for the horses, and once the horses had been tied up, they took some water from the well in the courtyard, filled the horse trough and then took a full bucket inside for Megan and the two Norman servants. Turold and Rufus accompanied Asger and Bjorn to see about supper. They did not have to penetrate too far into the forest before they could hear the snuffling of wild boar.

The men tried to get downwind of the animals but unfortunately, Turold had trod in something smelly and unseemly which distracted his attention and this, together with his muttering of, 'Oh blast, oh poo, ugh,' as he hopped about, gave his position away.

The dominant female raised her snout and smelt the air, and with Turold now being still upwind, the boar soon smelt his presence, but rather than running away or attacking him, she just started running towards him gently snorting. She soon caught up with the fleeing Turold and commenced rubbing up to him. Turold decided to stand still and try and stay calm, and began stroking and scratching what seemed to be the leader of the pack which resulted in snorts of contentment, and he was soon surrounded by her family.

The three men looked on and were amazed by what they saw. As soon as they approached the boars, they all treated them as a threat so the men decided to keep their distance. Turold carefully turned towards the lodge and walked slowly back, followed by his new friends. Nothing could be done. Into the courtyard Turold went, at the head of the procession. He took them over to the trough and they contentedly drank the water, then all moved into the corner and rested in the shade. Asger requested that Turold choose one for their supper, but he just could not do it. Asger was exasperated but decided not to antagonise the animals, so he and Bjorn disappeared back into the forest, and soon returned with three dead wild piglets. They presented them to Megan who looked at them for a while, not knowing what to do with them. The Norman servants took over cooking duties, being experienced in roasting meats. One of the Norman servants volunteered to skin the piglets and the other servant then dismembered and hung the meats over the fire where they cooked slowly. Turold and his boys gave their new boar family the offal. The twins were very excited and were soon doing good impersonations of wild boars with their father.

Rufus said to Turold, 'At least you have found one four-legged creature that likes you. It explains why the horses dislike you so much. They must think you are an oversized male wild boar intent on harming them.'

Turold had to agree that there was just something about his scent that the boar liked. In addition, he had an affinity with them. In many respects they seemed better behaved than many humans he had met.

Eventually the meat was cooked and after deciding to keep one roast piglet for breakfast, all tucked into the other two. Any tough bits left over were fed to the boars, which had smelt the food and were all trying their best to get into the lodge. The cannibals seemed to have a passion for roast pig. They then all went back to their corner and settled down for the night. Bjorn did a final perimeter sweep and closed the courtyard doors.

The group settled down as best they could. They all slept fitfully and then, late into the night, they were awoken by howling outside, and from lots of snorting in the courtyard. A pack of wolves had laid siege to the lodge and had decided that they were not leaving until a kill or three had been made. The humans were in as much a state of blind panic as the boar, although Asger and Bjorn tried their best not to show it.

Asger and Bjorn eventually came up with a plan.

This would involve sacrifices, but as far as they were concerned if it was not them, then they were happy. Bjorn told the two Norman servants what they must do, and then pushed them out into the courtyard, quickly closing the door and securing it. Initially the Normans banged on the door, but as they could not get in, decided that their best course of action was to follow the plan. They went out into the courtyard, mounted two horses, drove the boar towards the courtyard gate, quickly opened the gate and then forced the boar out into the forest. Bjorn had followed them out. He quickly closed the gate before the wolves could get in. Outside, the two Normans and their horses panicked. The Normans fell off their mounts, and the horses galloped off. Both the men and the wild boar scattered throughout the forest, followed by the wolves. The screaming and squealing soon died down as the wolves took their pick of the frightened men and animals, and after a while peace descended.

Bjorn was very pleased with himself as he entered the lodge. He never did liked Normans. They were, well, not English and had no respect for the Viking gods. Also, they ate funny food.

Turold asked, 'Have the wolves gone? Are the Normans and boar alright?'

Bjorn replied, 'The danger is over, but there were casualties.'

Vital consoled Megan, Turold and the boys. Vital was just relieved to still be alive.

The party tried to sleep some more but none gained much from their effort. At daybreak they all gathered and thanked God for their survival. Asger and Bjorn also gave thanks to various Viking gods as well since they, along with many other housecarls, could trace their ancestry way back to the Vikings and still clung to their pagan roots and religion, taking the view that it seemed best not to lay all your reliance on just one religion when two were available. This, however, was yet another reason why God was so upset with the English. After eating the remains of the roast meat, and carrying out their morning ablutions, the cart was loaded and the party set off south towards the burgh of Lewis, followed by the remains of the herd of boar, which had lost their dominant female in their encounter with the wolves and saw Turold as their new leader. After a mile or so, they gave up the chase and disappeared into the dense undergrowth, much to the disappointment of the twins who were now very adept at mimicking their new friends.

Lewis was a fortified town built as part of Alfred the Great's plan to protect the areas of England he controlled. The whole group were looking forward to the relative safety of that town, and seeing the back of the dark and dangerous forest. Even Asger and Bjorn decided that they had endured enough excitement for at least six months and wished for a quiet alehouse where they could receive comfort. By midday they had reached the southern extremity of the forest and, to their relief, had only seen some deer during their journey. However, the deer took exception to the presence of Turold, and it took the sight and sounds of two charging Vikings to see them scatter away into the undergrowth. The rest of the journey to Lewis was very pleasant indeed, enhanced by the good weather, and by late afternoon they reached Lewis where the housecarls made arrangements for their overnight stay. Turold and his family stayed at the alehouse all night enjoying the food, ale, and soft beds. Asger, Bjorn and Rufus enjoyed much alcoholic liquid refreshment, while Vital, Wadard went for what they called a stroll, which seemed to comprise a review of the town's fortifications, the drawing up of a street plan of Lewis, and various notes, including a description of the Weald and its dangers, and a strong recommendation for any army to avoid it.

The next day the group finished their journey to the dilapidated fort at Pevensey, where the two housecarls left for their return journey to London via the relative safety of Kent and Canterbury. Both had decided to visit the cathedral there to pray to God, and give thanks and a donation. God, however, was no fool and had marked them down for special treatment at a later date. He would indeed teach them for worshiping Odin and Thor and all those other Viking gods.

IT'S SO NICE TO BE BESIDE THE SEASIDE

Pevensey turned out to be a very conducive place and all, in their own way, made the most of it. Rufus was delighted to be on the south coast of England again and was only too willing to act as guide for Vital and Wadard, who seemed very interested to see both the seashore and the land around the town. Firstly however, Vital and Wadard paced out the interior of the fort and calculated its dimensions, and drew diagrams all of which would prove very useful in the construction of one of the prefabricated forts that would be transported from Normandy. They told Rufus that they were interested in old Roman fortifications and would someday write a parchment on the history of Roman architecture. Rufus was not convinced.

Rufus met several of his old acquaintances and seafaring friends and helped out on some of the fishing boats. The two Normans even came out a couple of times, with Vital saying, 'Just to see the views and the beautiful coastline from the sea. Oh, and by the way, perhaps the captain can point out any navigational hazards just in case we decide to do a bit of restful fishing on our own.'

In the evenings Vital and Wadard spent most of their time making notes while Turold and Rufus and the others had some traditional nights out, which as always, finished with the ceremonial fight, where Turold's groin butts were well received one way or another. Turold also performed some of his acts for which he received free ale and food. The townspeople and sailors and fishermen had never seen such entertainment before and they were hungry for any such diversions as distractions from their hard, plain lives, which revolved around fishing and digging for salt in the marshes.

After a few days, Vital and Wadard requested that Rufus take them further into the countryside as it was so beautiful. On their list were Hastings and its environs, including the nearby Norman Fecamp estate, given to Norman monks by King Edward himself. Rufus helped with interpretations, but as they say, money talks, and the Normans soon met many influential Englishmen willing to sell their allegiances. Hastings was of great interest to Vital and Wadard along with the nearby cliffs. There, they decided, would be another good site for a fort. By then Rufus had been replaced by one of Matilda's agents living in the area and the three continued to reconnoitre the area north along the Roman road until it met the main road from Dover to London. These three Normans even took a journey up to Canterbury and down to Dover to review the defences. Vital and Wadard were very pleased. By the time they had completed their research, they should have all that would be required for a safe landing and invasion. As for Turold, the summer was a good one, but seemingly all too short for his liking.

HAROLD'S PILGRIMAGE

Meanwhile, King Edward, Earl Harold and his retinue were proceeding to Hereford via the great religious sites of St. Alban's Abbey, Oxford Monastery, Bath Monastery, Malmesbury Abbey, and Gloucester Abbey. Harold thought that this would be enough of a pilgrimage to save his soul. Other than their stay at Malmesbury, the journey was mainly uneventful.

King Edward insisted on a visit to Malmesbury, saying to Harold, 'My son and heir, we must go there. We must give homage at the tomb of our great Saxon King Athelstan, the first true Saxon king of the whole of England. That old and venerable flying monk, Eilmer, has also requested a meeting with me, as he has an important God-sent vision to relate to us both. Finally, you must sit with the scholarly monks living there and be guided by them regarding your future as king. They have much knowledge of the two great Saxon kings, Alfred and Athelstan. Oh, and coincidently, we can enjoy some hunting and feasting at the same time, as King Athelstan's magnificent hunting lodge still exists, along with his private chapel for our prayers and confessions. We will surely feed both our souls and pleasures at the same time, young Harold!'

Harold had been totally confused, and queried, 'Did you say 'flying monk', Your Grace?'

Edward sighed, and then said sternly, 'Be patient and all will be revealed! And don't drink so much!'

With those words, Edward left Harold alone, as he wished to find his special Athelstan Bible and casket. Edward suddenly had an inspired idea. If only he could remember where he had hidden those precious items. They were concealed in his luggage somewhere.

Harold sighed, thinking, *not another vision please,* and poured another glass of wine. He was not enjoying this pilgrimage and was definitely not looking forward to his marriage of doom at all, and yes, he knew he was drinking too much but it dulled his mental anguish.

Edward had made prior arrangements with Abbot Beorhtic for a service to be held in memory of King Athelstan, which would also celebrate Edward's rule, and finally ask for God's protection of Harold as the next king of England.

All went well for most of the service. Abbot Beorhtic and the monks were delighted to meet Harold in particular, since it had been he and his father who had intervened in Edward's decision of 1053 as to who should become the next Abbot. Prayers were said around the holy shrine of Saint Aldhelm, where Eilmer seemed to miraculously have his lameness cured. Further prayers were said at the tomb of King Athelstan, and finally at the High Altar where King Athelstan's two cousins, Alfwine and Athelwine were buried. They were two heroes from the great battle of Brunanburh, where Athelstan not only beat the Irish Norsemen but was also accepted as ruler of the whole of England. The service ended with prayers requesting that God protect Harold and England from those overseas rulers with envious eyes. At the conclusion of these prayers God seemed to answer. Suddenly a large jet-black cloud descended as from heaven, and from it a bolt of lightning flew down, hit and smashed part of the chancel's stained glass window depicting Saint Aldhelm, and hit the gold cross on the altar, sending shafts of yellow blinding light in all directions. A terrible crash of thunder followed that shook the ground and caused a statue of Athelstan to topple over and break into many pieces.

There was consternation amongst all present, but Abbot Beorhtic took command in his usual calm way. 'God has spoken, and His light has surely shone on Earl Harold Godwinson!' he exclaimed.

However, many thought otherwise, including Harold, and even Edward had his doubts.

While Harold had his studies with the monks, Edward spoke privately with the Abbot. 'I am truly pleased with your appointment. You have proved yourself to be a well-respected holy leader, unlike some of your predecessors, such as Abbot Beorhtwold who I understand collapsed and died at one of his many drunken orgies and whose body had to be exhumed from St. Andrew's Church when the church became infested with evil spirits. I understand that the unholy remains were taken with great ceremony to a nearby bog and thrown in.'

'Yes, indeed Your Grace, it took several days to cleanse the church of the devils that dwelled there!'

'Now I am nearing my earthly end, I wish to settle certain important matters. Firstly, here is a document signed by me which grants Malmesbury Abbey a general confirmation of all its possessions including 329 hides of land as detailed in the manuscript. In return, I must ask you to swear before God that you will undertake the solemn duty of protecting the holy remains of Saint Aldhelm and King Athelstan and also all the religious relics in the possession of the abbey. This task must be handed down from one abbot to the next, and if and when the time comes, the precious remains and relics must be taken to a secret place of safety where they can rest and where the ways of our old religion can continue unseen. I have received a vision from God that sometime in the future our religion will be swept away along with all that we hold so dear. As with other abbeys, I leave the future of our old religion in the hands of abbots that I can trust. May God protect us all!'

'Amen, and with God's will it shall be so!' replied the abbot.

Later, Harold asked Edward what had been said between him and the abbot, as Beorhtic seemed to be unnaturally concerned about his future.

Edward put his arm around Harold's shoulders and replied, 'It's just a backup plan I have devised in case things do not go well for you. I'm sure you'll be fine, young Harold, but I must take precautions. I'm sure you understand! Now we must meet Eilmer.'

Harold would've preferred hunting, feasting, and drinking, but sighed and trudged down the corridor behind Edward.

Eilmer was a person able to bring an air of great optimism to any room. The old monk rose up out of his chair, smiled, chuckled, and bowed as low as he could to Edward. 'What an honour to meet you. And who's this, is it young Harold? No, it can't be, but yes it surely is! Let me see you close to. My eyes are not how they were!' and he continued chuckling as he grabbed Harold's right hand in his. Then he stopped, and his face seemed to change shape for a while before he spoke again. 'Oh well, young Harold, I'm sure, well, let's say, oh, just come here for a big hug!' The jolly monk hugged Harold, released him, and wiped a tear from his eye as he asked his guests to sit down.

Edward sat down first, in the most comfortable of the chairs with extra cushions provided by the monk, who understood only too well old men's posterior issues.

Edward turned to Harold and commanded, 'Come sit next to me, young Harold, and listen carefully!' Edward chuckled, then coughed, then laughed again.

Harold sighed, sat down, and sighed again. He hated being called 'young Harold' and he was already fed up with these two senile old chucklers. He knew he was doing too much sighing as well as drinking, but then what did he have to look forward to, and he did miss his family so much that it hurt his heart.

The sighing annoyed Edward. 'Stop sighing, young Harold, and just enjoy yourself for a change. Yes, let's hear some chuckling from you!'

Harold tried to laugh but it came out as more of a low pitched scream.

Eilmer took pity on him and intervened. 'He's only a young man, Your Grace, and you know what they are like at their age, just adolescent rebels.'

Harold felt like reminding the two of them that he was over forty and not fourteen, but just remained sitting with a silent sigh. The two old men looked at each other, and started laughing again. Harold looked at his boots.

Edward was first to stop laughing. 'Now Eilmer, I believe you have something to tell us.'

Eilmer wondered for a while whether he should say anything, then replied, 'I have had a vision. When I was a young boy there appeared in the sky a large bright star with a tail of light resembling a sword or a band of long golden hair. It was observed with horror and considered a bad omen sent by God himself as a warning to all Saxon-speaking peoples in England, and of course a new round of invasions by the Vikings occurred soon after, which led to Cnut being crowned king of England. God has revealed to me that this tailed star will return within the year and that there will be great battles, which will decide who God wants to be the rightful king of England!'

Both Edward and Harold remained quiet for a while as they digested this prediction.

At last, Edward spoke. 'I suppose that means that I have only months to live, but you must surely see, young Harold, that you are destined to defeat all invaders and become the greatest Saxon king of all time!'

Edward was absolutely convinced about his interpretation, but Harold just looked at his feet, wondering whether the floor would take pity on him and devour him.

Eilmer chuckled, then laughed, and then he stood up. 'If it pleases Your Grace, I have laid on some entertainment, so please follow me outside.'

Edward stood up, chuckling, then coughing, and then swaying a bit, so Harold had to hold him until he was stabilised. Eilmer led the way, now limping again, as it seemed the miracle had been very short lasting. Edward followed, coughing, and then plodded Harold. Outside it was sunny again, although there was quite a strong south-westerly wind. Eilmer gestured skyward, and the three ended up looking up at the Abbey's tall western tower, which Eilmer was pointing at enthusiastically with a smile on his face. A great crowd had assembled to see the advertised event, all of them hoping for a great deal of blood and gore.

'Now, in the year 1,000 I celebrated the 1,000 years since the birth of Christ by flying just like the Archangel Gabriel. I calculated that, with the will of God, I could design a contrivance that would enable me to jump off the tower into the wind and glide above the slope below, and across the river, to finish in the meadow beyond. It was composed of a rigid framework of ash, made in the shape of a diamond, covered with linen, to which I could be securely strapped. Here is a rough drawing.'

Both Edward and Harold looked at the drawing. Harold laughed incredulously, but Edward seemed to be taking the story very seriously, so jabbed Harold in the ribs and shook his head. Harold turned away and sniggered for a while before gaining his composure.

Eilmer continued to explain. 'With the whole of the population of the town present to see the miracle, I jumped off the tower. My take off was perfect, and the uplift of air towards the tower gave me sufficient lift. I was indeed flying! However, without a tail to my contraption, I started to lose control, and then the wind gusted. I was now in uncontrolled descent, and soon hit the river with such force as to break both my legs! God must have looked on in pity, and I survived, although he had punished me for my rashness and conceit. As you know, pride comes before a fall! I was later told that I had flown a distance of some 600 feet, and as a result, I became known as the flying monk!'

Edward slapped Eilmer on the back exclaiming, 'What a story! Did you hear that, young Harold? The first flying man!' and he burst out laughing and coughing.

Harold was thinking, *the first flying imbecile*, but nodded and smiled.

Eilmer continued to speak. 'Today, to honour your visit, there will be an attempt to improve on my achievement.'

Edward exclaimed, 'No, don't do it! At your age, well, it's suicide!'

Eilmer laughed loudly and said, 'Now, I'm not that stupid. My flying days are over, but my apprentice Oliver on the other hand is ready for the challenge. He was considered by all those present to be the town idiot, but in reality, I have found him to be just otherworldly and also a devout Christian ready to put his body and soul in the hands of God.'

Harold looked up at the top of the tower, where he could now make out a small young man strapped to a large sort of diamond shaped flag, with a tail. *Yes*, he thought, *a devout idiot, soon to become otherworldly.*

Eilmer concluded his explanation. 'You see it was a design fault that resulted in my downfall. As with all birds, my contraption needed a tail as well as wings!'

With those final words he raised his right arm, and an obliging monk shoved a reluctant Oliver off the tower.

Oliver's flight was not a disappointment as far as the crowd was concerned. Initially he screamed as he soared high above them like a huge majestic eagle. He was able to use the tail to create the correct flow of air so as to produce the required lift. Oliver began to realise that so far, his flight had gone well. He was now thoroughly enjoying himself, and started waving at the spectators as he tried a turn so that he could soar over the throng once more before turning back into the wind and heading down the steep bank towards the river. This enthusiasm was his downfall.

The strong wind caught him and propelled him towards the tower wall. Oliver could not turn. He hurtled towards the tower and hit the stonework with a thud, cracking his head in the process, before plummeting lifeless towards the ground.

Eilmer was inconsolable. Edward helped him walk over to the body, covered by the contraption as if covered by a bloodstained death shroud. Eilmer gave Oliver the last rites, and the monks carefully lifted him and carried him inside. The Abbott decided that Oliver would be buried in the abbey, with all the honour given to a martyr.

Meanwhile, the townspeople took away any parts of Oliver and his contraption that were left, as keepsakes or even religious relics if his future tomb produced any miracles. They were fully content with events that day, and it was talked about for months. Harold just looked and shook his head as he watched, wondering whether he was seeing what was going to happen to his body when he died. He was also pondering whether he would have preferred being Oliver rather than Harold, given his various possible fates.

The hunting and feasting that followed helped lift the mood, but Harold was starting to get very concerned about Edward's declining health.

HAROLD CONTINUES HIS PILGRIMAGE, AND IS MARRIED

The pilgrimage continued without any problems, but then full precautions were taken to ensure there was no chance of poisoning or ambush. In most places, King Edward was received with great rejoicing from the nobles and the general population since the south of England was under the control of Earl Harold, but there was, in places, an undercurrent of resentment from those with strong links to the Mercian nobility and from others with strong Danish or Welsh roots. It was apparent to both Edward and Harold that the kingdom was not a completely happy and united one by any means. The situation worsened as they neared Hereford where Harold's invasion of south Wales in 1063 did not sit easy with many, especially those with Welsh blood. There had been many deaths, including that of the Welsh king, and Harold soon discovered that his belligerent brother, Tostig, had in the past alienated and annihilated many. Harold was also hearing disturbing reports about his brother's actions in Northumberland, and decided that he would have to try one last time to make his brother see sense.

Harold conducted his pilgrimage rituals as required, and from the bottom of his heart, asked for God and Jesus to receive his soul when the time came. He could often be seen kneeling and praying in the churches, where he could calmly consider the events of the past year or so. A year ago, life had been so straightforward. He had been

Edward's right hand with no ambition of being his heir. But now King Edward and Duke William had changed all that. He was the victim of circumstances way beyond his control and he could still see no easy way out.

The Saxon cathedral at Hereford had been sacked and burnt by King Gruffydd and his Welsh army in 1055, and was now under reconstruction. Harold was able to pray in the cathedral, and although the sacred shrine of Saint Ethelbert had been destroyed, he was able to lay his hands on the saint's few remaining bones and see the great and ancient illuminated gospel book, known as the Hereford Gospels. Harold sat and contemplated. The Welsh had certainly caused mayhem over the years, and was it not he himself who had finally crushed their spirit and killed their one and only true king, whose widow he was now going to marry. Surely perhaps, he thought, God was indeed on his side and had great plans for him. Another thought sprang to his mind. Perhaps if he could remove the threat of that Duke William, then he could rightfully and safely become king. *Yes, but how?* he thought. Another dastardly idea infected his brain, *POISON, POISON! But how?*

At Hereford Harold met his bride-to-be, the widowed queen of Wales, Ealdgyth, daughter of Elfgar Earl of Mercia. He found her intelligent and likeable, although they both agreed that their marriage would be best maintained at a safe distance unless there was an emergency. They both hoped that their marriage would help maintain peace between the Mercians and the Wessex royal family. Edward was very happy after the marriage ceremony since it would cement the support of the Mercian nobility and help Harold rule England upon his death. As far as Edward was concerned, his plans would ensure the safety of his realm. But only time would tell.

Harold and Edward also managed some hunting and Edward was well enough to kill a few startled and defenceless animals. The journey back from Hereford was arduous and by the time they returned to Westminster, the king was in poor health. His cough was back with a vengeance and he became increasingly tired. He knew his time was near but he was determined to continue working on his project, Westminster Abbey. Summer would soon turn to autumn and then winter, and with that would surely come the shadow of death. Edward knew that winter had a way of seeking out the sick, the frail, and the elderly, and he was all of those.

TOSTIG RECEIVES AN INVITATION

Upon his return, Harold invited Tostig to go on a hunting trip in Wiltshire. Tostig did not want to go, indeed he used any excuse he could to avoid King Edward's court. He had more allegiance to the king of Scotland than Edward, due mainly to the deep-rooted hatred for Edward for not only banishing his family, but also because he believed that Edward had something to do with the death of his dear father, and finally, Edward favoured his brother Harold more than he should. However, he was having continued trouble with the Northumberland peoples and knew that perhaps he should try and get the support of his brother in quelling any thoughts of rebellion. He needed Harold's army so he could teach them a harsh lesson.

Their meeting was destined not to go well due to two main factors. Firstly, Tostig tended to get very irrational and there was much slurring when he drank too much, and this happened all too often these days. Secondly, he had an expanding lump on his head that had recently started to press on his brain. This medical condition would result in an increasing number of side effects including even more irrational behaviour, hallucinations, and psychotic episodes.

RICHARD ARRIVES AT HOLY ISLAND

Richard and his dog, which he had now named Fang, had managed to escape various threats against their persons and were now sat on the seashore looking at Lindisfarne, otherwise known as Holy Island. From their viewpoint they could see the imposing abbey buildings. Lindisfarne Monastery had been founded by the Irish monk Aidan in 635, and continued to be an extremely important centre of Christianity in England, although by now a number of Viking raids had led to much destruction and death.

They had to wait for the tide so they could walk across the causeway, a journey that would take some two hours and so needed to be started two hours before low tide. They sat and ate their lunch. The weather was warm and sunny and both felt like enjoying their rest for the remainder of the day, but Richard knew he was already behind schedule, and that his contact had probably already given up all hope of seeing him, so start they must. Richard sighed, and Fang yawned and stretched his legs, then off they walked. Fang was excited by the strange smells and the birds and other wildlife. He ran in and out of the water barking at the seagulls, daring them to come close to his jaws. On they walked and sure enough, after just under two hours they reached the island. A monk stood waiting for them. He had been observing their progress in between his duties. Richard announced that he was Richard Longshanks and wished to see Monk Aidan.

The monk laughed. 'You are some three hundred years too late sir, but I know that one of the existing monks has been extremely vexed about your health. I will go and fetch him. He is at his work in the kitchens.'

The monk patted Fang on the head (an extremely risky thing to do but the dog was in a good mood), and headed off towards the monastery. Richard sat on a rock and waited, looking at the wonderful scenery. Then he closed his eyes and started daydreaming, while Fang relaxed on his back watching the white and grey squawky flying things.

Suddenly Richard received a tap on his right shoulder. It made Richard jump and that made the dog jump and growl. It took all of Richard's strength of mind and training to stop something nasty happening. The dog's mind was not so strong and it went for the offending arm, but was miraculously calmed by the monk attached to the arm.

'Come dear dog, take this offering and be still.' He threw the dog a bone and gave Richard some bread and cheese and water, then sat down next to him.

'You see, I look after the kitchens and things can easily fall into my deep pockets,' he said, finishing off a piece of fruit pie, and continuing, 'My colleague had warned me about the evil-looking hound you had and I came prepared. I am so glad to see you. I thought you must have drowned or had been the subject of some other terrible fate. However, you seem to have the protection of God, and here you are. I will thank God tonight.'

Richard looked at the monk. He seemed a jolly gentleman, perhaps too jolly to be a monk, but maybe all that time in the kitchens with all that food had something to do with it. His figure certainly suggested that he never missed his meals.

'I am indeed lucky to be here, sir, in fact if it was not for this dog, I probably would not be, although he has caused me problems on the way.'

The monk stroked the dog and was rewarded by Fang rolling onto his back and allowing him to tickle his belly. Richard was amazed.

The monk finally spoke. 'You will both stay in the guest cell. Tomorrow I will ask the abbot whether he will permit me to take you to a remote farmhouse near the market town of Wooler to meet the local resistance leader. He is a friend of mine, a devout Christian, who wishes to end the tyranny of that dastardly Tostig. Much suffering has descended upon the people since Earl Tostig's tight grip on Northumberland and his lack of action against the marauding Scots. It is time that direct action be taken against his rule, although of course I cannot encourage any blood being spilt, but then again, if it is the will of God, then who am I to defy His will!'

Richard could only nod, not yet knowing the facts in detail. He would assess the situation himself and then decide what could be done to inflame the rebellious local people.

VITAL AND WADARD ARE CONCERNED

Vital, Wadard, Rufus, Turold, and Megan sat around the table. Vital had requested they meet in secret. The two Norman knights had felt increasingly guilty about their clandestine activities and the potential consequences for Turold's family. They had both grown very attached to the family, especially as so much Norman blood flowed through Turold's sons, Peter and Paul.

'Now, you must both listen to me carefully, I have something important to discuss with you.' Vital was very commanding.

Turold and Megan had his attention.

'This is in strict confidence. Turold, your family may not be safe here next summer if Duke William does not get his way. I assume you know of his intentions regarding England?'

Turold nodded. Megan had no idea what was going on and shook her head.

Vital sighed and continued to speak, looking intently at Megan, 'As soon as King Edward dies, Duke William expects to be King William of England. If this doesn't happen peaceably, then it'll happen by force. If there's to be war, this town will not be a safe place to be.'

Megan was now white in the face, shocked by this news.

Turold consoled her while Vital continued, 'We've a plan to save you, Megan, and your sons. We will make arrangements for you to be taken by ship from here to

Normandy, where you will be with Turold, and under Duke William's protection.'

Turold was both happy and concerned. He knew only too well what William's protection could mean, possibly an indefinite stay at his pleasure in the palace or worse. However, on balance, anything was better than his family being in a war zone, as he knew only too well that rampaging European knights tended to create a great deal of collateral damage.

Turold looked intently at Megan. 'I think, in the circumstances, it would be for the best if we agree. I know both Duke William and his wife only too well, and if God is on their side, they will surely succeed.'

Megan thought for a while. She liked it here. She had made some good friends and her life was much improved compared to her existence in London. She also knew that London was still suffering from the plague and totally unsuitable for her boys and the new life that was forming in her belly.

She sighed. 'I agree. It'll be for the best for the twins and my unborn child or children.'

Turold fell off his chair and slid under the table. He awoke from his faint with a glass of brandy in his hand and three grinning faces looking down on him.

Wadard shook him by the hand saying, 'Well done, Turold you old dog. It must be the herbs she puts in your food.'

Turold was dazed and confused, but not enough to miss the chance of some brandy.

After gulping it down he replied, 'What herbs pray?'

Wadard's face went red and so did Megan's.

TOSTIG SLURS A LOT

Harold and Tostig sat around the table.

Tostig was drunk again and slurring and swearing. 'And another thing, why am I still up in Nowthumblyland. I hate it. It's cold and wet and as for the local wilergews, well I would have them all dealt with if I could. They are tewible people, bwother Hawold. I cannot contwol them, none of them like me, and I have had to recwuit mewcen... Eh meawcende... eh men from Flandews and Euwope to help me. No one will pay any blumin taxes bwother Hawold. Please do not send me back.' Tostig started sobbing.

Harold offered Tostig some water, but he pushed it away and filled his flagon with more ale, 'and what about stupid King Egghead. He's useless. We need a stwong king not some wishy washy weligious dweamer. I suggest my fwiend King Malcolm of Scwotland for the job.'

Harold looked around at the servants. They were all a-gasp at this blatant treachery towards Edward. 'What a joke, dear brother,' he said while putting his hand over Tostig's mouth. He looked at the servants. 'You are all dismissed for the night. My brother is unwell with a fever.'

The servants all left quickly, only too willing to spread what they had heard to the rest of the household.

Harold let go of Tostig. 'Brother Tostig, do not say such things or you will end up like our father.'

Tostig burst out crying. 'Ah, I miss him so, the old beast. Now he was a man, unlike Egghead who is a semidwuid saint. Father should have been kwing, then I would now be a pwince.'

Harold thought, *oh no, not Mother next please.*

'Then there is Mummy, she hates me. Why is God against me? Why is God so bad to our family? What have we done that is so dwedful? I hate God, I hate Egghead, I hate England, and I hate you. Why are you evewyone's favouwite? Why does no one like me?' Tostig rubbed the lump on his head and then buried his head in his arms and wept.

Harold could not handle this at all. *All that praying and shuffling on my knees for what? Tostig's blaspheming and other outbursts have probably cost me any chance of getting out of my difficult situation.*

'Listen bother Tostig, things will get better I promise. Edward will probably not see the year out and it seems I am to succeed him. I will then be able to improve your lot. In the meantime, get back to Northumberland, keep quiet, and don't antagonise its peoples.'

'I'll antagonise them alwight! I'll cwush any rebellion, even if it means getting my fwiend King Malcolm to help!'

Tostig raised his head. He looked livid. He had just realised what Harold had said. 'What, you as my kwing? I will not bow down to you! I would wather die. I want to be kwing too.' He started weeping again as he staggered out of the room.

Harold sat talking to himself, 'That could have gone better, methinks. I must deal with him sooner wather than later. Oh dear, he's got me slurring now.' He poured himself another wine. *Now, where's my damp towel, my head hurts again!*

RICHARD AT HOLY ISLAND

Richard and Fang sat at the dining table with the other monks. The two were in a blissful haze of peace and tranquillity with as much food and bones as they could eat. Who could ask for anything more? There had been two sticky moments when things could have gone back to the normal life of mayhem and danger. One was when the abbot refused the monk's request to take the two of them to the rebels. However, this was soon resolved peaceably when Richard donated a significant sum to the abbey roof fund. It seems that Duchess Matilda had foreseen the need for much bribing during his assignment. The second was when one of the monks had suggested to Fang that he was more like a docile pregnant bitch rather than a proper dog, but Fang just rolled on his back, allowing his tummy to be tickled with his tongue hanging out of his mouth while seemingly laughing. Fang did not mind his doghood being questioned if it meant a lot of pampering and bones.

After the meal, Monk Aidan asked, 'When are we going to Wooler?'

Richard replied sleepily, 'Who's Woller?'

'Do you not remember? It's not a who it's a where.'

It all came flooding back to Richard. *Ah yes, the mission. Oh, blow the mission*, he thought. *I want to stay here. In any case why do Duke William and Duchess Matilda want England? It's a strange backward place full of people from migrant ancestors. I've not yet met a real native Briton. I've heard that there are still some in the west but most of the population are now Angles, Saxons, Danes, or northern Vikings. Each dislike the other to some degree and most are ambivalent as regards which king ruled them, since most just ignore their King and carry on regardless. Then there are the peoples of Mercia and the north east of England. They just plain and simply dislike King Edward. In my opinion King Edward is too weak a ruler. Perhaps England deserves a cruel and ruthless ruler like Duke William! No, I'm not in the mood to do any work!*

So, he tried to change the topic of conversation and replied, 'I think it is time for evening prayers.'

The monk looked at him seriously. 'We must depart tomorrow for our meeting with the rebels!'

Richard smiled meekly and said, 'I think God would prefer me to become a monk and give my life to Him! Are there any qualifications required, or exams?'

Aiden sighed and shouted, 'Richard, focus!'

'I know, Fang and I could both become monks and then we could protect the monastery from any Viking raids. Do you have some robes for a dog?'

'Richard, just—'

The bell rang for prayer. *Saved by the bell* thought Richard, and stood to leave. The monk sighed and went with him.

WHAT TO DO ABOUT TOSTIG

King Edward and his counsel sat around the table. 'I am uneasy about having this meeting without Earl Harold of Wessex present.'

'Your Grace, it is because of the subject of this meeting that we think it best that he is not,' one of his counsel replied.

'Alright, carry on. My bladder can only last so long before needing relief, and as for my backside—'

'Your Grace, Earl Harold's brother Earl Tostig is creating problems in Northumberland. He seems to be favouring the Scots at the expense of your own subjects. As you know, these lands are difficult to control at the best of times, but Earl Tostig's bad management is likely to lead to an all-out revolt against him and therefore you. He has been ineffectual at securing the borders with Scotland and this has led to many attacks on your lands, and now he has hired foreign mercenaries to keep control of the population and that has led to resentment, atrocities, and high taxes. The local population are at this moment planning direct action against the local authorities. Luckily our spies have advised us that the dissenters are disorganised and without a real leader.'

Edward scratched his beard, and shifted his bottom. 'I will not tolerate revolting peasants. If the situation is as you describe, then Earl Harold of Wessex will take an army north and deal with them.'

Another counsellor spoke. 'Your Grace, in our view, we must humbly suggest that the easiest option would be to replace Tostig with a more reasonable man who can calm down the situation. An internal struggle at this time would surely attract the attention of those abroad looking enviously at your kingdom.'

Edward thought hard – they were right. 'I will consider your advice, but it will be Earl Harold, as my right hand, who will carry out my final decision on this matter. Now be gone, I must rest, this is all too much for me.'

He coughed for several minutes, the product of which did not look too healthy at all. The Witan rose as one and left Edward to his sleep. Edward was very angry and upset, and could not settle. His love of Tostig clouded his judgement, he knew this, but he could not tolerate revolt of any kind. He had spent too much effort keeping the country together and its foreign enemies away from its shores to have it ruined now. His anger boiled over. He tried to arise and call for his advisors, but suddenly got a searing pain in his head, and fell back into his chair. He had received a severe seizure leading to a blood clot on the brain. He had suffered a stroke. Over the next few days, he had further seizures. This was surely the beginning of the end.

GOD SPEAKS TO RICHARD

Richard was enjoying his meditation in the chapel while the monks conducted their service. The monks were intent on praising God and improving their souls while he enjoyed the feeling of well-being it gave him.

All of a sudden God whispered in his right ear, or was it his left? It did not matter. The words were clear. 'You must complete your mission. I require you and your furry angel of death to undertake the organisation of the rebels, not for the sake of any duke or duchess, but for My sake. This country is destined to become a great nation but first it needs to be purified and unified. Now pray to me, and then leave this place and do my bidding.'

Well, thought Richard, he and Fang had God's work to do. He gave thanks to God for giving him the clarity of mind to see his part in the destiny of England, and waited for Monk Aidan outside the chapel.

When the monk eventually came into view, Richard said to him, 'God has spoken, it is time to go and unite the rebels.'

Aidan was shocked. He had no idea that God was interested in the project. It seemed as if it was to be God's will that they were to succeed. Aidan was both joyful and apprehensive.

ARRIVAL AT WOOLER

Richard, Fang, and the monk had reached their destination, an isolated farmhouse in the middle of the Cheviot Hills above Wooler. The Northumberland men who had gathered there looked suspiciously at Richard, and even more so when he started talking with a strange accent. They did not like foreigners or southerners.

The leader looked at the monk and asked, 'Why have you brought us this soft southerner? What good can he do?'

Richard spoke. 'I was sent to Lindisfarne by a high authority. While there I received the word of God and He has told me that I am to be His instrument and help you remove that terrible Earl Tostig forever, and bring back justice and the Danish customs of your ancestors.'

The leader grunted, wiped the drizzle off his nose and replied, 'Fine words indeed. Is this true, monk?'

The monk nodded and said, 'It is sir, you can believe his words as he has God by his side.'

Looking and pointing at Fang, the leader responded, 'Well, that's a strange-looking god alright.'

The rest of the rebels laughed as Fang growled and showed his full set of sharp teeth.

'No, I assure you all, God has chosen this man,' the monk insisted.

There were many gasps from the assembled men. They were all Godfearing men and held the monastery on the Holy Isle in great regard, as it was one of their holiest places. This must surely be the sign they were waiting for.

Richard continued to speak. 'I'm here to help you fight the oppressors, and to advise you. I understand that there are several factions of disgruntled men ready to fight, and that there is indeed some animosity between them. To defeat the oppressors, you must be united.'

The leader laughed and agreed. 'You are right, we of the Northumberland Shepherds and Goat Herders Association hate the Northumberland Fishermen's Liberation Army nearly as much as that dastardly Tostig and his foreigners. They smell bad and fight like wenches.'

Richard sighed. 'I advise that all the leaders are gathered together for a meeting where your various differences can be overcome and unity can prevail.'

The leader, Eric Black Goat, shook his head. 'They'll not come, since they'll think it's a trap.'

Richard thought for a while and said, 'I'll show you and the others what I'm capable of, and convince you all of my abilities and my honesty.'

Fang looked angrily at Richard, and Richard corrected himself quickly, 'and my dog will also prove his worth.'

The whole assembled locals laughed until they cried. Eric was the first to regain composure. 'Eh, Lad, what can one man and his dog do other than herd sheep?'

The men started laughing again. Richard thought to himself, *I need to keep control, and mustn't do anything hasty.*

Suddenly two men who had been keeping watch on the hill behind the farmhouse rushed into the farm.

Both were breathing heavily but one managed to talk. 'Eric, we're betrayed, some twenty of Tostig's men approach from the south.'

Eric looked accusingly at Richard and took out his sword, but then saw in the corner of his eye, Shepherd Anund looking rather sheepish. Anund made a run for it but Eric shouted, 'Hold the traitor Anund!'

Anund was grabbed just as he had his hand on the door handle. *Oh, sheep's entrails and droppings*, he thought.

Eric looked again at Richard. 'Well, lad, it seems your time to impress has come. I'll give you and your dog first pickings!' And with those words, he pushed the two of them outside.

Some nervous laughter followed their departure as the not-so-brave rebels hid in a corner of the farmhouse.

Eric addressed his men. 'I suggest we hide and pray with the monk for our deliverance.'

The men were only too willing to oblige.

THE FIGHT

Richard and Fang surveyed the ground outside the farmhouse. Richard considered his options and from the relentless training and knowledge of his abilities, decided on his best course of action. He prayed to God for help, and God listened.

The heavily armed men approached, and their leader stepped forward and looked at the two, rubbing his fine red beard and sniggering. 'Well, if it's not the rebel army, one strange looking man and his scruffy dog.'

His men laughed as if on cue.

He looked at the two again. 'Just a minute, are you the two outlaws wanted for various curious crimes that took place all the way from the Wash to York? Yes, I believe you are. Well, men it looks like we get both the traitors and the outlaws today. We'll certainly be feasting tonight.'

His men showed their appreciation by banging their swords and axes on their shields.

Richard spoke. 'I and my dog will deal with you as one, so if you could all gather together it'll make my task easier.'

The captain laughed, and his men joined in. 'Anything to help bring matters to a swift conclusion. We are missing important drinking time.'

His men laughed again. The soldiers were now assembled in four rows of four (the two rebel lookouts never could count). Richard closed his eyes, prayed, and hoped God was willing to help. The cold light drizzle was gradually replaced by wind and dark cloud. This weather phenomenon was extremely localised to where Tostig's Flemish soldiers stood. The wind started to spiral and seemed to captivate them as its intensity increased. It was now a surging whirlwind. The men in the farmhouse had been attracted to the windows by the noise and looked unbelievingly at the scene. The soldiers' feet were now a few inches above the ground and the column of wind moved up accordingly, giving Fang the opportunity to rush in and out of the maelstrom snapping and biting at their legs, resulting in much swearing, and screaming. The wind was ever increasing and eventually the men were some twelve feet above the ground. Much weaponry blew out of the whirling mass of bloody bodies, so that eventually Richard lost concentration as he dived to his left to avoid a sword projectile with his name on it. The wind stopped immediately and the soldiers fell to the ground, resulting in many broken limbs and a great deal of swearing and moaning.

Richard got to his feet, brushed himself down, went to the farmhouse door and opened it declaring to the trembling rebels, 'It's safe to come out. I'll leave you to deal with what's left. Has anyone got any ale, and possibly some mutton? I think we deserve some reward!'

Eric poked his head outside and made sure there was no danger, then turned to his men and shouted, 'Come on lads, time for some sport! In the meantime, lad, have whatever you can find.'

Richard sat in a chair by the fire with Fang beside him, sharing some well-earned food and ale that the monk had found, while the rebels took their revenge on the poor Flemish soldiers.

The monk spoke. 'I think, sir, that your demonstration has impressed. Something similar in full view of the local population should do nicely in convincing the various bands of men that you have all the qualifications to be their leader.'

Richard was sleeping when Eric and his men entered the room. All looked happy and content with their labours. Eric approached Richard and Fang growled, so he stepped back a few paces. Fang's growling awoke Richard.

He had had a dream. 'Ah, Eric, God has spoken. My demonstration will take place on the Feast of Saint Matthew the Apostle at Dun Holm. I have been told to march from Chester le Street, where the original shrine of Saint Cuthbert of Lindisfarne was kept, to the great stone church at Dun Holm, which, as you know, is his current resting place. God has requested that as many Godfearing true Northumberland people as possible join me in this pilgrimage. We will end our journey at the shrine and ask for a sign from Saint Cuthbert, and then we must all give thanks to God. We will all be like that Danish King Cnut who walked six miles barefoot to visit the shrine. However, I will leave my dog to do the barefoot walking, since I must preserve my body for the struggles ahead. Go and spread the word.'

Richard had given Eric and his men hope, strength, and bravery. They discussed plans to send word to the other factions to be at Chester le Street on September 21 to see the events unfold. It would surely be worth being there. Once rested, the monk and Richard said their goodbyes and left on their journey to Chester le Street. Outside, nothing remained as evidence of the fate of Tostig's men. The monk advised Richard that there were some caves nearby which probably now had silent occupants.

The monk spoke seriously to Richard. 'If this is a religious occasion you must not defile it with violence.'

Richard looked at Fang, and then the monk. 'We will not cast the first stone, I promise, but I will defend myself and my followers.'

The monk shrugged his shoulders. He was not happy about the answer, but if God was on their side, then as long as things did not get out of hand, God's wrath could surely be avoided.

SEPTEMBER 1065, NORTHUMBERLAND: THE PILGRIMAGE TO ST CUTHBERT'S SHRINE

The word went out far and wide like a spreading flood, centred on the village of Wooler. God has sent a warrior, his dog, and a holy man from Lindisfarne to rid Northumberland of the tyrannical Earl Tostig.

On the Feast of St Matthew, the Apostle, Richard the First would lead a pilgrimage from Chester le Street to the great church at Dun Holm where St Cuthbert was buried. Once at his tomb, St Cuthbert would provide a sign and God would bless the rebellion against Earl Tostig. All present hoped they would see a miracle that would change their lives forever. Large numbers of people were organising themselves for their journeys.

Unfortunately, Earl Tostig's officials also became aware of the march, and decided that steps must be taken to disperse the expected masses since they were afraid that large gatherings of people could well lead to an uprising. They made their own plans to ambush the marchers as they approached Dun Holm. They knew that the saint and the monks, who chose the setting for the building of the church, had indeed chosen wisely. Once on the island of Dun Holm, the pilgrims could easily defend themselves (Dun Holm, dear reader, is now known as Durham).

Richard, Fang the dog, and the Lindisfarne monk known as Aidan reached the outskirts of Chester le Street on September 19, and stayed at a safe house known by the rebels and the monk. The next day they went to the site of the original shrine of St Cuthbert and prayed to God for his protection during the walk ahead. The population of the town had already trebled and many others were also praying at the site. Some recognised Richard and Fang, and soon a large crowd had gathered at the shrine. The monk conducted a brief service, blessed the congregation, and requested they remain godly in preparation for tomorrow's pilgrimage.

Richard and the monk returned to the safe house, which was now no longer safe since they were being followed by several people asking for a miracle or healing. They would not take no for an answer. Some regretted touching Fang in hope of a miraculous cure. Their reward was merely a nasty wound on their hand. However, always looking for an opportunity to make money, a few were then selling their blood as a divine liquid, able to heal any illness.

Mayhem ensued in the resulting crush so Richard had to take command of the situation. He made a speech to them on the doorstep. 'Tomorrow you must show that you are worthy of God's protection. Your deliverance from the evil Tostig is at hand. Pray to God and then rest. I will see you all tomorrow, and you shall see the power of God and St Cuthbert before the day turns to night.'

His followers left, with a keen feeling of anticipation and hope. Richard, Fang, and the monk had some food and refreshments, and while the farmer helped the monk construct a cross, Richard meditated and Fang slept, dreaming of seagulls and the kitchen at Lindisfarne Abbey.

Richard awoke at dawn, and prayed to God for guidance. He had not received any more information from God and he was naturally worried. He had no idea what was going to happen that day and what miracle he had to perform. *Just a minute*, he thought, *I never know what is going to happen next so why am I worried? I must remain convinced that God is by my side. I will put my faith in God.* He laughed out loud and the others stared at him quizzically. Outside it was a young bright morning full of sun and peace. *Yes*, Richard thought, *nothing will go wrong as long as I remain a believer.*

Richard and his followers set off early for Chester le Street and soon their numbers were swelled by those who wished to join the pilgrimage. By the time they made the town's market place, their number had swollen to over 1500. They met several hundred more in the town, and there was a constant stream of new arrivals.

Eric was there already, and quickly drew Richard aside. 'I wish you to meet the other two important leaders of those groups wanting justice. This is Cuthbert, leader of the Northumberland Independent Ceorls, known as NIC, and this is Oswald, leader of the Northumberland Assertive Ceorls, known as NAC.'

Cuthbert shook Richard's hand and said, 'Why ay, hello yah nah.' And the other shook his remaining hand strongly. 'Ow do you do lad.'

Richard retrieved his two throbbing hands. Those two leaders, he concluded, had grips like vices.

Richard considered this information carefully, yet something still seemed a little confusing and awry. 'What is a ceorl, pray tell?'

Eric was first to reply. 'Good question, lad. We ceorls are the common people, the freemen, as it were, of this land although these days we don't feel free at all.'

Richard considered this reply and looked at the three leaders carefully. 'I assume their names, which just happen to be two of the saints laid to rest at Dun Holm, are not their real names, and nor is yours, so-called Eric, and as for your social standing as ceorls, I do not believe it, quite honestly. All three of you have the look of at least thanes and I suggest you are all indeed landed gentry.'

The three had a quick conversation and Eric spoke for them all in a more natural tone of voice. 'Yes sir, you're absolutely correct, we're indeed as you say, but we've been unjustly treated just like the others and pray for the return of proper law and order. We are sorry to have tried to deceive you but we find it easier to control the masses if we talk and act as they do.'

Cuthbert nodded in agreement. 'Yes, sir, we find it easier to keep up appearances at all times.'

Richard understood their reasoning. 'Now listen to me carefully. Regarding the march today, my only demand is that we stop at Pity Me on the way. God has requested that we all rest and pray there before proceeding to the church. The monk has informed me that this is where the monks dropped the coffin of St Cuthbert on the way to Dun Holm, and it is where it is said that St Cuthbert cried out to take pity on him and be more careful even though he was dead.'

Eric replied on behalf of the others, 'That is agreed. We will spread the word, and at the same time warn people not to stray from the path, as there are many dangerous bogs that would swallow a person within seconds and drag them down into hell. We have also made arrangements for three carts with provisions to accompany us. Our pilgrims will be more cheerful if their bodily needs are provided for.'

Richard nodded. 'Yes, tell them no straying from the one true path and no overindulging. God will only protect the righteous.'

Discussions concluded, they returned to the throng that had gathered, which was being entertained by Monk Aidan and several other monks who had materialised seemingly out of nowhere. They started chanting and praying, and then the decibels increased when a group of musicians joined in. Eventually the musicians started playing requests and many local folk songs followed, some of which were totally inappropriate, given the occasion.

At last, it was time to set off. The procession now consisted of over 2,000 men, women, and children. Monk Aidan held the cross aloft, and was followed by the rest of the monks, then the musicians, and then Richard, Fang, and the leaders, and finally the rest of the people. The leaders sent scouts ahead to ensure they would not be ambushed on the way. They had heard from spies that the local sheriffs and their heavily armed men were planning to stop them reaching their destination. Chester Moor was crossed without incident. And then it was on to Plawsworth, and finally Pity Me. At Pity Me, Aidan and his fellow monks conducted a short service and everyone knelt down and prayed on the spot identified by Aidan as the place where the monks stumbled and fell all those years ago. Indeed, the site had a spiritual feeling about it and many used the opportunity to pray to God for healing. One middle-aged and partly crippled woman swore afterwards that she had been healed. Most initially did not believe, but on seeing her dancing about crazily, knelt again and prayed for forgiveness for not believing in the power of the saint and God. Richard mulled these events over. *These northern people are indeed better Christians and seemingly less corrupt than those in the south of England. Perhaps God will deliver them from the hands of Duke William and his knights and thugs.* He sat down with a sigh and stroked Fang, then they had some food and drink with the others.

After the break, it was up and across Framwellgate Moor, where sadly a call of nature was the death cry for two men. They left the path and headed into the moorland where they stepped into a bog and were silently engulfed by the sticky mud, with their tights still around their knees. No one saw the mishap or heard them gurgling as they sank, so the happy procession continued.

As the pilgrims approached the bridge across the River Wear, some scouts returned and halted the joyful throng.

They gave a report to Eric, who then approached Richard. 'The local sheriff and his heavily armed men are on the bridge, and they're not there to welcome us.'

It seemed it was time for the main miracle of the day. Richard scratched his head and then scratched Fang's. He had no idea what to do. He knelt and prayed, more out of desperation than hope, and God stroked His beard and decided upon the nature of the miracle.

Richard stood up and tried to look resolute and determined. 'Pilgrims, kneel and pray and see what happens to the unjust.'

He marched off with Fang towards the bridge. The riverbank was soon covered by kneeling onlookers, all expecting a great show. The defenders on the bridge waved their weapons and jeered, shouting abuse and obscenities and showing their bare behinds. Richard held his hands heavenward and luckily for him, God having had enough of the blasphemy and wishing the pilgrims to reach their destination, decided to act.

It all started with much noise and the flapping of unseen wings. Slowly, an expanding dark screaming cloud spiralled above the bridge and blotted out the sun. Confusion ensued. The cloud then descended as it got louder and louder. Black feathers started to float down on the wind, and the onlookers realised that the dark cloud was in fact a massive flock of ravens, rooks, and crows. No one had seen the like before, or ever would again. The panicking pilgrims prayed passionately for protection. The birds circled lower above the sheriff and his soldiers on the bridge. The squawking screaming storm of stabbing darkness suddenly attacked. The bridge became a jumble of ear-piercing pecking and clawing birds, black feathers, high-pitched shouting men with bloody bodies and pieces of skin, eyes, ears, and anything else that had been ripped off. The sheriff lost both eyes within a minute. Witnessing this, many of his men took their chances, dropping their weapons and leaping into the river, only to meet a watery grave in the torrent below. With much swearing and screaming, the remaining men retreated towards the church, but the birds were relentless. They pursued their victims as if possessed (which of course, they were). Some men died where they fell, others staggered blindly about before plummeting over the bridge or river bank to be gleefully received by the fast-running river. Finally, the commotion ceased and the birds ascended as one, as if returning to God, and disappeared from sight. The pilgrims were left completely stunned but thankful to God for their survival.

Eric and the other leaders sent their men ahead to clear up the mess. The monks then purified the bridge through prayer and some holy water before the pilgrims were allowed to reach their destination. The whole congregation had witnessed the miraculous deliverance, and all were assured that God would be on their side in the forthcoming struggle. All the leaders ran to Richard and cheered.

Eric slapped Richard on the back. 'Well done lad! What a great spectacle!'

Richard shrugged his shoulders and replied, 'I have to admit that this time it was nothing to do with me. It was God's work.'

Eric and the other leaders were shocked. They could just about accept that Richard had certain abilities, but that this had been the visit of God's will, was very difficult to believe. Yet it had happened, so it must be true. With this epiphany, they were all true believers, and knelt to give thanks to God.

Richard sat with Fang's head on his lap, looking at the scene in front of them. An orderly queue had formed, which the priests were letting into the church to view, pray, give thanks, and ask for personal favours. Everyone was convinced that, given the circumstances, all of their prayers would be answered. God, Jesus, and the saints were listening, considering merits when deciding their fates. The people left the church as devout Christian pilgrims, but as usual, the devil immediately worked on their weaknesses. Soon many were overindulging themselves with much laughter and festivity. Seemingly out of nowhere, the local traders were taking advantage of the light-headedness of the throng, attempting to sell them food, beer, trinkets, relics, and anything else they could tempt them with. Richard despaired.

Suddenly Richard received a tap on his head. He jumped up and looked at the man with the offending finger. Fang had been thrown into the air by Richard's actions, and tumbled down the slope to end up yelping in the river.

Richard ran down to save him, removing his clothing as he went. He turned his head. 'I'll deal with you once I have retrieved my dog. He will surely have something to give you to remember him by as well.'

He dived into the cold, fast-flowing water. Fang was now some 100 metres downstream, struggling against the strong flow and currents. Richard swam as if his life depended on it while concentrating his mind on the water in an attempt to calm it. God was distraught, as He could see His instrument drowning before Him. He calmed the waters sufficiently so as to allow Fang to doggy-paddle towards the bank. The dog was swept into the bank behind some rocks where the water was calm enough for him to find the bottom with his paws. Richard joined him a few seconds later. He grabbed Fang and pushed as hard as he could towards the bank. The two then flopped on the bank, breathing fast and coughing up water. Fang was the first to recover. He stood up and violently shook his body, sending sprays of water in all directions, including Richard's.

'Thanks a lot!'

The dog replied by giving him a lick.

Richard stood up. 'Fang, it's time to deal with that stranger.'

Up the slope they struggled, with Richard retrieving all of his clothes other than his boots, that had quickly ended up for sale on a trader's stall. Eric challenged the store holder and swapped a promise not to throw him into the river, for the boots. All was settled quickly and the trader left before the crowd could show him the error of his ways.

Richard shouted, 'Eric, hold that strange cloaked fellow while I put my clothes on.'

'Ay, I would if I were you, since most women have not seen a body like yours in these parts. It could easily lead to unrest and revolution.'

Eric grabbed the black-cloaked man but he easily broke the hold, twisted behind Eric, and subdued him with a neck hold, and then pushed him onto his knees. 'Je 'ave this home at moi mercy, Richard, zo just calm down and call off your chien.'

Richard immediately understood who the man was. 'You work for you-know-who?'

The hooded ghoul nodded and replied, 'Yes.'

'Let's all calm down, including you, Fang. Let Eric go and we will have a civilised conversation.'

The ghoul's death grip was released.

'Eric, this is an acquaintance of mine, and he will now apologise.'

The face under the hood grimaced. He was not one for apologising but he knew of Richard's powers and knew that Duchess Matilda would not be amused if her plans were upset by any rashness.

He swallowed his pride and through his teeth replied, 'I am sorry for my actions; it will not 'appen again.'

Eric rubbed his neck and decided to accept the apology, but to remember the events in case he ever met the foreigner on his own. *The stranger will learn that we Northumberland men forget nothing and forgive little.*

Richard took the agent as far away from Eric as possible and found a private space behind the church, where they disturbed a courting couple. Fang soon put an end to their steamy passions.

Fang then started growling at the cloaked man, who then readied himself to kick him when Richard shouted, 'I wouldn't do that if I was you.'

But the growling continued. Fang went into stage two in an attempt to subdue his victim. He relieved himself on the stranger's boots, creating a cloud of steam.

'Mon Dieu, quelle chien!' Then he started jumping up and down and screamed, 'My boots are melting!'

'I would keep still if I was you, otherwise he will go into stage three and his fart is considered worse than his bite by most sensible people.'

The agent thought for a moment, then quietly removed the remains of his boots, and spoke. 'Here are the sealed orders from Duchess Matilda. I'm off tout de suite, but will see you again.'

The barefoot cloaked figure moved gingerly towards a pile of clothes taken from the bodies of Tostig's men and commenced his quest to find a pair of boots that fitted and still had some wear in them.

Richard sat down in the afternoon sun, with his back against a tombstone that announced Ralf Smithy of Bernicia was now at peace, beheaded but now whole. The sun warmed Fang's coat and his few remaining fleas (following their near-annihilation in the river). He rolled about on the grass and ended up with all four legs in the air, studying the big warm glowing thing above him. He soon closed his weary eyes and began dreaming. Richard read his detailed orders and scratched his head for a while. He had to think carefully about how he could accomplish this part of his mission. On the one hand he could not disobey Duchess Matilda, but on the other, he would not betray his new friends or put them in undue peril. He was sure that if he was subtle, this could be done. However, he would be the first to acknowledge that subtlety was not in his nature.

Richard got up and found Eric, who had one hand round a leg of lamb and another round a very comely woman. 'Can I speak to you? It's very important.'

Eric sighed and let go of the larger of his prizes. 'If you must.'

They moved away from the noise, the smell of sweaty bodies, and the goings-on of northern men and women who had never before been in the company of so many interesting human beings. A frank but friendly conversation took place whist both consumed some bread, meat and several flagons of ale.

RICHARD SOWS A REBELLIOUS SEED

'So, Richard, what do you want?' enquired Eric.

'Well, I will try and speak plainly, especially given the amount of beer that you have consumed.'

'It helps me think.'

Richard continued, 'At present Earl Tostig is with his brother and King Edward but once he hears about recent events, he will return with an army. In my view, you have the upper hand and should use this opportunity to resolve your various grievances.'

'What do you suggest? Rebellion?'

Richard tried to pick his words carefully. 'Change your allegiance. I suggest you approach the good Earl Morcar, brother of Edwin of Mercia. That family has strength and political standing almost equal to that of the house of Godwin. I understand that the Earl Morcar has a manor house at Eisicewalt (now known as Easingwold). Perhaps you and I together with some of your fellow thanes could visit there and discuss this possibility with his representatives.'

Eric thought for several minutes. 'You seem to know more than you should about such matters. It makes me rather suspicious, but you've made a good argument. I'll request a meeting of the Shire Moot to discuss this. We thanes must follow proper procedure in making important decisions. You should return to the farmhouse where you'll be well looked after and protected. I'll let you know the result of our meeting.'

Richard nodded. 'One further suggestion before I leave, I would humbly suggest that a force of some 300 men together with me and Fang would make short work of the defenders of York. As long as no clergy are included to hold us back, we'll take York and its weapons and supplies. If we hold York then the Earl of Mercia will undoubtedly take us seriously and join us.'

'Not so much 'us' Richard, but your advice will be considered.'

Eric gave a hearty laugh and slapped Richard on the back. Fang sprang into action and only a swift body tackle by Richard saved Eric from a certain lack of a lower leg. Eric laughed again, thinking *if that dog had done his worst, then I would only have had one leg to stand on when presenting my case to the forthcoming meeting of the Shire.* He also was hatching a plot to help subdue the dog when required by introducing him to a nice bitch. *That diversionary tactic certainly worked on bloodthirsty Vikings, so why not on a ferocious dog or even perhaps a miracle-working foreigner? It's a well-known fact that all males have a certain weakness that's easily exploitable.*

RICHARD HENRY'S MOTHER INTERRUPTS

Back in the year 2026, Richard Henry's mother was frantic with worry. She had phoned her son several times but kept being told by the network that the call could not be connected. It was now 3am. She picked up her phone yet again.

Richard Henry (Henry to his friends and family) was still fast asleep when his phone rang loudly. It startled the ghostly spirits more than Richard Henry. Duchess Matilda paused the dream. She and Priest Pierre led the ghostly apparitions out of the tapestry. With the help of God Matilda and Pierre had quickly become friends since their deaths.

As God said, 'After all, you were both fervent believers when flesh and bone!'

Unfortunately, for many of the others, they remained restless spirits, unable to face the facts or settle their differences.

As far as Matilda and Pierre were concerned, the presence of Richard Henry on the anniversary of the Battle of Hastings presented a unique opportunity to lay all the ghosts to rest.

Pierre went over to Richard Henry and blew a breath of ice-cold air over the mobile phone that sat on the bench next to the stirring young man. It stopped working.

Priest Pierre then whispered soothingly into Henry's left ear, 'Sleep young Richard Henry, sleep.'

Matilda spoke to all of the ghosts. 'Fellow souls, just as God sent me the two Richards, he has sent us this boy, the living descendant of those two heaven-sent beings. Please continue to let the truth be told through his dream.'

Harold was first to reply. 'But William keeps manipulating the dream to put himself in a better light, and he is trying his best to make me seem weak and unworthy!'

'No, I've not! It's not my fault if you are what you are!'

'Come here and say that! I'll crack your head with my axe!'

'You just try it! I'll slash your gut open with my special Welsh sword that was your deadly gift to me.'

Richard the First laughed. 'I'd like to see you two fight a duel, but unfortunately you do not have the flesh and bone to hold any weapons let alone fight with them!'

Matilda shook her head. 'Harold and William, why can you not be friends? You are both warriors. Stop and shake hands.'

William was sulking now. 'He started it, Matilda.'

'And I'll finish it. Shake hands or else!'

The two reluctantly tried to shake hands but of course without physical form, this proved impossible.

Harald Hardrada was getting impatient. 'You're wasting time! You've already used up half of the night. I want this boy to see my heroic deeds!'

Tostig was feeling very upset. 'You've made me look like some insane psychopath! I was not that crazy! Oh, by the way has anyone got a drink?'

Richard the Last laughed. 'You idiot, your dead! Any drink would just flow straight through you!'

Turold was getting bored. 'Just get on with it, oh, unless you want me to give you one of my jester performances?'

All the other ghosts spoke as one. 'No!'

Edward knelt in front of the others, saying, 'I confess, I must repent. Please hear my sins!'

All the other ghosts spoke as one. 'No!'

Matilda did her best to conclude matters. 'Why don't we play out the second half of the dream and see what happens. Pierre, please do what is necessary.'

Priest Pierre whispered soothingly into Henry's left ear, 'Sleep young Richard Henry, blessed above all others. Sleep and dream and all will be revealed!'

Pierre watched the now peaceful youth and smiled. Once he was sure that he was truly asleep, he turned to the others saying, 'Pray for this man and to God, and then continue. All is now well, but time is passing quickly, so please, no more shouting and arguing, and that means you too, William, and you also, Harold of England, and Harald of Norway!'

Richard Henry's mother managed to leave just part of her message before she was disconnected. 'Henry, I'm going to phone the police at seven if you have not phoned me by then. Father Rodut is here with me and he says that you are in great danger and to beware—'

Outside, across the street from the museum's entrance, a black BMW car was parked while a large Frenchman stood nearby smoking a cigar. Francois was hoping that this would be his last night of following the young English student. His associate, the Algerian, Farid, known as The Butcher, had told him that their surveillance could well end in the morning. It just needed one phone call from their master.

THE STORY MUST NOW PAUSE

Unfortunately, dear reader, we must leave the various players in this last great saga of early medieval Europe. The saga is half told. Harold seems destined to become the next king of England unless he can find a way of convincing either King Edward or the Witan, that Duke William would be a better choice. Richard the First is ready to sow discontent throughout Northumberland, and when the time is right his twin will undertake his mission to Norway. Duchess Matilda will continue to manipulate events so as to strengthen her husband's chance of winning the crown of England, since once he becomes king, she and God can cleanse the English Church and bring its flock closer to God. By so doing she hopes this will kill any lingering thoughts the peoples of England may have of worshiping any pagan gods. She is indeed convinced that with the assistance of the three men that she believes were sent to her by God Himself that her holy crusade will eventually succeed.

Finally, it seems that Richard Henry has more than ghostly apparitions to worry about.

All will become clear in Book Two: Four Men, One English Crown.

LIST OF HISTORICAL EVENTS

These are based upon historical records, but some of these documents are considered unreliable so some dates are subject to debate.

1036: Princes Edward's and Alfred's ill-fated invasions
1040: Spring, death of King Harold Harefoot
      Summer, Harthacnut becomes king of England
1041: Prince Edward invited by King Harthacnut to return to England and help rule the country
1042: King Harthacnut dies suddenly and Prince Edward becomes king of England
1051: Duke William becomes an ally of King Edward and according to Duke William, Edward promises him the crown if King Edward dies without issue. Duke William marries Matilda, daughter of Count Baldwin
1051 or 1052: Adeliza, daughter of Duke William is born
1053-1054: Duke William's wars with France and his neighbours. This includes the Battle of Mortemer
1063: England's war with Wales and the death of Gruffydd King of Wales
1064: Spring, Harold's journey to Normandy via Eu
1064-1065: Duke William's war with Duke Conan of Brittany
1064: Autumn, Earl Harold returns to England
1065: Summer, Earl Harold marries Ealdgyth the widowed queen of King Gruffydd
1065: Autumn, unrest in Northumberland leading to a revolt

HISTORICAL CHARACTERS

Duke William- bastard son of Duke Robert
Duchess Matilda- wife of William and of high status
King Edward- Saxon king who was rather weak
Queen Edith- sister of Harold and wife of Edward
Turold- there is historical evidence that he did exist
Earl Harold Godwinson- son of Earl Godwin
Edyth Swanneck- Harold's common law wife
Earl Tostig Godwinson- Harold's petulant brother
Earl Godwin of Wessex- Harold's devious father
Bishop Stigand- corrupt, excommunicated by the Pope
Vital- a Norman knight
Wadard- a Norman knight
Bishop Odo- William's half brother
Robert Count of Mortain- William's half brother
Adeliza- William's daughter
Count Guy- a not so noble lord
Wulfnoth Godwinson- brother of Harold held prisoner
Hakon- nephew of Harold held prisoner by William
Duke Conan of Brittany- foe of William
Count Artaud of Forez- Count of Lyon
Ealdgyth of Mercia- ex queen of Wales, marries Harold
King Gruffydd- the last true king of Wales
Abbott Beorhtic- well-respected Saxon cleric
Eilmer the Flying Monk- thought he could fly

All other characters are fictional, or were they?

PHANTASTIC REVIEWS- not to be taken seriously!

SAXON FOOTBALL PARCHMENT
'In the first half, the English Saxons were completely out-played by a dazzling display of Norman footwork. We hope for much better in the second half.'

NORMANDY OBSERVER
'What a ripping read! The Duke and Duchess are destined for greatness! Duchess Matilda's gowns were stunning!'

HISTORICAL TIMES
'It's history, but not as we know it. I never knew history could be so entertaining!'

MYSTIC HERALD
'As predicted, a magical read!'

KNITTERS WEEKLY
'After reading this book, we strongly advise all our readers have their knitwear exorcised before wearing.'

VIKING RUNES MONTHLY
'We can't wait for Book 2! King Harald Hardrada is bound to impress, especially when he goes berserk!'

ANIMAL RIGHTS QUARTERLY
'We hope no horses, dogs, squirrels, hedgehogs, boar, rats, birds or other animals were harmed during the writing of this book.'

THE ART OF JUGGLING
'Can't believe what Turold can do with his balls! What a performer! Anyone got Megan's recipe for that mysterious pottage of hers?

THE ART OF POISONING GAZETTE
'We would like to thank the Duke and Duchess of Normandy for their support and articles on potions.'

WEST WALES CHRONICAL
'Marwolaeth i'r Saeson! This book proves that our mighty King Gruffydd did not fall in a climbing accident in Snowdonia as the English reported, but was brutally murdered and decapitated by the wicked English Saxons. Revenge will be sweet and swift! We predict that one day, Welsh kings will rule England!'